The QuicKeys® 3 Book

Steve Roth
Don Sellers

Addison-Wesley Publishing Company

Reading, Massachusetts • Menlo Park, California
New York • Don Mills, Ontario • Wokingham, England
Amsterdam • Bonn • Sydney • Singapore • Tokyo • Madrid • San Juan
Paris • Seoul • Milan • Mexico City • Taipei

Many of the designations used by manufacturers and sellers to distinguish their products are claimed as trademarks. Where those designations appear in this book, and Addison-Wesley was aware of a trademark claim, the designations have been printed in initial capital letters or all capital letters.

The authors and publishers have taken care in preparation of this book, but make no expressed or implied warranty of any kind and assume no responsibility for errors or omissions. No liability is assumed for incidental or consequential damages in connection with or arising out of the use of the information or programs contained herein.

Library of Congress Cataloging-in-Publication Data

Roth, Stephen F., 1958–
    The QuicKeys 3 book / Steve Roth, Don Sellers.
       p. cm.
    Includes index.
    ISBN 0-201-40979-8
      1. Utilities (Computer programs)   2. QuicKeys.   I. Sellers, Don.
  II. Title.
  QA76.76.U84R673   1994
  005.4'3--dc20   94-36390
                                           CIP

Sponsoring Editor: David Clark
Project Manager: Joanne Clapp Fullagar
Production Coordinator: Debbie McKenna
Cover design: Barbara T. Atkinson.
   Front cover artwork was designed by CE Software, Inc. in
   West Des Moines, IA, and Creative Support in Allen, TX.
Text design: Joyce C. Weston
Set in 10 point Usherwood by CIP of Coronado

1 2 3 4 5 6 7 8 9 -MA- 9998979695
First printing, October 1994

Addison-Wesley books are available for bulk purchases by corporations, institutions, and other organizations. For more information please contact the Corporate, Government and Special Sales Department at (800) 238-9682.

Contents

Contents

■ ■

■ ■

Contents

Contents

■ ■

■ ■

A Book About QuicKeys?

A few years ago, one of my coworkers here at CE Software said that someone was writing a book about QuicKeys. I was confused by the concept. Why would someone do a book about QuicKeys? After all, *I* had no problem using QuicKeys. It was all crystal clear to me. Unfortunately, though, not everyone has the advantage of having written QuicKeys, and it turned out that a book could be pretty handy for everyone else.

Steve Roth and Don Sellers turned out a marvelous book, walking you step by step into QuicKeys and then giving you ideas and strategies to get the most out of the program.

Well, it's a few years later. Both QuicKeys and I have changed a bit over time.

The new 3.0 version of QuicKeys is more powerful than the last. This means there are vast, new opportunities to explore with QuicKeys, and Steve and Don have done it again!

One of the most marvelous discoveries I've made over the years is that QuicKeys gives people the chance to really customize their Macs. No two QuicKeys users will have exactly the same shortcuts. Steve and Don let their personalities show in this book. They've seen some possibilities that hadn't occurred to me. That's what I love about QuicKeys—you can do things even I didn't imagine!

This book is great. I found it thought-provoking and entertaining. Hang on to your hats. You're in for some fun!

Donald Brown
CE Software, Inc.; author of QuicKeys

Deceptive Simplicity

"Why would anyone want a book about QuicKeys? What's to say?"

"Well, there are actually a lot of nooks and crannies to the program, you know."

"Yeah, you know the other day I was building this big sequence…"

So we started talking. And then we talked some more. And the more we talked, the more we realized that QuicKeys is a deep, deep program masquerading as an easy-to-use utility (it's that, also, of course). There are hidden treasures in the program that we didn't find until we were writing the last chapter of this book. QuicKeys is deceptively simple, but when you start exploring it, you discover that it just keeps on going.

QuicKeys is one other thing: It is the best program available for increasing your across-the-board efficiency on a Mac. So we are always surprised when we meet someone who owns a Mac but doesn't know about QuicKeys. We're doubly surprised when we meet someone who owns QuicKeys but doesn't take full advantage of it.

Why We Wrote This Book

This book is a revised and expanded edition of a book titled *The Little QuicKeys Book*, published by Peachpit Press. We've updated the material extensively for QuicKeys 3 and System 7.5 and added dozens of tips and techniques that we've discovered in the years since we wrote the first edition.

We wrote this book because we're crazy about QuicKeys. It's integral to our day-to-day keyboard pounding. When we happen to sit down at a Mac that doesn't have QuicKeys (or *our* shortcuts) installed on it, we fumble around, grumble imprecations, and generally make annoyances of ourselves. QuicKeys has become so integral to how we work that we can't seem to use our Macs anymore without it.

But you have to set up and use QuicKeys correctly to make it worthwhile. Although the QuicKeys manual is very good, it doesn't tell you the tactics and strategies that result from years of working with the program. The manual doesn't mention the foibles and inconsistencies that you may encounter (that's right, we're in love, but we're not blind). The manual doesn't include passels of application-specific shortcuts that expert users have developed and refined.

That's what this book is about. We designed it to be both a teaching tool and reference guide. It is our hope that after reading it, your efficiency will have improved so much that you wish someone had written it years before. (We wish someone had, so we didn't have to.)

How to Use This Book

We've tried to make this book as transparent as possible. You don't need a reference to little icons to figure out what's going on, nor do you need to use the book in any order. You can get at the information in several ways.

- Read it from beginning to end.

- Browse through.

- Refer to it in times of crisis.

Reading the book from beginning to end is our favorite recommendation, but we're not fooling ourselves. Browsing is another great method, and we've tried to provide a lot of ways to browse through the book. Peruse the heads, jump into the figures, and jump from them to the figure references in the text (the references always precede the figures).

For those seeking a point of reference, we offer three methods.

- **Table of Contents.** It includes chapter titles and first-, second-, and third-level heads.

- **Index.** This is the tool to use if you have a specific question about QuicKeys.

- **Shortcut Functions.** This is the way that the chapters are arranged. Each chapter covers certain shortcut types arranged by function. See the next paragraphs for a description of the contents of each chapter.

How This Book Is Organized

There are four main parts to this book.

Using QuicKeys. The first four chapters lay out QuicKeys, the program. They explain how to build shortcuts, how to use them, and how to bend QuicKeys to your will.

Shortcuts. Chapters 5 through 16 go into detail on each of the shortcut types, organized by function (what you want to do with the shortcuts).

The Sequence represents such a powerful tool in QuicKeys that we devote two chapters to it: the first (Chapter 14) explains how to record and edit Sequences, and the second (Chapter 15) describes the functional shortcuts that are used mainly as steps in a Sequence. Chapter 16 gives you the best succinct rundown of Apple Events we've ever seen (you can see that modesty is not among our strong points).

Aids. Chapter 17, *Keystroke Strategies*, provides details on creating arrangements of shortcuts and how to assign them easily remembered keystrokes. Chapter 18, *QuicKeys Utilities*, gives the lowdown on the four QuicKeys utilities.

Applications. Chapters 19 through 23 describe useful (and in a couple of cases, ingenious) shortcuts for various popular applications.

That's the rundown. Now here are the blow-by-blow, chapter-by-chapter, shortcut-by-shortcut details.

Chapter 1: What's New in QuicKeys 3? If you're a long-time user looking for cool new stuff, this is the place to begin.

Chapter 2: The Old Kit Bag. When you install QuicKeys, you end up with lots of little pieces scattered around your hard disk. This chapter explains what all those pieces are and why you should care.

Chapter 3: The Gateway to QuicKeys Knowledge. In this chapter we build our first QuicKey shortcut, talk about the most sensible approaches to building shortcuts that work (and keep working), and explain how QuicKeys works with sets of shortcuts.

Chapter 4: The QuicKeys Cockpit. Here's where you lay your hands on all the controls that make QuicKeys fly. From the menus in the QuicKeys main editor window to configuring QuicKeys Toolbox, this is mission control for QuicKeys pilots.

Chapter 5: Shortcuts That Launch and Open. Launch shortcuts help in opening applications, documents, and folders.

- **File Launch (formerly File).** You'll probably use file launch shortcuts more than the other shortcuts in this category. A file launch shortcut can open a file or an application.

- **Transfer.** The Transfer shortcut (on the Specials menu) launches an application or document that you choose after you trigger the shortcut.

- **Folders (formerly Location).** The Folders shortcut (an extension) takes you to a particular folder when an Open File dialog box is active.

■ **StuffIt Stuff.** The Stuff and UnStuff shortcuts (extensions) compress and decompress files in conjunction with the archive application StuffIt Deluxe.

Chapter 6: Shortcuts That Control Windows. Here's where you manipulate the standard Mac window. Window Control has five subgroups.

■ **Document Windows.** The first and largest set of window control shortcuts affect document windows. They are all Mousies (Line up, Line down, Page up, Page down, Home, End, Column left, Column right, Page left, Page right, Close window, Zoom window).

■ **Application Windows.** The application window shortcuts, both from the Specials menu, let you choose which window of a particular application is on top and active.

■ **Menu Selection.** The Menu Selection shortcut (formerly called Menu/ DA) selects menu items.

■ **Pop-up Menu.** The new Pop-up Menu shortcut (an extension) selects items from pop-up menus, like the process of selecting a font from a pop-up font list in PageMaker.

■ **Buttons.** Button shortcuts click buttons and checkboxes.

Chapter 7: Shortcuts that Mimic the Keyboard and Mouse. Here's your chance to fool the Mac into thinking you're hard at work on your keyboard and mouse, when you're actually lolling on the beach.

■ **Keyboard.** An Alias Keystroke shortcut can make the Mac think that one keystroke (plus modifiers) is any other keystroke (plus modifiers).

■ **Mouse.** A Click shortcut can mimic any mouse movement and clicks (plus modifiers).

Chapter 8: Shortcuts That Control the Mac System. The System Control shortcuts manipulate some basic functions of your Mac.

■ **Switches.** Switch shortcuts (they're Specials) turn the machine off and back on.

■ **Picture and Volume.** The Picture and Volume shortcuts (both extensions) access the Monitor and Sound control panels to let you change the color depth and sound volume of your display.

■ **System 7 Specials.** System 7 Specials switch Balloon Help and file sharing on and off, and toggle between open applications.

■ **ProcessSwap.** The ProcessSwap extension switches between open applications without requiring the use of the Application menu.

■ **FKEYs.** FKEY shortcuts are not to be confused with function keys on an extended keyboard. FKEYs are special utilities available on early Macs that have hung around and are still used by some folks. This QuicKey type accesses any FKEYs your machine may have.

Chapter 9: Shortcuts for Networks and Devices. These shortcuts allow you to control your modem, telephone, and network connections.

■ **Choosy.** Choosy (an extension) selects any of your available printers.

■ **Mounty.** Mounty (an extension) mounts and dismounts AppleShare volumes.

■ **NetModemChoosy.** NetModemChoosy (a new extension) switches between a NetModem controller and NetSerial controllers.

■ **Phone Dialer.** The new Phone Dialer extension supports the automated dialing of speaker phones, modems, and desktop telephones from your Mac.

Chapter 10: Shortcuts for PowerBooks. This chapter describes an updated extension that provides shortcut tools especially for maintaining PowerBooks. At the end of the chapter, a section introduces the sets that come with QuicKeys intended for PowerBook users.

■ **PowerBook Specials.** These extensions supply you with battery-saving tools, such as sleep and spin down, for extending battery life on your PowerBook.

■ **PowerBook Sets.** Two ready-made sets of shortcuts enhance the power of QuicKeys for PowerBook users.

Chapter 11: Shortcuts for Sight and Sound. These extensions play sounds and show movies.

■ **Sound.** Sound (an extension) plays a sound from your System file.

■ **Speak Ease.** The new Speak Ease extension uses the MacPlainTalk system extension and new multimedia Mac to provide synthetic speech for your Mac.

■ **QT Movie.** The QT Movie extension plays QuickTime movies.

Chapter 12: Shortcuts That Manipulate Text and Graphics. If you want to do anything with text or graphics, use one of these shortcuts.

- **Text.** This is the progenitor of the category. Text shortcuts type the text you want into documents, dialog boxes, and windows.

- **Scrap Ease.** A new extension called Scrap Ease incorporates the functions of the three old extensions, Grab Ease, Type Ease, and Paste Ease, letting you copy to and paste from multiple clipboards.

- **Date/Time.** Date/Time shortcuts, not surprisingly, type the current date or time in a variety of formats.

- **Quotes.** Quotes shortcuts (they're Specials) type curved quotation marks and apostrophes.

- **Display Text (formerly Display).** The Display Text shortcut is an ingenious little word processor, disguised as a QuicKey extension.

Chapter 13: Shortcuts That Control QuicKeys. The shortcuts that control QuicKeys are the knobs and valves that let you control aspects of QuicKeys itself.

- **QuicKeys Editor.** QuicKeys Editor (a Special) opens the QuicKeys Editor window, the main area for building and controlling QuicKeys.

- **Toggle QuicKeys On/Off.** This Special makes the QuicKeys program go to sleep until you wake it again.

- **QuickReference Card.** The QuickReference Card (a Special) shows you a list of the shortcuts in either or both of your two active sets. Your shortcuts can be activated directly from the QuickReference Card.

- **SoftKeys.** The SoftKeys extension puts your shortcuts on Palettes you can display. From the Palettes, you can trigger shortcuts.

- **Sequence Switches.** These two types (Specials) start and stop the recording of two different categories of shortcuts: real-time and Sequence shortcuts.

Chapter 14: The Sequence. This chapter explains everything you need to know to create the ultimate shortcut: the Sequence.

Chapter 15: Shortcuts For Sequences. Most of these shortcuts are only useful within Sequences.

- **Wait.** The Wait extension delays a Sequence until certain conditions are met. The multiple, old Wait shortcuts (for example, WindowWait and MenuWait) have been combined into this new simplified shortcut.

- **Branchers.** The two branchers (both extensions) allow a Sequence to proceed in one of two directions, depending upon circumstances.

- **Pause.** The Pause extension stops a Sequence for a period of time or until the user restarts it.

- **Repeat.** The Repeat extension replays part of a Sequence or another shortcut a predetermined number of times.

- **GoSub.** The GoSub extension shifts the execution of a Sequence to another shortcut and then back to the original Sequence.

- **Message.** Message (an extension) displays a message and can wait for input before proceeding.

Chapter 16: Apple Events and Scripting. Apple Events extensions can control program function and information sharing through Apple Events. The scripting extensions can run AppleScripts or application-specific scripts. The chapter also introduces QuicKeys Script, the internal scripting language of QuicKeys.

- **Apple Events.** The Apple Events extension sends Apple Events to running applications. The extension contains sophisticated implementation, including the ability to query a target application to find out what Apple Events it handles.

- **Finder Events.** The Finder Events extension can send six different Apple Events to the Finder. These events will switch to the Finder and display the Clipboard, put a PowerBook to sleep, display a file's Get Info window, display open folders, open files, or print documents.

- **Scripting shortcuts.** The AppleScript extension runs scripts written in AppleScript, Apple's universal scripting language for the Mac. The DoScript extension sends application-specific scripts to the appropriate application for execution.

- **QuicKeys Script.** QuicKeys Script is the OSA-compliant internal scripting language of QuicKeys.

Chapter 17: Keystroke Strategies. This chapter gives tips on how to build a cohesive, consistent stable of shortcuts. Included in the chapter are suggested functional groups of shortcuts, strategies for keystrokes, and memory aids.

Chapter 18: QuicKeys Utilities. Four utility programs come with QuicKeys to provide various support services—from helping you create a passel of shortcuts customized to your Mac, to printing out templates of your shortcut keystrokes.

Chapters 19-23: QuicKeys and Popular Applications. In these chapters we show you how you can use QuicKeys shortcuts to enhance your use of some popular applications: Word, PageMaker, Excel, FileMaker Pro, and QuarkXPress.

Appendix: Resources. Resources provides information on where you can acquire products mentioned in the book.

Acknowledgments

Many people helped create this book. We'd like to start by thanking our editor at Addison-Wesley, David Clark, who was always a pleasure to work with.

Rita Lewis. Rita Lewis took on the task of updating the Little QuicKeys Book when the new version was just a glimmer in CE Software's eye. Rita's an expert at learning new software on the fly and at translating technical information into lay terms after 13 years of technical writing that includes writing four Macintosh books on diverse topics. Rita's ability to work closely with CE Software was a great help in keeping the book on track.

CE Software. We could never have attempted a project like this without the support of CE Software.

Don Brown, QuicKeys' creator, willingly gave time out of his busy schedule to diffuse the mist that sometimes obscured our understanding of his program. His insights on the ramifications of QuicKeys were especially fascinating, and his foreword graces the front of this book.

Matt Kramer, Product Line Manager for Personal Agents at CE Software, lent avid support to the project by pointing us to the proper resources at CE and helping us to maintain a close working relationship with them.

Despite the support from CE, any errors or omissions in this book are ours, not theirs.

Dave and Patti Loverink. Dave Loverink, a former QuicKeys development manager (now with Now Software), and Patti Loverink, co-author of the QuicKeys documentation, reviewed the book for technical accuracy. Dave was a constant source of information and enlightenment for the first edition of this book, so we felt lucky to have him and Patti read this version. Their immediate, thorough, and expert criticism was extraordinarily helpful.

Acknowledgments

■ ■

Contributors. Three people contributed their words to the original version of this book. Much of their material has been rewritten, but substantial portions remain. Howard Hansen of The Oasis Group in Seattle wrote significant portions of the chapter on Excel, as did Joe Kroeger, editor of *The FileMaker Report,* of the FileMaker chapter. Don Munsil, programmer *extraordinaire* at ElseWare, wrote the seven-page section on Apple Events in the book's first version. One sentence of that original chapter remains in what is now the longest chapter in the book. Don, if you can tell us which sentence is yours, we'll buy you a pint of Pike Place ale.

Glenn Fleishman, Steve's managing editor at Open House, contributed his extensive knowledge by reviewing and rewriting parts of the PowerBook and FileMaker Pro chapters. Glenn's wide-ranging expertise and support ("Glenn, why can't I link to Steve's Mac?" "Glenn, you can't assign keystrokes to styles in Word, can you?" "Glenn, why is the server so slow?") are also reflected throughout the book.

We'd like to offer our thanks to these four writers. They contributed a great deal more than their time.

Others. David Blatner provided insights into the mysteries of QuarkXPress, especially its scripting. David also loaned Don enough equipment so he could have two Macs running (so while one was rebooting, Don could work on the other). Ole Kvern offered his usual extraordinarily competent sheaf of perceptions on PageMaker and Apple Events.

Finally, thanks to Susie Hammond for giving us Jesse and Dia and doing without Steve; and to Lucy, Sam, and Tom for stoically surviving many evenings and weekends alone while Don was hard-a-working.

Steve Roth
Don Sellers

■ ■

1 What's New in QuicKeys 3?

In computing, a few years is a lifetime. Look at what is happening in the Mac universe: new Macs every three months; new technologies such as speech recognition, CD players, Newtons, wireless LANs, open collaboration environment, and open scripting architecture (and whatever has been announced while this book was in press). QuicKeys has had to grow up to meet the challenges of working in this sophisticated computing environment. In this chapter we review what's new in QuicKeys 3. New users may want to skip to Chapter 2, *The Old Kit Bag*.

CE Software has totally redesigned the program from the inside out (with improvements to QuicKeys Toolbox, CEToolbox, and QuicKeys itself, and with newly designed windows, menus, and commands). QuicKeys now requires System 7 and will not operate under System 6. QuicKeys 3 can handle up to 64 open applications. An internal scripting language has been added, and Apple Events integration has been improved. Although the program still looks basically the same, you get a lot more power under the hood. QuicKeys 3 offers

- an enhanced, simplified, and more intuitive interface

- new extensions (which fill in some of the annoying gaps in the program) and improvements to many old extensions

- more sophisticated Sequence recording

- improved accessibility and performance of its utilities

The QuicKeys Editor Window

The QuicKeys Editor window, your home base for creating and editing shortcuts, has been redesigned to provide easier access to your shortcut sets. The window can be made larger and, in addition, QuicKeys 3 introduces a color interface to help the user differentiate shortcut categories. Buttons replace pull-down menus, providing easier switching between the views of your shortcuts.

In the QuicKeys Editor window and elsewhere, CE Software has changed some of the program's terminology to make it more intuitive. What were termed keysets are now simply called sets. Each individual macro was called a QuicKey but is now called a shortcut. We can only follow CE's lead (after all, we sure complained enough), so we conform to the new terminology in this book.

Let's take a closer look at the new QuicKeys Editor window.

File Menu

The File menu remains basically unchanged, although the command names have been reworded to better describe their function in opening, closing, and saving sets. In addition, a Make Icon command has been added that replaces the QK Icon utility's function of creating stand-alone applets (small programs) out of shortcuts. Applets can now operate with their shortcut information imbedded in the icon so that they work even if you move them to another Mac (provided QuicKeys is installed on it) or delete the shortcut on which they're based.

Edit Menu

The only change to the Edit menu is the addition of the Select All command, which does just that. It's an overdue addition, useful for copying and pasting the contents of entire sets.

Define Menu

The guts of the QuicKeys Editor reside in the Define menu. This menu has been rearranged to make shortcuts easier to find. Some shortcuts have been renamed to better reflect their functions; for example, Alias' new name Alias Keystroke differentiates it from System 7's Make Alias command, and File's new name File Launch better describes its function. Other, deeper changes have occurred in the Extensions submenu, which used to be a full single list, making it difficult to find and select a shortcut. Now, individual extensions have been organized into categories.

- File Tools

- System Tools

- Network and Device Tools

- Text Manipulators

- Sequence Tools

- Scripting Tools

- 3rd-Party Tools

Using the Extension Manager (see Chapter 18, *QuicKeys Utilities*), you can place the extensions that you use most often above and outside these categories for easier access.

Sets Menu

The Sets menu replaces the Keysets menu in the QuicKeys Editor window. Sets are organized into three categories.

Active sets. The Universal Set and the set for whichever application is currently in front.

Application sets. All the sets in the QuicKeys Keysets folder. Usually, each set contains shortcuts specific to a certain application. QuicKeys creates an application set for you when you launch a new application, but you can also store sets that you've built yourself in this folder.

Temporarily opened sets. If you open a set that isn't stored in the Keysets folder, QuicKeys displays it at the bottom of the Sets menu. These sets only stay on the menu while you have the QuicKeys Editor open. When you close it and reopen it, you have to reopen those storage sets as well.

QuicKeys puts a check mark beside the name of the set currently displayed on the Shortcut list.

Options Menu

The Options menu has been reworked so it's less a grab-bag of leftover commands and more a place to go if you want to configure your QuicKeys components, find out how well your shortcuts are performing (using the new Memory command), or reorganize your shortcuts via the various sort commands.

Utilities Menu

A Utilities menu has finally been added to give easy access to QuicKeys' four utilities from the QuicKeys Editor.

Extensions

New extensions, improved extensions, extensions that are no more. The new extensions may be either brand new or combinations of many old extensions into one shortcut (a welcome simplification). Most old extensions have been improved to enhance utility and reliability. A few have been relegated to the QuicKeys 2 Hall of Fame—they're gone. Here's a rundown of the most significant news.

■ **Pop-up Menu (New).** At last! This was probably the greatest failing of previous QuicKeys versions—the inability to select items from pop-up menus. Now QuicKeys can access items in most pop-up menus and record selections from pop-up menus as part of a Sequence.

■ **Phone Dialer (New).** This extension dials the phone using a speaker, modem, or desktop dialing add-on. It may seem unimportant, but we love it (especially the ability to dial a number from the Clipboard).

■ **Jump (New).** Jump improves Sequence control by jumping a certain number of steps forward or backward in a Sequence.

■ **Gosub (New).** Gosub improves Sequence control by jumping to another shortcut from a Sequence and then returning.

■ **NetModemChoosy (New).** The NetModemChoosy extension switches between NetModem and NetSerial setups.

■ **Speak Ease** (**New**). This extension lets you enter text that the Mac can then speak using the new PlainTalk system extension (part of Apple's multimedia Macs).

■ **Scrap Ease (New).** Grab Ease, Type Ease, and Paste Ease have been combined into a single extension.

■ **Decision (New).** Decision replaces the Cursor, Menu, Button, and Window Decision extensions. Used only within a Sequence, Decision branches to other shortcuts based on user-defined conditions.

■ **DoScript (New).** The DoScript extension lets you send a script to a specified application (via the DoScript Apple Event).

■ **AppleScript (New).** The AppleScript extension lets you send an AppleScript for execution.

■ **Apple Events (Revised).** The redesigned Apple Events extension supports more Apple Events, such as object-based events, and provides a more intuitive way to design your own Apple Event parameters.

■ **PowerBook Specials (Revised).** The PowerBook Specials extension has added screen dimming, processor resting, and a Caps Lock indicator for PowerBooks.

■ **Message (Revised).** You can now enter text in a message dialog box. QuicKeys can access the text entered. This provides a way to prompt the user for more information and act on that feedback within a Sequence.

- **Wait (Revised).** The new Wait extension now incorporates the functions of Button Wait, Cursor Wait, Menu Wait, and Window Wait. Waits are automatically recorded as part of a Sequence when used with the new floating Recording palette.

- **Choosy (Revised).** The revised Choosy incorporates the WhichPrinter functions.

- **Mounty (Revised).** The Mounty extension now lets you both mount and dismount volumes by incorporating the DisMounty functions.

- **Folders (Location) (Revised).** Hallelujah! Location has been renamed Folders, which better describes its function. It can now open folders in the Finder.

- **Display Text (Revised).** The Display extension has been renamed Display Text, and you can now print from its text window.

- **(Removed)** Panels, DisMounty, WhichPrinter, and Frontier extensions have been discarded.

Sequence Recorder

The Sequence Recorder now has an expanded variety of shortcuts that it can integrate into Sequences. It now records Wait steps in most Sequences, increasing the reliability of the Sequence. The recorder's controls have been improved, particularly with the addition of floating Recording and Playback Palettes. With the Recording Palette you can pause the recording of Sequences and manually insert shortcuts into the Sequence during the recording session.

QuicKeys Utilities

QuicKeys provides redesigned utilities to install new extensions and shortcuts, print a template of triggering keystrokes, and create Shortcuts. We discuss these utilities in more detail in Chapter 18, *QuicKeys Utilities*. Here is an overview of the revisions to the various utilities.

Instant QuicKeys

Instant QuicKeys provides a tutorial for learning QuicKeys and also gives you a running start on creating your own shortcuts. Instant QuicKeys can now be chosen from the Utilities menu. The program has been redesigned to present a HyperCard-like environment so you can navigate through areas that explain different functional categories of QuicKeys in which you can create various shortcuts.

Shortcut Installer

In the bad old days, transferring sets of shortcuts from one machine to another was an onerous task fraught with potential disaster. Now, the new Shortcut Installer provides an easy method to install sets and extensions. Like the Extension Manager, the Shortcut Installer supports drag and drop, but the Shortcut Installer can also be started with a script.

Extension Manager

The Extension Manager has been redesigned to make it easier to use. The Extension Manager now lets you drag and drop new extensions to install them. Clicking on the new Get Info button displays information about selected extensions. You can also use the Extension Manager to turn extensions on and off.

The Extensions Manager also lets you customize the placement of extensions within the Extensions submenu of the Define menu of the QuicKeys Editor window. Clicking an extension's Preferred checkbox makes the extensions appear above the categories in the Extensions submenu.

QK Template Printer

The venerable Template Printer has received a facelift and a new name—QK Template Printer. The utility still prints templates of your shortcuts and their triggering keystrokes.

2 The Old Kit Bag

It's best to start on any journey fully prepared, and the path to QuicKeys nirvana is no exception. CE Software has outfitted you with two jam-packed disks, a traveler's kit bag that's chock full of items—so many items that, in some cases, you might question why they're included.

In this chapter, we check out the QuicKeys package. We investigate what you need to know about installing QuicKeys on your Mac. We describe how QuicKeys lives inside your machine by revealing the crannies and corners where you can find QuicKeys. And we dump out the entire contents of the QuicKeys kit bag and sort through what's inside.

Inside Your QuicKeys Package

This chapter discusses the installation of QuicKeys 3.0.1, the most recent version of the program. Although the 3.0.1 installation differs substantially from that of QuicKeys 3.0, what gets installed is pretty much the same. So if you have the older version, the bulk of this chapter should still make sense to you. However, if you have a version older than QuicKeys 3.0, this chapter won't do you much good, and you should seriously consider springing for an upgrade.

The newest QuicKeys performs all sorts of tricks that previous versions can't (see Chapter 1, *What's New in QuicKeys 3*), and CE offers a variety of upgrade plans depending on how old your copy of QuicKeys is. So far the company has supported perpetual sanctuary (it's always possible to get an upgrade rather than buy a whole new program), but that can't be guaranteed to go on forever. So if you have version 2.1.3 or earlier, give CE Customer Service a call (see Appendix, *Resources*) and a rep will tell you how to come in from the old.

▪ ▪

The standard installation puts a variety of applications, folders, and files on your hard disk. At first glance, you might wonder what all this stuff is doing there: some you didn't know you were getting, some you may never use, and some you won't find referenced in the manual.

This bounty is due to CE's "be prepared" corporate policy. Standard installation includes just about everything included on the two installation disks, so you get whatever you might possibly need on your hard disk, ready to use. Plus, the wizards at CE constantly upgrade their product and include changes on their disks more quickly than they can publish support literature. Instead, they include Read Me files within different folders to explain what's what. It's great to have the most advanced features, but if you're like us, you don't relish trudging through the mire of Read Me files; you want to jump right in and get to work. To do that, you must first install QuicKeys.

▪ ▪ ▪ ▪ ▪

QuicKeys Installation

The Installer places the QuicKeys elements you need where you need them. The installer automatically either updates an old version of QuicKeys (and its related paraphernalia) or installs a new version if none's already installed.

If you are updating, the Installer removes all old extensions and replaces them with new versions, and it converts old shortcuts to new ones, as needed (for instance, it deletes shortcuts based on Panels, WhichPrinter, DisMounty, and so forth, and replaces them with shortcuts based on new extensions that perform the same functions). In addition, the Installer calculates the memory size your specific QuicKeys configuration needs and allocates that much memory and no more.

The installer gives you very few options, and it makes up for this by being fairly smart. For example, the PowerBook Specials extensions are only installed on PowerBooks; there is no option to install them on a desktop machine, even if you want to (we can't think of why you would, unless you like your Caps Lock key to click when pressed).

Installer. The Installer is located on Install 1. When working with any master disk like this, the cardinal rule is: Don't. Lock the master and then copy it. Forever after, work with the copy.

Insert the copy of your master disk and open the QuicKeys Install icon. The first window introduces you to the Installer and suggests you use the standard installation. Pressing Continue opens a scrolling window that contains the text of the Read Me file (this is a separate file on the disk and can also be read with any text editing program). It's probably

▪ ▪

a good idea to browse through the Read Me file, especially for known conflicts and last-minute information.

Pressing Continue in this window gives you a window with Install and Custom buttons, so you can finally start the installation (see Figure 2.1). This is the place to decide whether you want to perform the recommended standard installation that loads all of QuicKeys and its paraphernalia, or to perform a custom installation where you choose what you want installed from a list. Either choice elicits a dialog box informing you that you will have to restart when the installation is complete.

Figure 2.1
QuicKeys Installer
dialog box

If you are running virus protection, you may need to remove it from your system before you start the installation process because virus scanners and installers do not mix very well. (Remove the virus protection program's icon from your System:Extensions folder and drag it onto your desktop. Restart your Mac and open the Installer again.) Indeed, some setups require you to turn off all your system extensions (restart your computer while holding down Shift) to get QuicKeys to load properly, although this is less of a problem with the new installer than it was with the old one.

Standard installation. Pressing the Install button begins the process of installing the total QuicKeys program without letting you select parts of the program not to install. With the standard installation, QuicKeys takes up the most room on your hard disk, since just about every extension, utility, supporting application, and whatnot is installed. So, if you have limited storage space, consider using the custom installation procedure discussed in the next section. Neither type of installation lets you choose where things go, which makes sense for the guts of the program that get installed in various places within your System folder. With the standard installation you also receive a mega folder (QuicKeys Tools) on the top level of your startup hard drive. It's stuffed with odds and ends (none is required to make QuicKeys function, but some may be very useful to you).

Custom install. The QuicKeys Installer provides you with a Custom button, which brings up the Custom Install window (see Figure 2.2), in which you can select parts of the program and related materials to install. The components are grouped into three sections.

■ **All QuicKeys software.** The top section has one option that installs essentially everything. This option gives the same results as if you had used the standard installation.

■ **Basic components.** This section includes QuicKeys, the four QuicKey utilities, CEToolbox (a support program that QuicKeys needs to operate), basic and additional extensions, DialogKeys (a control panel device with which you can navigate through dialog box options with keystrokes), and speech support.

■ **Supporting materials.** This section includes Support Tools (some small applications that can identify problems you may have with QuicKeys), Example Sets (predefined sets and some Apple Event information), Special Documentation (scripting QuicKeys and integrating QuicKeys with HyperCard), and Keyboard INITs (for third-party keyboards used with a Mac Plus).

Figure 2.2
The QuicKeys
Custom Install
Dialog Box

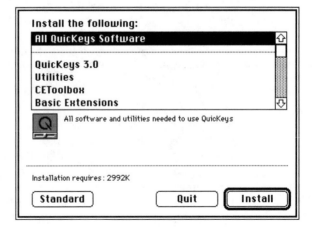

10

The Custom Install option can be useful when you want to tweak the installation, but not as useful as it could be. Even though the standard installation will undoubtedly install something you won't use, trying to include just the items you want with the custom installation probably won't work because the components aren't divided into enough options. So you will likely want to follow CE's suggestion of using the standard installation and then getting rid of items you don't need. This is fairly simple because almost all extraneous material installed will be in the large QuicKeys Tools folder, where it is easy to deal with. Don't know what to keep and what to throw out? Refer to "Thumbs Up/Thumbs Down" later in this chapter.

Confirming the installation. After you install QuicKeys on your Mac and restart, you might notice something—there isn't much to notice. QuicKeys sits invisible in the background of your computing environment. However, there are a few ways in which you can reveal that QuicKeys actually lurks inside your computer, waiting to do your bidding.

■ **Check the Apple menu.** You can verify that QuicKeys is installed and active on your machine by pulling down the Apple menu and seeing if QuicKeys is there.

■ **Activate a shortcut.** Type in an activating keystroke combination for a shortcut. If you have none available yet, see the next chapter, *The Gateway to QuicKeys Knowledge*.

■ **Notice the Startup icon.** If QuicKeys is loaded, its icon appears during startup.

Where Does It Go?

Here's a quick rundown of where everything goes. You will find a complete description of each item in "The Necessary" and "The Helpful," later in this chapter.

Control Panels folder. The Control Panels folder resides in the System, or "blessed," folder. The Installer places the main component of QuicKeys, the QuicKeys control panel, here.

Extensions folder. The Installer places CEToolbox and QuicKeys Toolbox here. On AV machines, you'll also find the files Speech Handler and Speech Rules here.

Preferences folder. The Installer creates a CEToolbox Preferences file in the Preferences folder. In addition, the Installer creates a QuicKeys

■ ■

folder here that contains many QuicKeys program elements in several sub-folders. This folder's size will increase as you create more shortcuts.

QuicKeys folder. The QuicKeys folder acts as the central repository of many QuicKeys elements. Unless you are curious, you should never have to visit this folder. Don't move or remove items in these folders unless you are really sure you know what you are doing.

The Installer places the QK.HELP file (which contains Balloon Help) in the top layer of the QuicKeys folder. After you create preferences for QuicKeys and use the QuicKeys Template Printer, their preference files will also go here. A small application, QuicKeys Registration, that initially confirms your serial number, also lives here (until you kill it; see "The Helpful," later in this chapter).

The QuicKeys folder also contains a number of other folders.

■ **Clipboards.** Contains the text or graphics that you save as clips for use with the ScrapEase extension.

■ **Extensions.** Contains the QuicKeys extensions that have been installed (note that these are different from System extensions; these are additional types of shortcuts that you can create via QuicKeys' Define menu).

■ **Keysets.** Contains the different sets of shortcuts. (In previous versions, sets were called keysets, and the name change hasn't made it over to the folder name.)

■ **Macros.** Contains Real Time shortcuts. No one knows why the name is called Macros.

■ **Sequences.** Contains Sequence shortcuts.

■ **Templates.** Contains the templates for different keyboard types that the QK Template Printer uses.

■ **Utilities.** Contains the four QuicKey utilities.

QuicKeys Tools folder. A standard installation puts a 600 + K folder on the top level of your startup disk. The folder contains seven other folders. Here's what's inside.

■ **Keyboard INITs.** Contains some small system-level aids for using third-party keyboards with the Mac Plus.

■ **QuicKeys Example Sets.** Contains different QuicKeys sets. Also includes documentation illustrating examples of integrating QuicKeys with applications using Apple Events.

■ ■

■ **QuicKeys Programmer Files.** Includes documentation and examples for those who want to program the Shortcut Installer or write QuicKey extensions or programs that trigger QuicKeys shortcuts.

■ **QuicKeys Script Info.** Contains documentation and examples for using QuicKeys Script, QuicKeys' internal scripting language, with OSA (Open Scripting Architecture).

■ **QuicKeys Support Tools.** Contains two small applications: one for configuring CEToolbox and the other for checking sequence integrity.

■ **QuicKeys XCMD.** Contains some code that can be added to HyperCard to enable it to trigger QuicKeys shortcuts.

■ **TAA.** The Technical Assistance Assistant is a small diagnostic aid to help determine what might be interfering with your QuicKeys shortcuts.

Thumbs Up/ Thumbs Down

Some items your QuicKeys package includes are necessary, some are merely helpful, and some are only required for specialized applications. Here's a rundown of what you paid for.

The Necessary

These files are necessary to make QuicKeys function. Be sure to check out "The Helpful" to ensure you have everything that allows QuicKeys to work at its best within your configuration.

QuicKeys program. The main QuicKeys program comes in the form of the QuicKeys control panel. This is what you thought you were buying. You have to restart your Mac after installing QuicKeys, because the Mac loads control panels only during startup.

CEToolbox. CEToolbox is a system extension, a little program that loads during startup. As with the QuicKeys control panel, you have to restart your Mac after it's installed. Several CE programs take advantage of CEToolbox; it handles these tasks.

■ Makes QuicKeys show up on the Apple menu or on the menu bar in a variety of configurations.

■ Enables File Launch shortcuts to work (so you can launch programs and open documents with QuicKeys).

■ Enables keystrokes to be displayed and edited in the QuicKeys Editor window.

■ Watches for keystrokes that trigger shortcuts and tells QuicKeys when it see them.

The Installer places CEToolbox into the Extensions folder in your System folder. If for some reason it isn't there, you'll get a message when you boot. You can only operate QuicKeys in a crippled form without CEToolbox; that puts it on our necessities list.

We discuss the CEToolbox options in more detail in Chapter 4, *The QuicKeys Cockpit*.

QuicKeys Toolbox. We put the QuicKeys Toolbox in "The Necessary" because IAC (inter-application communication), also called Apple Events, is one of the *big* evolutions of the Mac, and QuicKeys Toolbox helps QuicKeys take great advantage of it. We used to list this system extension (when it had another name, CEIAC) in "The Helpful" because in those days most applications weren't Apple Event aware. Now enough players in the Mac environment have adopted this technology to make it useful.

QuicKeys Toolbox is the *gateway* through which the Apple Event *messages* (or commands) are sent to and from QuicKeys. For Excel to send an Apple Event message to QuicKeys to trigger a shortcut, for instance, it sends the message to QuicKeys Toolbox, and QuicKeys Toolbox passes it on. QuicKeys Toolbox is also required to use QuicKeys Script. QuicKeys Toolbox is copied into the appropriate folder in the System folder when you install extensions such as DoScript, AppleScript, Apple Events, or Finder Events that require QuicKeys Toolbox to function.

Extensions. Extensions are additions to the QuicKeys program that perform various specialized functions. You can think of extensions as the citrus juicer or the dough blade attachments for your Cuisinart (or the hole cutter, circular sander, or grinding wheel attachments for your electric drill, if you're of that persuasion). They're extras that work with the same mother machine to make it more versatile. The sublime aspects of extensions are that CE and outside programmers produce more of them all the time, and (so far) they are inexpensive or free.

Extensions should reside in the System:Preferences:QuicKeys: Extensions folder. QuicKeys can only access extensions that are in the Extensions folder.

Extension Manager. The Extension Manager is a little application that lets you install and control your QuicKeys extensions. The Installer only installs those extensions that came with the original program; you need to use the Extension Manager to install any new extensions that you subsequently receive, as well as any third-party extensions that you may acquire. Although you can probably get away with just dragging new extensions into the Extensions folder inside the QuicKeys folder, to avoid possible memory troubles, you should use the Extension Manager, which is why we deem it necessary.

Read Me files. These files contain the latest information on the particular version of QuicKeys that you received, so they're worth glancing through to see if anything important pertains to your system configuration. You never know what earth-shaking item will show up in a Read Me file. So you should definitely take a look at "Read Me (QuicKeys v3.0)" on Install 1 and the other Read Me files in The QuicKeys Tools folder.

QuicKeys Registration. QuicKeys Registration is a little (30K) application that starts automatically when you first launch QuicKeys. It asks for your serial number and name and then blesses your copy of QuicKeys so you won't be queried again. Oh yes, it also sits in your QuicKeys folder, wasting 30K of disk space, so after it has fulfilled its role, you can get rid of it. If for some reason you need it again, just re-install QuicKeys.

The Helpful

These items aren't absolutely critical to make QuicKeys function. But you will probably want to use some of them. The others you may want to get rid of to conserve disk space. They are always available on your original QuicKeys installation disks. Three of these helpful items (Template Printer, Instant QuicKeys, and Shortcut Installer) are described in detail in Chapter 18, *QuicKeys Utilities*.

DialogKeys. DialogKeys is a control panel that serves as a natural accompaniment to QuicKeys: it puts keystroke control into dialog boxes—just dialog boxes. When DialogKeys is active, you can tab through the buttons in the dialog box and choose the one you want by pressing a key—a function that usually requires the mouse.

DialogKeys comes with three keystrokes preset for its four functions (Click performs two functions: starts DialogKeys and clicks the blinking button). You can change these presets through the DialogKeys Control Panel (see Figure 2.3).

Because QuicKeys can accomplish many of the same things DialogKeys does, Don doesn't install it. Steve uses it intermittently, and there is no doubt that DialogKeys works well for those who want to be able to click buttons without resorting to a mouse.

The standard installation does not install DialogKeys. You must use the custom installation and choose DialogKeys from the scrolling list of installation options to install it.

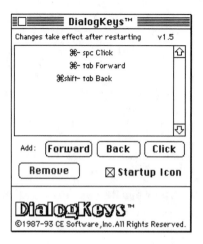

Figure 2.3
DialogKeys cdev

QK.Help. QK.Help is the Balloon Help file. Balloon Help isn't too help-ful for us, but CE views it as providing hints, and it does that well. If you are just learning QuicKeys, it may untangle some of your conundrums. The QK.Help file isn't very big (34K), so we leave it in our QuicKeys Folder for grins.

Template Printer. Using the Template Printer application, you can print a schematic of your keyboard with the names of your QuicKeys located right on top of their appropriate activation keys.

You definitely don't need this, but it can come in handy if you want to look at your shortcut keystroke distribution patterns (ours seem to bunch up on the left and right sides of the keyboard). However, if you don't intend to print templates, consider moving the 228K Template Printer from the Utilities folder to the Trash. And don't forget the Templates folder that holds the different keyboard templates the Template Printer uses.

Instant QuicKeys. CE Software created the very cool (albeit somewhat confusing) Instant QuicKeys utility application to try to solve the perennial problem with QuicKeys: people bought the program and then didn't use it. Instant QuicKeys leads you through the task of building a stable of handy shortcuts that work for your unique computing environment. We applaud the intent, even though the execution might be tweaked a bit.

Consider trying Instant QuicKeys (see Chapter 18, *QuicKeys Utili-ties*), but if you don't need help figuring out which shortcuts you need, and you do need more disk space, consider sending the 298K applica-tion (in the Utilities folder) to an instant end in the Trash.

Shortcut Installer. Another QuicKeys utility, the Shortcut Installer, helps the process of moving sets of shortcuts from one machine to another. It is deemed only helpful because it is possible to install shortcuts without it. However, it comes in handy and it will run from a script, which is great—great enough to stay in our Utilities folder.

Example Sets. In the QuicKeys Example Sets folder of the QuicKeys Tools folder, CE has provided a potpourri of set examples, some of which you may want to incorporate into your own environment. You can use the Shortcut Installer (see Chapter 18, *QuicKey Utilities*) to install these sets on your Mac. Three folders within the QuicKeys Example Sets folder contain these example sets.

- **Misc. Examples.** The Misc. Examples folder holds a diverse variety of sets. Two sets (Alias Keystroke set and Extended Keyboard Alias set) contain Alias Keystroke shortcuts that map keyboard keys to themselves. These can come in handy when you want an application set to lock out any keystrokes that trigger Universal Set shortcuts. Also, the extended keyboard set can supply useful keystrokes to Macs (for example, PowerBooks) that don't have them. The More Universal Shortcuts Set contains shortcuts that CE thinks you might want to include in your Universal Set. They're worth checking out, as are the remaining sets that give a few specialized shortcuts. These sets are small, so we have left them on our machines.

- **PowerBook Sets.** The PowerBook Sets folder holds two sets of short-cuts for PowerBooks. One (Calculator Set) contains shortcuts that make up a virtual keypad on the PowerBook's abbreviated keyboard. The other set (PowerBook Universal Set) contains the virtual keypad shortcuts and more. If you don't have or intend to have a PowerBook, you can get rid of these. If you do have a PowerBook, see Chapter 10, *Shortcuts for PowerBooks,* for more on these sets.

- **QuickMail Sets**. These two sets do what you expect: provide shortcuts for use with QuickMail. We use QuickMail so we find them useful. If you don't, you won't.

The Specialized Well, aren't you special? If so, you might need one of these. If not, consider unloading them.

Keyboard INITs. We had a lively discussion trying to guess how many people might actually have a use for these INITs. To need them you need a MacPlus with a third-party keyboard (and you must be running

System 7 with this Plus or you can't use QuicKeys 3). Of course, if CE left them out, someone would be bound to complain. For the rest of you, chuck 'em—they're in the QuicKeys Tools folder.

Apple Events Examples. Inside your QuicKeys Example Sets folder you'll find Apple Events Examples, a MicroViewer-based application that gives examples of sending Apple Events between QuicKeys and FileMaker Pro, and between QuicKeys and HyperCard. If you want to familiarize yourself with the techniques of sending and receiving Apple Events with QuicKeys, you'll want to read this document, even though you may be disappointed at how little AppleScript is mentioned. See Chapter 16, *Apple Events and Scripting*, for a description of using Apple Events with QuicKeys.

QuicKeys Script information. Many programs contain their own internal scripting language, and QuicKeys is no exception. With QuicKeys Script you can write script-based shortcuts using any OSA-compliant script editor (OSA stands for Open Scripting Architecture—Apple's method of sending scripting languages via Apple Events). Extensive documentation and a few examples for such state-of-the-art scripting are included in the QuicKeys Script Info folder.

Programmer files. One of the nice things about QuicKeys is that it constantly evolves—not only through the efforts of the people at CE, but also through the work of independent programmers. These programmers create new extensions and, so far, have generously made them available to CE to distribute to QuicKeys owners.

To promote and support this arrangement, CE includes the QuicKeys Programmer Files folder in the QuicKeys Tools folder. If you weren't, aren't, and never intend to be a programmer, you can ignore or throw out this folder. It contains aids for developing extensions and installer scripts including icons, source code in both C and Pascal, and documentation.

QuicKeys XCMD. This folder contains an XCMD and its companion Read Me file. An XCMD is a small HyperCard extension that you can copy into your HyperCard application (using a resource editing or copying program). It gives your HyperCard program the ability to access QuicKeys directly from its scripts. If you don't program in HyperCard (or any other program that supports XCMDs), you won't need this; your usual shortcuts will work in HyperCard with normal keyboard activation.

TAA. When we first saw this, we had some fun creating possible meanings for this acronym, but we never came close to the real root—Technical Assistance Assistant. TAA (rhymes with FAA) inspects your entire Mac system from head to toe. It checks out certain important system files, memory, system extensions, control panels, fonts, drivers, and more.

Why would you need it? Most people don't. CE includes it as an aid for its technical assistance staff. If you experience a problem with QuicKeys and petition CE technical support personnel for aid, they will sometimes ask you to send them a TAA report.

QuicKeys support tools. This folder in the QuicKeys Tools folder is a companion to the TAA folder; it contains a tool, QK Disconnect, that you can use to check the integrity of Sequences, and Configure CEToolbox, that you can use to determine where you can set options for the CEToolbox, including where the QuicKeys menu appears. We haven't found a use for QK Disconnect yet, but keep it around in case a call to CE Technical Support elicits a request for its use. We keep Configure CEToolbox around in case we need to change the QuicKeys menu location after we have hidden CEToolbox.

Beyond This Point

Now that you know how to install QuicKeys and where all its components go, you are ready to start the adventure of learning about the parts of QuicKeys, as well as some common rules for working with shortcut sets that will make your search for QuicKeys nirvana that much smoother.

3 The Gateway to QuicKeys Knowledge

I f you don't have much experience with QuicKeys, read this chapter. It explains the conceptual underpinnings of the program—how QuicKeys works, where you'll most likely use it, and what you ought to know before you begin. This chapter will familiarize you with some of the sights and sounds you'll encounter on your ever-accelerating journey to QuicKeys nirvana.

QuicKeys Nirvana

What is QuicKeys nirvana? It's increasing your efficiency, going home early, mesmerizing your boss with flying fingers and flashing screens, feeling the heady pride of capturing the potential speed that's been lying dormant within your Mac.

Ultimately, like any good nirvana, what you find when you achieve it all depends on what you're after. QuicKeys, like any computer tool, only provides you with help in accomplishing something—how wisely and creatively you use QuicKeys as a tool is up to you. Luckily, you sought the right help (us), and we're going to make it easy for you to maximize your relationship with QuicKeys and minimize the pain.

QuicKeys is based on shortcuts—small programs that automatically perform various tasks. You usually create your most valuable shortcuts yourself, because they will be customized to your setup and your needs. But you may also find a use for those shortcuts that CE Software has included in the package. We have described many incredibly useful and creative shortcuts in this book; all you have to do is enter them into the program and you'll be ready to go. Shortcuts are also available from online services such as CompuServe and America Online (see Appendix, *Resources*).

■ ■ ■ ■ ■
**A Useful
Shortcut**

The best way to illustrate how QuicKeys works in real life is to build a simple shortcut to open a file. Opening a file is simple stuff, but it can be the basic building block for a whole slew of other shortcuts when you link shortcuts together to form Sequences. We'll discuss building Sequences in more detail in Chapters 14 and 15.

**Creating and
Triggering a
Sample Shortcut**

We'll start by creating a shortcut that opens a Microsoft Word file.

1. Choose QuicKeys from the Apple Menu. The QuicKeys Editor window, similar to that shown in Figure 3.1, appears.

Figure 3.1
QuicKeys Editor
window

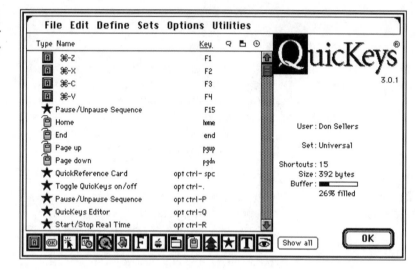

2. Make sure that Universal Set is checked in the Sets menu. If it isn't, then select it.

3. Choose File Launch from the Define menu (see Figure 3.2).

4. The Open dialog box appears. Navigate to the file you want to open. My target file is called QK-Gateway.wrd (the Word document for this chapter, in fact).

5. Select the document you want to launch by double-clicking on it.

6. The shortcut edit dialog box for File Launch appears (see Figure 3.3). Note that your selected document's name is already entered in the pop-up menu and that the file's type and creator are listed below the name.

7. Enter a keystroke combination in the Keystroke box (click in the box, then press the key combination you want to use to trigger the shortcut). We'll use Control-Option-L.

8. Click on the Include in QuicKeys Menu checkbox if you want to access this shortcut from the QuicKeys menu.

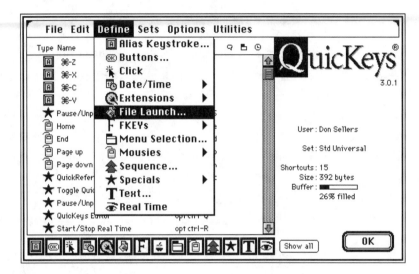

Figure 3.2
Choosing File Launch from the Define menu

Figure 3.3
File Launch edit dialog box

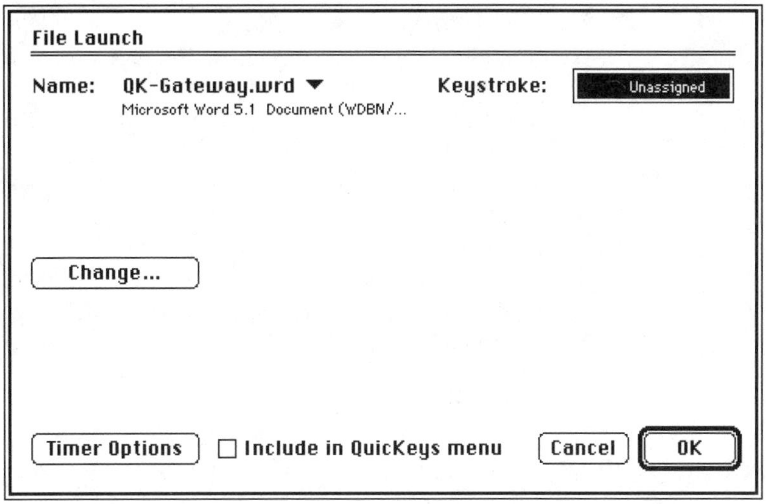

9. Click OK. The QuicKeys Editor window returns with your new short-cut displayed in its Shortcut window next to a File Launch icon. Click OK again, and you're finished.

Now that you've created a shortcut, there are (at least) three ways to trigger it.

■ Press the invoking keystroke that you typed in step 7.

■ If you clicked the Include in QuicKeys Menu checkbox in step 8, you can choose your shortcut from the QuicKeys menu (on the Apple menu, unless you've changed its position by configuring CEToolbox).

■ Open the QuickReference Card from the QuicKeys menu, and click on the shortcut.

The Ugly Macro

Before we go any further, we need to point out that there are shortcuts, and then there are shortcuts. There are good, bad, and ugly ways to construct shortcuts.

Chris Wallace, the technical support guru at CE Software, told us about a call he once received. The caller (let's call him Bob) had built a shortcut for opening a particular file. Bob understood that macro programs are sup-posed to automate what he does when operating his Mac. Bob wanted to open a Microsoft Word file that was buried in a series of folders. He wasn't exactly sure of the best way to accomplish this, but he knew that QuicKeys had a special feature that could help him, the Record Sequence function.

So to open his file, Bob selected Record Sequence from the QuicKeys menu and then double-clicked on his folder, Bob's folder. That folder opened to display a lot of other folders. He then double-clicked on the Miscellaneous folder and then on the file, Do Immediately!, he had stored there.

QuicKeys recorded and interpreted Bob's actions. When Bob tried to open the file by invoking the shortcut, it worked—until he decided that the Do Immediately file should be moved to another folder. Bob moved his file, but when he tried to open it with his old shortcut, another file opened instead! Bob called Chris Wallace for help. (If you tap out your own resources, CE Software Support likes to be called early in the morning—9 to 11 A.M., Central Time; that's when their lines are least busy, and their minds least boggled.)

QuicK and Dirty

Chris Wallace realized that Bob's shortcut looked something like the shortcut in Figure 3.4.

Figure 3.4
Bob's shortcut

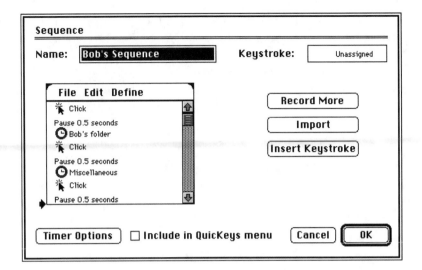

The Record Sequence feature had interpreted Bob's actions of opening his file as three double-clicks in different areas of the screen and had dutifully recorded them, along with some special timing steps in between. Now that Bob's target file was moved, there was no way to simply edit his shortcut to retain its function.

The Elegant Macro

Bob's shortcut worked, but it was the wrong shortcut type for his job. A shortcut needs to be tailored to the specifics of its task, and it also needs to be adaptable to normal changing conditions within the Mac environment. You can fulfill both of these requirements by using the right tool.

In the case of Bob's shortcut, he could have used the File Launch shortcut type—the same one we used for the sample shortcut at the beginning of the chapter—instead of a Sequence made up of double-clicks. Because File Launch shortcuts keep track of their target files via System 7's Alias Manager, he could then move the target file anywhere on his hard disk, and the shortcut would still find it.

Using the Sequence Recorder

Even though Bob's Sequence didn't work as well as it could have, don't consider this a universal condemnation of the Sequence Recorder. It's often the easiest way to create a simple shortcut quickly, and it can be a sophisticated tool for helping you create Sequence shortcuts. We use the Sequence Recorder all the time.

Especially helpful for creating simple shortcuts is a variant of the Sequence Recorder on the QuicKeys menu: Record One Shortcut. This command creates a shortcut out of the next single action you perform. Don uses Record One Shortcut so much, he has created his own Menu Selection shortcut to trigger it.

Recording Palette. What's that panel of strange icons that appears when you start the Sequence Recorder? It's the Recording Palette (see

Figure 3.5
Recording Palette

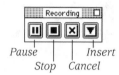

Pause   *Insert*
    Stop   *Cancel*

Figure 3.5). It lets you pause, stop, or cancel recording (options also available on the QuicKeys menu) and insert another shortcut in your Sequence. For more on the Recording Palette, see Chapter 14, *The Sequence*.

The Right Tool

The key to choosing the right tool for your job is to first consider how the Mac goes about doing the job you want it to do. Hang on. You don't have to know the specifics of how the ROM talks to the ADB in the entire Mac family; you just need to have a sense of some of the Mac's broad functions.

There are two main ways to make QuicKeys work for you: use the right tool, and take advantage of available shortcuts in applications and the operating system.

Choose your category. When you make a shortcut, ask yourself which category your tool is in. We cover each of these categories in a chapter, as outlined in the Preface.

Use existing shortcuts. After you have the right tool, use it well. Incorporate *existing* keyboard equivalents into your shortcuts wherever possible.

■ Command-Up arrow in Open and Save dialog boxes moves you up a folder level.

■ Enter is the same as OK or the outlined default button in most dialog boxes.

■ Command-. (period) is often the same as Cancel, especially in Open and Save dialog boxes.

■ Use command-key equivalents that are built into your applications (use the Alias Keystrokes shortcut type to access these built-in commands).

■ Use Alias Keystrokes instead of Text shortcuts in Sequences, where feasible.

■ Use DialogKeys in Sequences with Alias Keystroke shortcuts.

■ Use your word processor's keyboard cursor-movement and selection keys to manipulate text.

These are just a few examples of how you can use functions that are built into the Mac and your software to improve your shortcuts. Keep an eye out for others, and you'll find shortcut building a lot easier.

Sets

Different shortcuts are stored together as sets in QuicKeys. QuicKeys automatically creates a set for each application as you open it and maintains a set for each application for which you create a shortcut. For example, if you are working in Microsoft Word and you create a shortcut that enters some specific text, that shortcut is saved in the Microsoft Word set which QuicKeys automatically created, ready for you to use.

Universal set. QuicKeys also has a special set that is open whenever QuicKeys is running. This is the all-powerful and appropriately named Universal Set. It contains the shortcuts that you might want to trigger from *any* application. For example, if you want to standardize Command-S as the Save command for all your applications (some of them aren't designed that way; we don't know why), you include that shortcut in the Universal set.

The Sets menu. The Sets menu in the QuicKeys Editor window helps clarify the organization of your sets and shortcuts, listing currently usable sets and inactive sets through their placement on its menu (see Figure 3.6). The Sets menu has three sections. A check mark indicates the set whose shortcuts are currently displayed in the QuicKeys Editor window.

■ **Active sets.** There are only two active sets at any one time: the Universal set and the current application (the application window in

Figure 3.6
Sets menu

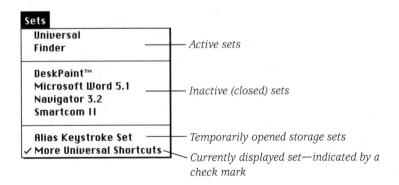

front) set are listed on top because they are the only sets that are active. Shortcuts can only be triggered if they are in an active set.

■ **Inactive sets.** The second section lists, in alphabetical order, all sets residing in your Keysets folder. When an application that has the same name as an inactive set is opened and on top (active), QuicKeys makes the application's shortcut set active. So an inactive set doesn't necessarily mean that its corresponding application isn't running, just that it isn't on top.

■ **Storage sets.** The last section displays sets that you open manually using the Open Set command from the File menu. Shortcuts in a storage set can be copied and pasted into either inactive or active sets. Storage sets are useful for transferring sets between machines. The names of these manually opened sets only remain on the menu until you close the QuicKeys Editor.

Copying and Pasting Shortcuts

If you have a shortcut in one set (for instance, your Microsoft Word set) and want to copy or move it to another set (for instance, PageMaker's), it's a simple matter of cut and paste.

1. Use the Sets menu to open the set containing your shortcut.

2. Click on the shortcut to select it, and cut or copy it (you can use the Edit menu, or the standard Mac shortcuts: Command-X and Command-C). You can select multiple shortcuts for cutting or copying by holding down the Shift key and clicking or dragging on the shortcuts you want. Use Select All from the Edit menu (or Command-A) to select all shortcuts in the set.

3. Open the set you want to put the shortcut into, and paste it in (from the Edit menu or with Command-V).

You can remove shortcuts from a set using the same techniques. Just select the shortcut(s) you want to remove, and use Cut, Clear, or Delete.

These techniques also work within the Sequence editor dialog box (see Chapter 14, *The Sequence*), so you can copy and paste shortcuts between sets and Sequences, and vice versa.

Set Clarity

Sets can be confusing, since they seem to appear out of nowhere. We provide some set clarity rules here to help you master sets and dispel this confusion.

Set Clarity Rule One

At any one time there are only two active sets from which you can trigger shortcuts.

- **The Universal set.** This set is always open and its shortcuts are always available for activation in any application.

- **An Application set.** This set becomes active automatically when you activate an application of the same name. Each application set is a specialist, targeted to a specific application.

So where do you put your new shortcut? If you want to be able to access it from any application, put it in the Universal set. If it is application-specific (designed to work only with a specific application), put it in that application's set.

Our shortcut that called up the chapter document went into the Universal set because we might access it at any time. It could have also been placed in the Microsoft Word set. To place a shortcut in an inactive set, select the set from the second section on the menu. The shortcut you build will automatically be saved in that set when you eventually click OK to close the QuicKeys Editor window (or select Save from the File menu).

Set Clarity Rule Two

An application set's shortcuts are only available for activation while its companion application is active.

When you open an application like Microsoft Word, QuicKeys automatically makes its Microsoft Word set active. If you build some shortcuts and put them in this set, they are available to be triggered whenever you are working in Microsoft Word. When you close Word, QuicKeys closes its set. When you open Word again, that set will again be available. QuicKeys takes care of all this housekeeping in the background.

QuicKeys finds an application set for each application as you open it because QuicKeys names the set with *exactly the same name* as the application and then puts it in a folder labeled Keysets (the path to this folder is System Folder:Preferences:QuicKeys folder:Keysets).

You can name any set in the Keysets folder with exactly the same name as an application, and it will act as that application's set. But don't let two applications or two sets have identical names, because QuicKeys won't be able to distinguish between them.

One implication of this exact-naming convention: if you upgrade to a new version of a program or change the name of the application (from Microsoft Word to Word, for instance), QuicKeys won't open that application's set anymore. The names are different, so it creates a new empty set with the new application's name. There are two simple ways to solve this problem. Choose one.

■ In the QuicKeys Editor window, open the old set. Select all the shortcuts (hold down Shift and drag across all of them, or press Command-A, or use Select All from the Edit menu), copy them, switch to the new set, and paste them.

■ Rename the old set so its name matches the new application's name exactly.

Set Clarity Rule Three

Shortcuts cannot be triggered directly from storage sets, but they can be transferred to sets from which they can be activated.

CE Software has included some sample shortcut sets in your package (see "Example Sets," in Chapter 2, *The Old Kit Bag*). One of them, More Universal Keys, is a good example of a robust set. You can open it from the QuicKeys Editor window by selecting Open Sets from the File menu (or pressing Command-O). A standard Open dialog box will appear. Select the More Universal Keys set from the file list by either double-clicking on it or highlighting it and clicking the Open button. More Universal Keys appears on the bottom of the set's menu list, and the Shortcut window of the QuicKeys Editor window fills with a list of this set's shortcuts.

You can copy shortcuts out of the More Universal Keys set and paste them into the Universal Set or any application set.

Set Clarity Rule Four

An application set's triggering keystrokes take precedence over the Universal set's triggering keystrokes, which take precedence over the application's triggering keystrokes.

Whew! What does that mean? First, let's just take the case of the application set and the Universal set. If you have two shortcuts, one in either set, that have identical triggering keystrokes, the one that will be triggered is in the application's set. So if Control-C is the trigger in the Universal set for launching Disk Copy, but Control-C is also the command in your terminal emulation application for triggering a QuicKeys Sequence that closes a session, when you press Control-C in the terminal emulation application, you get close session, not Disk Copy.

Simple. The application-specific shortcut overrides the Universal shortcut. But what if the terminal emulation program has a built-in Control-C keystroke that internally triggers a Cancel command? It will never get triggered, because either the application shortcut or the universal shortcut will override it.

In practice, this works out well. In fact, the application set can be used to protect applications that have keystrokes identical to those in the Universal set. Let's change the previous example slightly: say you still have the Universal set's Control-C trigger for Disk Copy, but now you have removed the shortcut in the application set with that same keystroke. Now, when you are in the terminal emulation program, you press Control-C, hoping to get its Cancel command. But instead, the Universal set shortcut confounds you by opening Disk Copy.

So you put an Alias Keystroke shortcut in the application set that maps Control-C to Control-C. Now when you press Control-C, the application set's Alias Keystroke shortcut triggers, passing Control-C to the application. The application sees Control-C and triggers its Cancel command.

Triggers and Targets

Before we make our way through the final gateway to QuicKeys nirvana, we'd like to pass through two other portals—triggers and targets. While it might sound like we're talking about semi-automatic weapons, we're actually talking about another kind of automation: how you trigger your shortcuts and what they act on once you've triggered them.

Triggers

Most people think of shortcuts as being triggered by a keystroke, but in fact there are at least nine different ways to trigger shortcuts.

Keystrokes. You most commonly trigger shortcuts with keystrokes. For example, Don triggers his QuicKeys Editor shortcut with Control-Option-Q. Steve launches Microsoft Word with Control-W. You can assign a keystroke to a shortcut in the QuicKeys Editor window or in the Shortcut Edit dialog box for the shortcut.

QuickReference Card. You can trigger a shortcut by clicking on the shortcut in the QuickReference Card. You can display the QuickReference Card by selecting it from the QuicKeys menu (or triggering the QuickReference Card shortcut; see Chapter 13, *Shortcuts That Control QuicKeys*). We discuss the QuickReference Card in more detail in Chapter 4, *The QuicKeys Cockpit*.

QuicKeys menu item. If you have the Include in QuicKeys Menu checkbox selected for a shortcut, you can trigger the shortcut by selecting it from the QuicKeys menu. You can also put a shortcut on the QuicKeys menu by clicking in the menu column of the QuicKeys Editor's shortcut list. For more on configuring the location of the QuicKeys menu, see "Configuring QuicKeys" in Chapter 4, *The QuicKeys Cockpit*.

Timer. You can set shortcuts to trigger at a certain time or at intervals. You can set up timed triggering by clicking in the Timer column of the QuicKeys Editor's shortcut list or by clicking the Timer options button in the shortcut's Edit window. We discuss time-based triggers in more detail in Chapter 4, *The QuicKeys Cockpit*.

SoftKeys Palette. You can build a SoftKeys Palette which can be used to trigger up to 10 different shortcuts. You'll find the rundown on SoftKeys Palettes in Chapter 13, *Shortcuts that Control QuicKeys*.

QuicKeys icon. Shortcuts can be made into little applications that can be run by double-clicking in the Finder, like any application. For more on QuicKeys Icons, see Chapter 4, *The QuicKeys Cockpit*.

Speech. If you have a correctly equipped Mac (like a Quadra 660av or 840av), you can trigger shortcuts with speech.

Apple Events. Programs that can send Apple Events, such as AppleScript, HyperCard, and Frontier, can trigger shortcuts by talking to QuicKeys via the QuicKeys Toolbox. All the excruciating details are waiting for you in Chapter 16, *Apple Events and Scripting*.

XCMDs. If you incorporate the XCMD that comes with QuicKeys into a HyperCard stack, that stack can then trigger shortcuts as part of its operation.

Targets

Some shortcuts only influence one target. For example, a File Launch shortcut opens one specific file. So it is likely you will have lots of File Launch shortcuts—different ones to open each of your important applications and documents. The same is true of AppleScript shortcuts; each one targets a particular application and possibly a particular document.

Other shortcuts are untargeted—affecting no specific object. These untargeted shortcuts may display a dialog box that allows you to select the target-of-the-moment. Usually, you only need one representative of an untargeted shortcut in your sets. The Transfer shortcut is a good example of an untargeted shortcut type. When you trigger the Transfer shortcut, a dialog box appears asking you what file you wish to open.

Achieving Nirvana

Now that we've decided where we're going (QuicKeys nirvana, of course), in the next chapter we'll check out the resources available to succor the pilgrim (that's you, pilgrim) on the way.

4 The QuicKeys Cockpit

Before we wander farther along the path to QuicKeys nirvana, we'd like to familiarize you with the lay of the land. In this chapter we introduce the QuicKeys Editor window. It's QuicKeys' home port—the place where you'll start creating shortcuts and where you'll always return after creating them. We'll also introduce the QuicKeys menu bar and its many uses, as well as point out strategies for placing sets and utilities on different menus.

The QuicKeys Editor Window

The QuicKeys Editor window—what you get when you select QuicKeys from the Apple menu—is the central control room for working with QuicKeys. From here, you can access almost every other piece of the sprawling complex that is QuicKeys. Some features in the QuicKeys Editor window you use frequently, others seldom. Some of its controls are intuitive, and others...well, we'll explain how they work.

A Stroll Through the QuicKeys Editor Window

Let's take a look at the QuicKeys Editor window (see Figure 4.1). The middle area is blank if you haven't got any shortcuts in the set it is displaying.

When the QuicKeys Editor window is open, you can't do much except work within the QuicKeys environment. The QuicKeys Editor window is a modal window; it essentially deactivates everything else on your desktop. Many QuicKeys Editor window's areas are active—you can perform some operations by clicking on them.

It looks pretty straightforward, but the QuicKeys Editor window's simple appearance belies its complexity. Here are its main features.

Figure 4.1
QuicKeys Editor
window

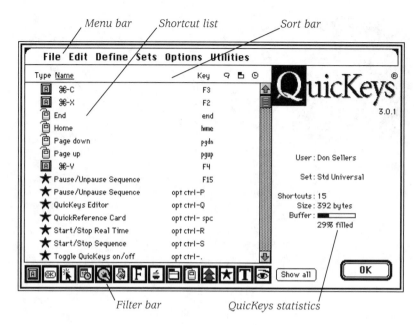

Menu bar   Shortcut list   Sort bar

Filter bar   QuicKeys statistics

Menu bar. The Menu bar is functionally similar to that used in most Mac applications, although this menu bar is at the top of the QuicKeys Editor window rather than at the top of your screen.

QuicKeys statistics. QuicKeys 3.0 has replaced the Memory Indicator bar of previous versions with a series of statistics displayed directly on the QuicKeys Editor window beneath the QuicKeys logo. This section of the window provides data on the currently selected set—its name, the number of shortcuts within the set, the storage size of the set, and the amount of buffer space available for your use. The current version of QuicKeys is displayed directly beneath the logo.

Sort bar. The Sort bar controls the order in which your shortcuts are displayed in the shortcut list that's right below it. Click on any of the three titles to sort the list. The Sort bar gives you three ways to display your shortcuts.

- **By Type.** This displays shortcuts in the order shown along the Filter bar.

- **By Name.** This displays shortcuts in alphabetical order. Numerals and special characters are sorted in the usual ASCII manner. Shortcuts without names are listed last.

- **By Key.** This displays shortcuts with function keys first, then most extended keyboard keys (except keypad keys), then numerals and keypad keys, and finally alphabetic characters.

We usually sort by key because that is how we delineate the different shortcuts in our heads. When we want to sort another way, we can choose it from the Sort bar or use a keystroke combination listed in the Options menu (for example, Command-T to sort by type).

The other three (or four) icons on the Sort bar aren't active; clicking on them does nothing. They are significant, however, when you're working in the Shortcut list which we discuss next.

Shortcut list. The shortcut list displays the shortcuts in the set checked on the Set menu. You can edit shortcuts quickly by clicking on different parts of this area.

- Double-click on the icon or the name of the shortcut to bring up its edit dialog box.

- Click on the keyboard shortcut and press a different keystroke combination to change the triggering keystroke.

- Click in the comment column (⌨) to view, edit, or add a message to the shortcut.

- Click in the menu column (📂) to add the shortcut to the QuicKeys menu (or to take it off, if it's already there).

- Click in the timer column (🕒) to set up the shortcut for automatic activation at a preset time.

- If you are operating an AV Mac with speech-recognition software installed, click on the Speech Recognition column to set up your shortcut to open using your voice.

Filter bar. The Filter bar causes the shortcut list to display specific subsets of shortcuts. Clicking on any Filter bar icon will show the shortcuts for that particular type only. By holding down Shift, you can select multiple types from the bar. Clicking the Show All button returns you to the default mode that lists all shortcuts in the chosen set. Choosing the appropriate type for the bar appreciably cuts down your shortcut listing and your search time.

■ ■

The Menu Bar of the QuicKeys Editor Window

Here's a quick rundown of each menu in the QuicKeys Editor window. For the nitty-gritty details, just keep reading.

■ The first two menus, File and Edit, are familiar to anyone who has had any experience with a Mac. They let you open and save sets, and cut, copy, and paste shortcuts.

■ The Define menu is the primary control for creating a shortcut.

■ The Sets menu lets you view different sets of shortcuts.

■ The Options menu holds display and configuration controls.

■ The Utilities menu provides access to such QuicKeys utilities as the Extension Manager and Template Printer, as well as Instant QuicKeys.

The File Menu

Most of this menu (see Figure 4.2) allows you to control sets. Its operation is self-evident, except in a few areas. Those of you familiar with earlier versions of the program should note that several commands have been renamed to better reflect their function: New becomes New Set, Open becomes Open Set, Close, becomes Close Set, and Save becomes Save Set.

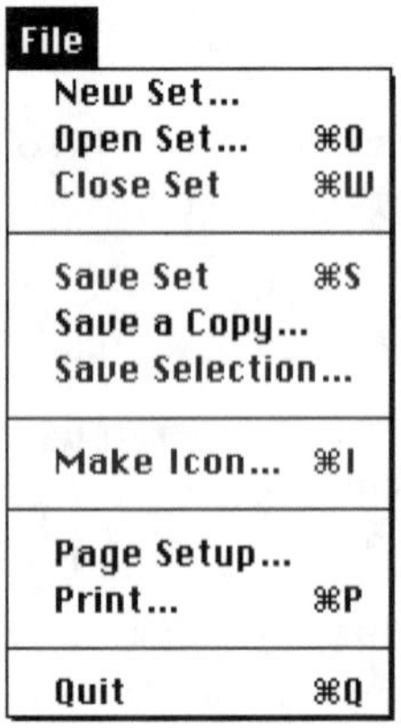

Figure 4.2
The QuicKeys
Editor's File menu

File
New Set...
Open Set...   ⌘O
Close Set   ⌘W
Save Set   ⌘S
Save a Copy...
Save Selection...
Make Icon...   ⌘I
Page Setup...
Print...   ⌘P
Quit   ⌘Q

Save a Copy. The Save a Copy command is used to save the contents of a set. This command is useful when you want to transfer a shortcut set to another Mac. We discuss transferring shortcuts and sets more thoroughly in Chapter 17, *Keystroke Strategies*.

Save Selection. The Save Selection command lets you save highlighted shortcuts in the shortcut list in their own set. Use this command to create storage sets of shortcuts.

■ ■

Make Icon. A totally new command, Make Icon, causes QuicKeys to make a QuicKeys icon (a little standalone application that triggers the shortcut) for each selected shortcut in the displayed set. Once you've created this applet, you can run the shortcut just as you would any other program—double-click on it in the Finder, put it in the Startup Items folder, whatever. (QuicKeys must be loaded for the icon to work; it's not a *completely* standalone app.)

To make a shortcut into an icon, select the shortcut (or shortcuts) and choose Make Icon from the File menu. QuicKeys prompts you with a standard Save dialog box, where you can choose the name and location of the application (or icon) you're creating.

The only thing you may find curious is Save Shortcut Data in QK Icon options. If you *don't* check this option, the icon just looks for the shortcut in your Keysets folder and executes it. If you delete the shortcut or send the icon to another Mac, it won't be able to find the shortcut or execute the instructions in it.

If you *do* check this option, all necessary shortcut instructions are saved in the Icon file itself. As long as QuicKeys is loaded, the Icon should perform as expected. There are a couple of options about how icons are displayed on the desktop, which we cover in "Configuring QuicKeys" later in this chapter.

Print. Print the currently displayed shortcut listing. As of this writing, printing from the QuicKeys Editor window doesn't seem to work with LaserWriter driver 8.1.1. If you want to print your sets, you'll either need to use the Template Printer utility, or find a copy of LaserWriter 7, put it in your System:Extensions folder, and select it from the Chooser (or use a Choosy shortcut to switch printers).

Quit. The Quit command is redundant; it does the same thing as the OK button in the QuicKeys Editor window.

The Edit Menu

The Edit menu (see Figure 4.3) follows Mac interface standards, so it doesn't have many surprises. Note that this new version of QuicKeys includes the Select All command.

- Delete is active when at least one shortcut is highlighted in the main window.

- Undefine and Modify are both redundant with operations that can be effected with the mouse in the shortcut list. Undefine deletes a keystroke combination from a highlighted shortcut. You can accomplish the same result by clicking on the keystroke and pressing the

Figure 4.3
QuicKeys Editor's
Edit menu

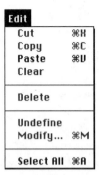

Delete key. Modify opens the edit dialog box of a highlighted short-cut; double-clicking on the shortcut in the shortcut list opens the Edit window, too.

■ Note there is no Undo in this menu. Since that is so and since QuicKeys has an automatic save feature when it's closed, when a shortcut is deleted or modified, it's forever.

The Define Menu

Here's something different—the Define menu (see Figure 4.4). In Chapter 3, *The Gateway to QuicKeys Knowledge*, we used the Define menu to make our sample File Launch shortcut. The first objects that probably catch your eye when you open the menu are the peculiar little icons that precede the shortcut names. Many of the same icons are repeated in the Filter bar (below the shortcut list). Each icon (sort of) represents a different *type* of shortcut. We discuss each shortcut type extensively in Chapters 5–16.

To create a new shortcut, choose one item from the Define menu. QuicKeys brings up the Shortcut Edit dialog box for that type of shortcut.

Figure 4.4
QuicKeys Editor's
Define menu

The Sets Menu

Using the Sets menu (see Figure 4.5), you can organize your shortcut sets to quickly open those sets that contain the specific shortcuts you need for every project.

Figure 4.5
QuicKeys Editor's
Sets menu

The Sets menu has three sections: The Universal and current (or front) application sets are listed in the top section of the menu, indicating that they are the active sets. The second section alphabetically lists all sets in your Keysets folder (in the QuicKeys folder in the Preferences folder of the System folder—whoof!). The last section lists any sets that you've opened that are not located in your Keysets folder.

For more on sets, see Chapter 3, *The Gateway to QuicKeys Knowledge.*

**The Options
Menu**

The Options menu (Figure 4.6) lets you configure the different QuicKeys components—the QuicKeys engine, QuickReference Card, and CEToolbox. You can also compress shortcuts and check out how much memory they use, and sort the shortcuts in the window via menu commands.

The first three items on the Options menu mimic the Sort bar, but include keystroke combinations you can sort with. The other options are more interesting.

Figure 4.6
QuicKeys Editor's
Options menu

Options	
Sort by Type	⌘T
✓ Sort by Name	⌘N
Sort by Key	⌘K
Memory Usage...	
Compress sets	
Configure QuicKeys...	
Configure QuickReference Card...	
Configure CEToolbox...	
About QuicKeys®...	

Memory Usage. The Memory Usage command is more accessible in QuicKeys 3; it provides a dialog box that displays the current buffer size and memory use for all opened sets. A total of 64 sets can be displayed along with their set sizes and shortcut storage sizes (see Figure 4.7). You can also invoke the Memory Usage dialog box by clicking on the Statistics section of the QuicKeys Editor window.

Figure 4.7
Memory Usage
dialog box

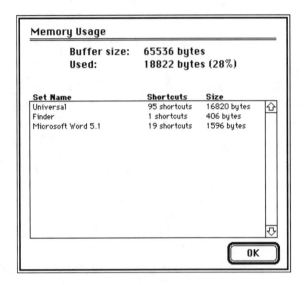

Sometimes QuicKeys starts acting a little befuddled when the memory used becomes a large percentage of that allocated in the buffer. There is no magic percentage at which increasing your memory buffer is necessary, but it must be pretty high. The Configure QuicKeys option on the Options menu lets you reset the memory buffer size used by the program to best fit your level of QuicKeys use.

Compress Sets. To understand the Compress Sets command, you need to understand a little about how QuicKeys stores shortcuts on disk. Most shortcuts are simply stored in the Keysets folder. Each set is a file. When you add or delete a shortcut, QuicKeys adds it to or deletes it from the appropriate set. Simple.

Sequences and Real Time shortcuts are a little trickier. QuicKeys stores a shortcut in the appropriate set file for each Sequence or Real Time shortcut, but stores their actual guts separately—Sequences in the Sequences folder, and Real Times in the Macros folder.

When you delete a Sequence or Real Time shortcut in the QuicKeys Editor, QuicKeys deletes the shortcut from the set file, but it doesn't remove the supporting material—the actual Sequence or Real Time code that's stored in a separate file. QuicKeys cleans up this material at startup if the Compress Files Automatically on Startup option is set in the QuicKeys Options dialog box. If the option isn't set, as you go through life, your Sequence and Macros folders just keep getting bigger and bigger, fuller and fuller.

The Compress Sets command removes those Sequence and Real Time files if their invoking shortcuts have been deleted. Optionally, you can also have QuicKeys check during compression to be sure that the target files for all File Launch QuicKeys are where they're supposed to be (see "QuicKeys Options" later in this chapter). Compress Sets will also clean up empty space inside files that resulted from editing or moving lots of shortcuts or sequence steps.

Configure QuicKeys. This command lets you control several aspects of QuicKeys' behavior, including positioning of the QuicKeys menu, memory allocation, and playback speed. We discuss it in more detail in "Configuring QuicKeys" later in this chapter.

Configure QuickReference Card. The QuickReference Card (a display that lets you view and trigger shortcuts) can be invoked from the QuicKeys menu or through a Special shortcut. We discuss the QuickReference Card in more detail in "The QuickReference Card" later in this chapter, and we discuss the QuickReference shortcut in Chapter 13, *Shortcuts That Control QuicKeys*.

Configure CEToolbox. This command invokes the Configuration dialog box for CEToolbox. CEToolbox is a resource that QuicKeys and QuickMail (another CE application) call on for menu positioning and System extension handling.

You can also access CEToolbox from the Apple menu and then press the Configure button to bring up the Configuration dialog box, but this is quicker and more integrated with the program. We discuss CEToolbox in more detail in "Configuring QuicKeys" later in this chapter.

The Utilities Menu

The Utilities menu (Figure 4.8) lists all of the contents of the Utilities folder (located in your System folder in a path labeled System folder:Preferences:QuicKeys folder:Utilities folder). The utilities that come with QuicKeys include the Extension Manager, Template Printer, Instant QuicKeys, and Shortcut Installer. Selecting one of these utilities

Figure 4.8
Utilities menu

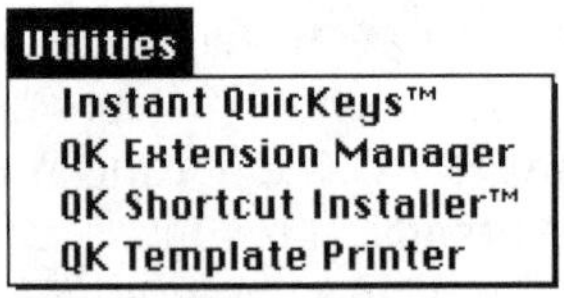

```
Utilities
Instant QuicKeys™
QK Extension Manager
QK Shortcut Installer™
QK Template Printer
```

closes the QuicKeys Editor window and launches the selected program. We cover these utilities in Chapter 18, *QuicKeys Utilities*.

You can also access the Utilities menu from the QuicKeys menu (or you can hide that Utilities menu, via the Configure QuicKeys menu item in the Options menu of the QuicKeys Editor window).

Configuring QuicKeys

Configuring QuicKeys can seem more confusing than it is, because you can get at the various configuration controls in various ways. In fact, you only need to consider four dialog boxes.

- Configure QuicKeys
- QuicKeys Options
- Speed Settings
- CEToolbox

Configure QuicKeys

There's only one way to get to the Configure QuicKeys dialog box (see Figure 4.9): via the Configure QuicKeys command from the QuicKeys Editor's Options menu. Here's a rundown of the four sections in the dialog box.

Figure 4.9
Configure QuicKeys dialog box

```
Configure QuicKeys

Hide menus:                    QuicKeys Opens To:
  ☐ QuicKeys Menu                ○ Universal Set
  ☒ QuicKeys Utilities           ○ Current Application Set
                                 ● Remember Univ/App Setting

Make Icon:                     Expand:
  ☐ Use Bullets in Name          ☒ QuicKeys Window
  ☐ Use Custom Icons             ☒ Sequence Editor Window

  [ Set Buffer Size... ]  [ Speed Settings... ]  [ Cancel ]  [ OK ]
```

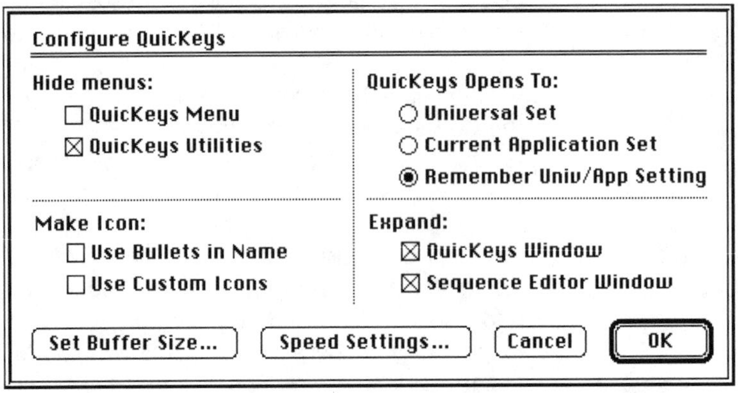

Hide menus. Do you want the QuicKeys menu to appear as part of the CEToolbox group of menus? We usually do, because we trigger some of our keystrokes and do some of our sequence recording and playback work from that menu. How about the tools available in QuicKeys' Utilities folder? Do you need access to them from the menu? We don't use them much, so we turn this option off and access them from the QuicKeys Editor window if we need them.

Make Icon. The two options in this section just control how the little applications look when you turn a shortcut into an icon (see "Make Icon" earlier in this chapter). Do you want the shortcut type to be reflected in the look of the icon, or do you want a generic QuicKeys icon? Do you want bullets bracketing the name of the icon? You can see the difference in Figure 4.10.

Figure 4.10
A QuicKeys icon
for a Sequence
shortcut

SCSI Mount

Without bullets and
custom icon turned on

•SCSI Mount•

With bullets and custom
icon turned on

QuicKeys Opens To. When you open the QuicKeys Editor, what set do you see? We always choose Remember Univ/App Setting (the default), because we're probably jumping in and out of QuicKeys to get a short-cut working right and want to hunt around for the shortcut as little as possible.

Here's how we'd *really* like it to work: when you open the QuicKeys Editor, you automatically jump to the set you were working on before, with the shortcut you were working on highlighted and ready for editing. Oh well. Maybe next version.

Expand. If you want the biggest editing windows possible on your screen, check these two options. Since both the QuicKeys Editor window and Sequence Editor window are modal (you can't work on anything else while they're open), we don't see much reason to minimize their size. And while we suppose it could be a pain to work with huge windows on a really big screen, we don't have that problem.

Set Buffer Size and Speed Settings buttons. Each of these buttons brings up another configuration dialog box. Set Buffer Size brings up QuicKeys Options (go figure), and Speed Settings brings up Speed Settings (now *that* makes sense!). We cover those two dialog boxes next.

**QuicKeys
Options**

There are two ways to get at the QuicKeys Options dialog box (see Figure 4.11).

■ Click the Set Buffer Size button in the Configure QuicKeys dialog box.

■ Click the Configure button in the QuicKeys control panel.

The options in this dialog box let you control memory usage and QuicKeys' shortcut-compression behavior.

Figure 4.11
QuicKeys Options
dialog box

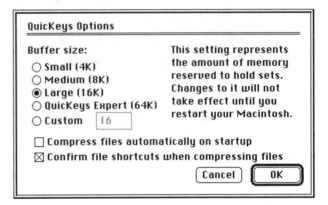

Buffer size. The Buffer Size options determine how much room to allocate in memory for your shortcuts. Question: How many shortcuts does it take to fill a 4K space? Somewhere between one and a whole lot. Shortcuts come in different sizes. Alias Keystrokes can be very small, and long Sequence shortcuts can be large—or relatively large; our largest is 19K, and its a Real Time shortcut. So how big does your QuicKeys buffer have to be? It's best to set it bigger than big enough. 32K is plenty for all except the most fanatic QuicKeys user.

You should only need to change the buffer size if the percentage indicator in the QuicKeys Editor's statistics section is nearing 100 percent or if QuicKeys pops up a notice warning you that the buffer size is exceeded (be aware that every time you open an application you open its associated set, potentially pushing the buffer limit). Bigger buffers mean less memory available for other things, like running applications.

Shortcut compression. Selecting the Compress Files Automatically on Startup checkbox activates the Sequence and Real Time compression routine discussed earlier in the chapter. We leave it off because with all the sets and sequences we have, it's a time-consuming procedure and, using a lot of beta software, we restart somewhat more than we would like. We also use lots of system extensions and control panels, so startup is long enough as it is. We prefer to compress files occasionally, using the Compress Sets command on the Options menu in the QuicKeys Editor window. However, CE recommends leaving on this option (and the one that we discuss next) to help keep everything running smoothly.

Confirm File Shortcuts When Compressing Files. Selecting this checkbox activates a feature that checks your File Launch shortcuts (the ones that open files for you) to verify the location of the files they call. By selecting Confirm File Shortcuts, you ensure that QuicKeys won't attempt to call a nonexistent file—which would happen if you make a File Launch shortcut and then delete the target file.

If it can't find the target file for a File Launch shortcut, QuicKeys displays a dialog box asking if you'd like to go looking for it (either manually, via a normal file open dialog box, or automatically, via QuicKeys).

Speed Settings

There are two way to get into the Speed Settings dialog box (see Figure 4.12).

- Click the Speed Settings button in the Configure QuicKeys dialog box.

- Click the Configure button in the QuicKeys control panel, bringing up the QuicKeys Options dialog box, and click the Speed Settings button (who says it's inconsistent?!).

However you get to the Speed Settings dialog box, you're probably wondering why you'd want to.

Sometimes you run into an application or Mac configuration that can't keep up with QuicKeys' clicking, dragging, and Real Time and

Figure 4.12
Speed Settings
dialog box

Speed Settings

Adjust QuicKeys' drag speed by:	Adjust QuicKeys' click speed by:	Adjust QuicKeys' sequence speed by:
○ 1/16	○ 1/16	○ 1/16
○ 1/8	○ 1/8	○ 1/8
○ 1/4	○ 1/4	○ 1/4
○ 1/2	○ 1/2	○ 1/2
◉ 1x ←Normal	◉ 1x ←Normal	◉ 1x ←Normal
○ 2x	○ 2x	○ 2x

Cancel   OK

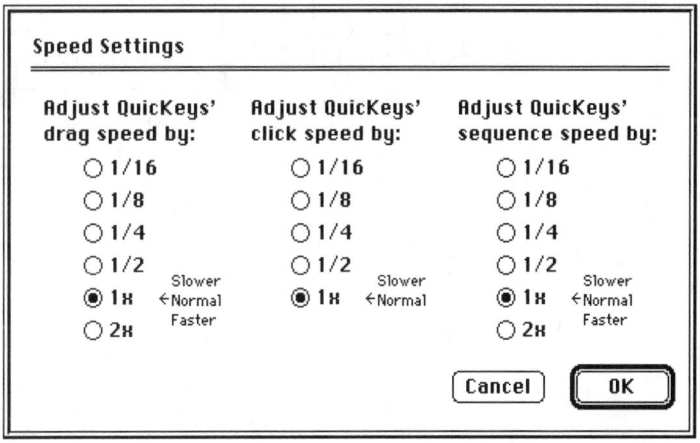

Sequence execution. Clicks, drags, and Sequence steps seem to get lost while the application goes about its business. While the best solution is usually to insert strategically placed Pause shortcuts into your Sequences, that doesn't work with Real Time shortcuts and it doesn't address a more general Mac speed problem.

If you run into these kinds of problems, try slowing down different aspects of QuicKeys' operation in the Speed Settings dialog box. We're sorry to say that the only way to do this is via trial and error, by changing the settings and seeing if your shortcuts work with the new settings.

CEToolbox

There are (at least) three ways to get into the CEToolbox dialog box (see Figure 4.13).

■ Choose the Configure CEToolbox command from the Options menu of the QuicKeys Editor window.

■ Choose the CEToolbox command from the QuicKeys menu or the Apple menu (in a bit of recursive logic, where the command is located depends on how CEToolbox is configured).

■ Run the Configure CEToolbox application, located in the QuicKeys Support Tools folder inside the QuicKeys Tools folder.

There are two sections in the CEToolbox dialog box that control where CE menus (including QuicKeys menus) appear and another section of miscellanea.

Figure 4.13
CEToolbox
dialog box

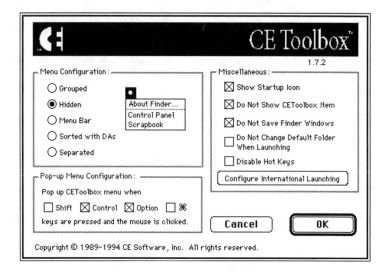

Menu configuration. Where do you want CE's various menus (including the QuicKeys menu) to appear? Should they be grouped together or scattered about on the Apple menu? There are five options.

■ **Grouped.** All the CE-related menus are in their own little section at the top of the Apple menu.

■ **Hidden.** None of the CE menus show (though you can still access them via the pop-up menu discussed in the next section).

■ **Menu Bar.** This option adds a menu to your Mac's Menu bar, just to the left of the Balloon Help icon.

■ **Sorted with DAs.** The various CE menus are arranged alphabetically on the Apple menu.

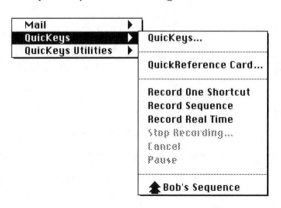

■ **Separated.** All the CE menus are available as sub-submenus off a Tools option on the Apple menu. We find this configuration too buried but apparently CE received many requests for it.

Pop-Up Menu Configuration. This tricky little option is the gateway to one of the best ways to trigger shortcuts. Set up some keys here (we use Control-Option), and your QuicKeys menu will be waiting for you, right at your mouse pointer, whenever you want it. Hold down Control-Option and the mouse button, and there's the menu, listing any shortcuts you've put on it (see Figure 4.14).

Figure 4.14
QuicKeys pop-up
menu

Hold down the appropriate keys plus the mouse button, and this menu pops up wherever your mouse pointer is.

This is a *great* way to trigger shortcuts without having to remember a keystroke or wander through the Apple menu.

Miscellaneous. When you can't figure out where to put it, call it miscellaneous. None of these items really pertains to QuicKeys, so we'll give some advice that we rarely give: turn on Balloon Help, and take a look at each item's Balloon Help to find out what they do.

The Shortcut Editor Dialog Box

So far in this chapter we've talked about different tools and methods for working with QuicKeys—the program—and for manipulating sets of shortcuts. Now we get into the nitty-gritty—editing the shortcuts themselves.

Action central for editing shortcuts is the shortcut edit dialog box. Although every shortcut type has a different edit dialog box to satisfy its particular requirements, almost all edit dialog boxes have six features in common (see Figure 4.15).

Type of shortcut. In the preface, we introduced the myriad types of shortcuts provided by the program and showed you how QuicKeys categorizes them for easier access. Two shortcut categories, Mousies and Specials, have their own special edit dialog boxes where the type of

Figure 4.15
A generic shortcut edit dialog box

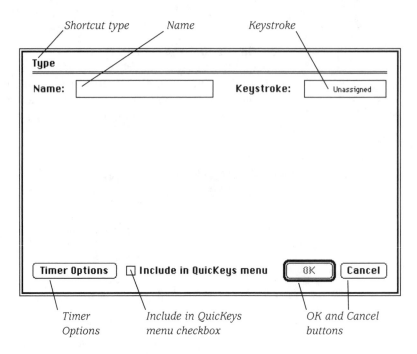

Mousie or Special shortcut is not displayed on the top of the box, but rather is accessed from a pop-up menu in the shortcut edit dialog box.

Name. All shortcuts can have a name. In most cases, you can name a shortcut whatever you want, but some shortcuts have a built-in naming process; the name depends on the function of the shortcut. For example, defining a Menu Selection shortcut automatically names it with that menu item; a File Launch shortcut's name is identical to its target file's name.

Keystroke. You can activate a shortcut with any regular key, with or without modifier keys (Shift, Option, Command, and Control). You can also build a shortcut with no invoking keystroke, for instance, if you want to call it from the QuicKeys menu or trigger it with a timer.

You can use the Tab, Enter, Delete, and Return keys on your keyboard as invoking keystrokes, but to enter them in the shortcut edit dialog box, you need to have the mouse key pressed. To assign some of the dead-letter keys (which put accents on the next character you type), you need to press them twice while entering them in the dialog box. (We can't imagine why you'd want to do this.) Here's a list of dead-letter keys.

- Accent grave (`): Shift-`
- Accent ague (´): Option-E
- Circumflex (ˆ): Option-I
- Enye (˜): Option-N
- Umlaut (¨): Option-U

Also be careful when you assign keystrokes that you do not override Mac keystrokes you may want to use. Mac guidelines reserve certain keystroke combinations for special purposes. Those applications that follow these guidelines to the letter use these keystroke combinations for common tasks.

- Command-O for Open
- Command-W for Close
- Command-N for New
- Command-P for Print
- Command-Q for Quit
- Command-X for Cut
- Command-V for Paste

- Command-C for Copy

- Command-Z for Undo

We go into a lot more detail on recommended keystrokes in Chapter 17, *Keystroke Strategies*. For now we can say this: if you use keystroke combinations that include the Control key, you're pretty safe. Few applications rely on that key for any of their built-in shortcuts.

Timing triggers. Clicking the Timer Options button invokes the Timer options dialog box (see Figure 4.16). There are three (well, two and a half) options.

- **Mac or application start.** This option triggers a shortcut a set time after you start up your Mac or launch an application (depending on whether the shortcut is in the Universal, Finder, or an application set). If you want your Mac to check your email every time you start up or initialize your modem every time you launch your communications software, this is the timer for you.

- **Preset value.** You can trigger the shortcut at any time you want by filling in the date and time. QuicKeys automatically fills in the present time as the default. You can make this work as a not-so-quick-but-dirty reminder system.

- **Repeat option.** If you have checked the previous option, you can repeat the invocation at a set interval. For example, you could have a

Figure 4.16
Timer Options
dialog box

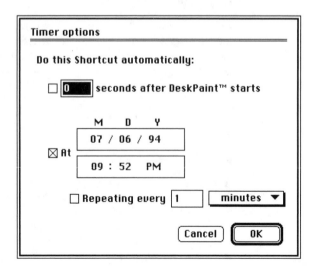

shortcut beep at you every day at 5 P.M. Don uses this to remind him to focus out the window every fifteen minutes or so to avoid monitor-related eyestrain.

Include in QuicKeys Menu checkbox. We used this option in our sample shortcut in Chapter 3. It puts your shortcut on the QuicKeys menu, so you don't have to remember a keystroke. Steve uses this option for his Choosy shortcuts: he can choose a printer on the network from the QuicKeys menu (it works especially well with the pop-up menu option discussed under CEToolbox earlier in this chapter).

OK and Cancel buttons. You figure. Yup, you're right.

The QuicKeys Menu

In the discussion of CEToolbox earlier in this chapter (see Figure 4.14), we detailed all the different ways (and places) you can get at the QuicKeys menu. Now it's time to look inside that menu to see what's there.

QuicKeys Editor. The first option is simple; it brings up the QuicKeys Editor window. You can avoid the submenus by simply choosing QuicKeys. The submenu pops up, but you don't have to travel out to that submenu. Just let go of the mouse button, and the QuicKeys Editor window pops up. Of course, we find it easier to use our keystroke shortcut (that triggers the QuicKeys Editor shortcut) to achieve the same result.

QuickReference Card. The QuickReference Card, discussed in more detail later in this chapter, lets you view your active sets and trigger shortcuts from those sets.

Record One Shortcut. The easiest way to create a single-step shortcut is to choose Record One Shortcut and then perform a single action. The edit dialog box for your single-step shortcut then appears and you can assign the shortcut a triggering keystroke.

Record Sequence. This is the easy way to create a Sequence. Choose Record Sequence, perform the actions you want included in the Sequence, and then choose Stop Recording. Up comes the Sequence edit dialog box, where you can fine-tune the Sequence. If you mess up while you're going through the Sequence steps, choose Cancel instead of Stop Recording. Note that you can tell that recording is occurring because the Apple icon changes to a blinking microphone during the recording process and the Recorder Palette pops up on screen.

For more on creating and editing sequences, see Chapter 14, *The Sequence.*

Record Real Time. This menu option lets you create a special kind of shortcut: a Real Time shortcut. Choose Record Real Time, and go through the steps you want included in the recording, again using the handy Recording Palette to control your recording. When you've finished, choose Stop Recording. As with Sequences, you can get out of the recording if you mess up by choosing Cancel instead of Stop Recording. For more on Real Time QuicKeys, see "Start/Stop Real Time" in Chapter 13, *Shortcuts That Control QuicKeys*.

Cancel. This command cancels the recording or playback of a Sequence or Real Time shortcut. Recording or Playback is appended to the Cancel command in the menu, as appropriate, when these activities are occurring. When QuicKeys is not recording or playing back a shortcut, the Cancel command is grayed out. This command is duplicated on the new Recording Palette for easier access during a recording or playback session.

Pause. This command lets you pause or continue (unpause) in the middle of recording or playing back a Sequence or a Real Time shortcut. You can start recording, then pause, and do other things without including those things in the recording. Select Pause again to uncheck it and continue recording.

This is also a key tool for working with Sequence shortcuts that require your intervention: you insert a Pause shortcut in the Sequence, so it stops its operation in the middle. You can perform actions, then uncheck the Pause option (or use a keystroke to unpause), so the Sequence continues on its merry way.

Recording or Playback is appended to the Pause command in the menu, as appropriate, when these activities are occurring. When no activities are occurring, the Pause command is dimmed. This command is also duplicated on the new Recording Palette for easier access during a recording or playback session.

Your shortcuts. Beneath the bottom line on the QuicKeys menu you'll see any shortcuts you've created and chosen to put on the menu. You can put your shortcuts on the menu in either of two ways.

- In the edit dialog box for the shortcut, turn on the Include in QuicKeys Menu option.

- In the QuicKeys Editor window, click next to the shortcut in the Menu (■) column. This turns on the Menu icon.

If you're including a shortcut on the menu, you may not even need to assign it a keystroke. Just call it from the menu when you need it. Since your shortcuts are listed on the menu alphabetically, you can customize the menu with different functional shortcuts by naming members of a group with the same initial letter (all your printer Choosy shortcuts could start with P, for instance).

The QuickReference Card

We mentioned the QuickReference Card a few sections back. Select it from the QuicKeys menu (or call it with a QuickReference Card Specials shortcut), and up it comes (see Figure 4.17).

Figure 4.17
QuickReference
Card

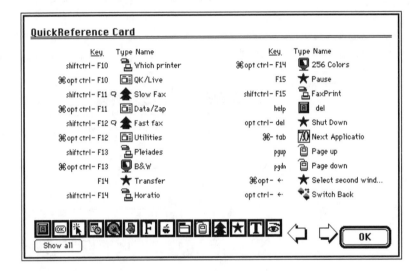

Our QuickReference Cards are set up to display all the shortcuts in our open sets; you can control this via the Configure QuickReference Card command off the Option menu in the QuicKeys Editor window (see Figure 4.18).

The QuickReference Card is actually more than a reference. If a shortcut has a comment, the comment icon lets you know. Press on the shortcut, hold down the mouse button, and the comment is displayed (see Figure 4.19).

Even better, you can trigger shortcuts from the QuickReference Card by clicking on them. This is a great way to trigger shortcuts whose keystrokes you can't remember. For more on the QuickReference Card, see Chapter 13, *Shortcuts That Control QuicKeys*.

Figure 4.18
QuickReference
Card Options
dialog box

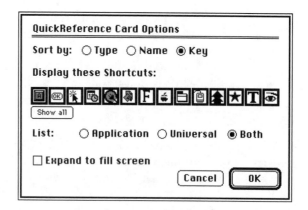

Figure 4.19
QuickReference
Card comment
display

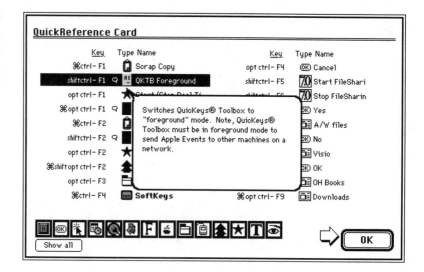

The QuicKeys Control Panel

There are a few controls for QuicKeys in its control panel (see Figure 4.20), some are redundant with other methods of doing the same things.

- Click the appropriate radio button to turn QuicKeys on or off.

- Click the Open Editor button to go into the QuicKeys Editor window.

- Click the Configure button and you will be rewarded by the QuicKeys Options window that we described in the Options menu section of this chapter. This is the same dialog box you can launch using the Configure QuicKeys command.

Figure 4.20
QuicKeys control
panel

- Check and uncheck the Show Startup Icon checkbox to control whether an icon displays at the bottom of the screen when QuicKeys loads on startup. We leave it on, because we like to know what's happening.

Beyond the Basics

In the previous three chapters, we reviewed the theory of how QuicKeys can make your Mac life simpler and smarter by creating shortcuts for common or repetitive tasks. We've also introduced our first shortcut and walked you through what makes a good or bad shortcut. And in this chapter, we've introduced the components that comprise QuicKeys— The QuicKeys Editor window with its menus, the QuicKeys menu, and the various configuration tools.

The next series of chapters investigates shortcut types in detail so you'll know their particular personalities and quirks.

5 Shortcuts That Launch and Open

The process of opening applications and documents is automated neatly in QuicKeys. The only trouble might be the abundance of launching and opening tools—File Launch, Transfer, Folders, and the StuffIt extensions. You'll most often find yourself using File Launch as the launching tool of choice. Transfer and Folders give you finer control over launching or opening in special situations.

Note that you can also use the Open option of the Finder Events extension instead of File Launch to open multiple documents (see "Finder Events" in Chapter 8, *Shortcuts That Control the Mac System*). And Menu Selection can be used to launch items on menus, although File Launch usually presents a better choice. The two extensions, Stuff and UnStuff, enhance the popular compression utility, StuffIt Deluxe (see Appendix, *Resources*) to squeeze and unsqueeze your files.

This chapter covers these shortcut categories and types.

- File Launch

- Transfer

- Folders

- Stuff

- UnStuff

File Launch

The File Launch type, formerly called just File, opens an application, document, control panel, font, or folder (or will play a sound file). Don has 25 File Launch shortcuts on his Mac. While working on this chapter, he generally used a File Launch shortcut to open it.

Choosing File Launch from the QuicKeys Editor's Define menu brings up an Open dialog box from which you can choose a file or a folder (see Figure 5.1). A Select button has been added to the bottom of the dialog box to facilitate your selection. The highlighted file's or folder's name will appear on the Select button. Use standard Mac techniques to move around your volumes and folders to find your target. When you have selected the file or folder you want, clicking the Select button selects the highlighted file and opens the File Launch edit dialog box with the document or application title you've chosen displayed (see Figure 5.2).

Type the keystroke you want (Don uses his function keys for often-used files), and when you invoke your File Launch shortcut, its target opens. You usually put your File Launch shortcuts in the Universal set so you can access them at any time.

Figure 5.1
Open dialog box

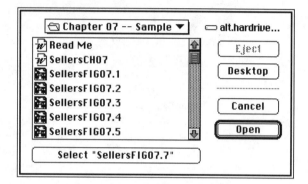

Figure 5.2
File Launch edit
dialog box

Pressing the Change button displays an Open dialog box that you can use to change your target application or document.

File Launch Considerations

You can sometimes use other types of shortcuts to launch applications, but usually File Launch gives the best results. For example, you can use a Menu Selection shortcut to launch an item on the Apple menu. But a File Launch shortcut for the same application works faster.

The File Launch shortcut has just a few potential bugaboos.

Files with no application. When you choose File Launch from the Define menu, the Open dialog box gives you a choice of *every* file that exists within a volume or folder, even files that have no application to open them. We know that you would never be silly enough to target one of these files, but if you do, you'll get an error message when you try to invoke it (see Figure 5.3).

Figure 5.3
Unopenable file
error message

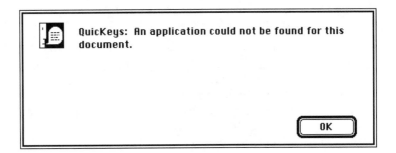

Misplaced files. QuicKeys tracks a file well if you change its location on a particular drive, but if you move it to another drive, QuicKeys will lose it. If you trigger a File Launch shortcut whose target has been deleted or moved sufficiently so that QuicKeys cannot find it, the program displays an alert box stating that the file can't be found.

Also, if the correct options are chosen in the QuicKeys Options dialog box (Compress Files Automatically on Startup and Confirm File Shortcuts when Compressing Files), on startup QuicKeys automatically searches for the targets of all your File Launch shortcuts to ensure they are where they should be. If QuicKeys finds a problem, a dialog box is displayed (see Figure 5.4) that gives you the option of tracking down the errant target yourself or letting QuicKeys do it (you can also choose Cancel, which leaves the situation unresolved).

Figure 5.4

Lost target dialog
box

**File Launch
Tactics**

*Use a File Launch Tool as your first choice to launch an application or open
a document.*

Here's an example of a typical File Launch shortcut. Don keeps a permanent Microsoft Word file titled To Do. He modifies it during his workday (and sometimes work night) as he completes tasks and takes on new ones. He has a File Launch shortcut in his Universal Set to launch the file, and he has it on a timer, so it opens his To Do file after his computer boots.

File Launch shortcuts generally break down into two classifications: permanent and short term.

Permanent. You can access your applications with a keystroke by making a File Launch shortcut for each. Most QuicKeys mavens use a keystroke strategy consisting of a modifier keystroke (like Control or Control-Option) and a letter key that corresponds to the first letter (or an easily remembered alternative letter) of the application's name (see Chapter 17, *Keystroke Strategies*). For example, Control-W opens Microsoft Word, Control-P opens PageMaker.

Short term. Documents that you work with intensively but briefly can be accessed with a File Launch shortcut. Keystroke strategists often use function keys to invoke these files (see Chapter 17, *Keystroke Strategies*). If you're working on a longer document, for instance, you could assign the first 12 function keys to the first 12 chapters.

■ ■ ■ ■ ■

Transfer

Transfer shortcuts open applications or files that you choose with an Open dialog box that appears when the shortcut is invoked. Transfer leaves the present application open whenever it switches to another application or file.

Transfer is a Special shortcut that essentially functions like half of a File Launch shortcut: it opens applications or files, but it doesn't have a built-in target; you must choose the target file whenever a Transfer shortcut is invoked. To construct a Transfer shortcut, you can choose Transfer from the Specials submenu of the QuicKeys Editor's Define menu; the Transfer edit dialog box appears (see Figure 5.5). Assign a keystroke, and you're all set to go.

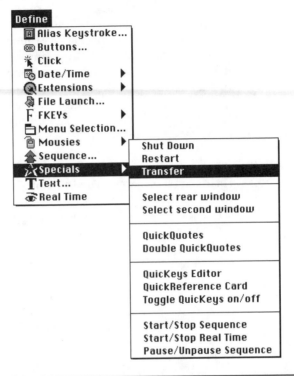

Figure 5.5
Transfer edit
dialog box

Transfer Tactics and Considerations

Use the Transfer shortcut to open applications or documents that don't have their own dedicated opening shortcuts.

Transfer tactics are simple, because you only need one Transfer shortcut. You can keep it in your Universal Set, ready to open files that have not been assigned to specific File Launch shortcuts. It is easier to open these untargeted files by using Transfer than by going through the alternatives (choosing the application or the Finder from the Application menu, then opening the file). Command-Option-O (for opens anything, a hierarchical level above Command-O for open) is a possible keystroke for your Transfer shortcut. Don finds his Transfer shortcut so useful that he has assigned his function key, F14, to it.

Folders

Folders was formerly called Location; its new name makes more sense. A Folders shortcut jumps to a preselected folder. You usually use a Folders shortcut when you are working in an application and want to open or save a document. An Open or Save dialog box is displayed with a folder—seldom the folder you want—already selected. Invoking a Folders shortcut changes the selected folder in the Open dialog box to a folder you've preselected.

One nice aspect of this shortcut is that the Open dialog box doesn't have to be open for it to work—you can invoke your Folders shortcut, *then* ask your application to open a document, and the dialog box will

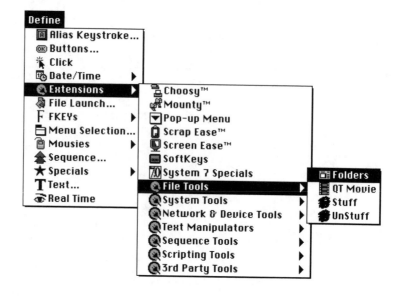

appear with your target folder selected. But the super aspect of this shortcut is that if you have a folder that is targeted on an unmounted drive, invoking Folders mounts the drive automatically. A big bow to Don Brown, Marsh Gosnell, and the other programmers at CE for such elegance and power!

To construct a Folders shortcut, you can select Folders from the Extensions submenu on the Define menu—the Folders edit dialog box appears (see Figure 5.6). The box contains two radio button choices.

Figure 5.6
Folders edit dialog
box

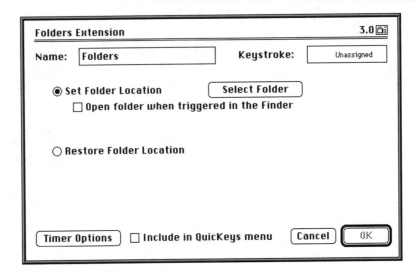

Set Folder Location. This makes the Folders shortcut jump to the folder you preselected using the Select Location button. You'll choose this option, which assigns a specific folder to the Folders shortcut, almost exclusively. Clicking on the Open Folder When Triggered in the Finder checkbox opens the folder when you are in the Finder. This convenient feature is not as powerful as targeting the folder with a File Launch shortcut, which will switch to the Finder and open the folder when you are in an application. However, it gives the advantage of using a single keystroke for both jumping to a folder in an open dialog box and opening the folder while you're in the Finder.

Restore Folder Location. This makes the Folders shortcut return to the file location that was current when you invoked your first Folders shortcut. Since this shortcut has no set target, you only need to make one of these. Many people have no use for this option—they just want to jump to preselected folders, not back to where they were. A Folders shortcut with this option selected will remember the last-used Folders shortcut until you restart. After you restart, invoking this key just selects the startup disk.

To create a Folders shortcut, choose Set Folder Location and then press the Select Folder button. A Select Folder dialog box like that in Figure 5.7 appears. It gives you access to all available folder choices.

Figure 5.7
Select Folder
dialog box

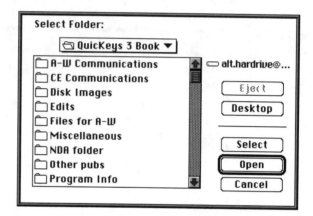

When you work with the Select Folder dialog box, you might think that highlighting a folder and then pressing Select will give you that folder as your target. It won't. Pressing Select chooses the folder that is displayed at the top of the Select location dialog box, even if you have a folder highlighted. You must *open* your desired target folder (not just highlight it) to select it as your target.

Folders Tactics and Considerations

Use Folders shortcuts to select your most often used folders.

Those of you with Now Utilities' SuperBoomerang probably realize that Folders merely mimics a capability you already enjoy. For the rest of you, remember it is easy to let the surgical-strike power of File Launch shortcuts make you overlook the broad strengths of Folders. Folders is a great asset if your work is set up so that you often access only a few different folders for a multitude of files. Folders is the perfect tool for desktop publishers—those tiny-file and many-folder freaks. When we wrote this book, we took a number of screen shots. We didn't want shortcuts that opened each one separately (we'd have run out of key-stroke combinations) but a shortcut that instantly took us to their folder—we used that one shortcut repeatedly.

Stuff and UnStuff are two extensions that integrate QuicKeys with the third-party compression utility, StuffIt Deluxe, to compress and expand your files.

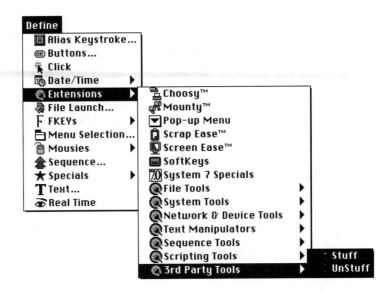

You can use the Stuff and UnStuff shortcuts to process preselected target files, or you can create generic StuffIt shortcuts that will ask you which files you want to process. Some people just stuff files to be transmitted over a telecommunications network. Others, especially those short on disk space, use StuffIt Deluxe as an integral part of their file storage and retrieval process.

Don (the curmudgeon) didn't want to discuss these extensions in this book, because a third-party program is necessary to make them function. Steve said that everyone should know about StuffIt (ubiquitous in the world of file transfer), and those poor souls who didn't want to could just skip this section. Guess who won.

In a nutshell, StuffIt Deluxe works like this: to stuff a file, you must first choose it. After the file is stuffed, it becomes an archive that you name. It is traditional and good practice (but not necessary) to designate a stuffed file with the suffix .sit (for example, 5.1.1.sit or Pix.sit). Unstuffing an archive is even easier than stuffing a file: you only have to choose the archive to unstuff. The unstuffed file automatically names itself with its previous name.

Stuff

When you select Stuff from the 3rd-Party Tools category of the Extensions submenu of the Define menu, you are rewarded with an edit dialog box (see Figure 5.8). The non-generic controls are ordered a bit illogically (for us), so we'll discuss them in the order we prefer.

Figure 5.8
Stuff edit dialog box

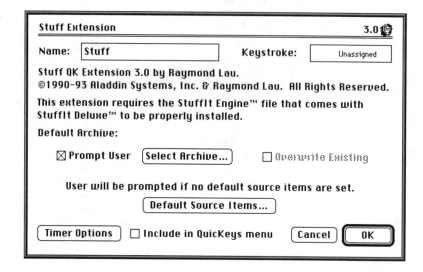

Default Source Items button. Near the bottom of the edit dialog box is the Default Source Items button, with which you can select the file (or files) to be archived. If you don't press this button, you will be asked what you want to archive when you activate this Stuff shortcut. So don't press this if you want to make a generic Stuff Anything shortcut.

Prompt User checkbox. This checkbox deals with the name the archive will have—a check mark here means that when you activate the shortcut, you will get an Open dialog box prompting you for the archive name. If you want to create a generic Stuff Anything shortcut that will also ask you for the name that the archive was saved under, then check this box.

Select Archive button. Click this if you want the Stuff shortcut to save your compressed file in a preselected archive. Clicking this button will display an Open dialog box from which you can choose the archive you want. Note that although this control is an alternative to the Prompt User checkbox, it remains active when that box is checked. However, as soon as you select an archive here, the Prompt User checkbox automatically unchecks itself.

Overwrite Existing checkbox. The Overwrite Existing checkbox on the Stuff edit dialog box remains dimmed until you select an archive with the Select Archive button. Then it becomes potentially active, so if you check this, the Stuff shortcut recreates (rewrites) its target archive every time the shortcut is activated. If you leave this box unchecked, then any Stuff command you direct to an already extant archive will elicit a dialog box asking if you want to replace the archive with the new compressed file. In other words, this feature avoids the annoyance of going through the warning dialog box, if you know you want to replace the old archive with the new one.

You cannot use a Stuff shortcut to *add* a file to an archive (a feature accessible through StuffIt Deluxe itself).

UnStuff

UnStuff is a bit simpler than Stuff. Choosing UnStuff from the Extensions submenu of the Define menu conjures up the UnStuff edit dialog box (see Figure 5.9) This dialog box has only three unfamiliar controls.

Figure 5.9
UnStuff edit dialog box

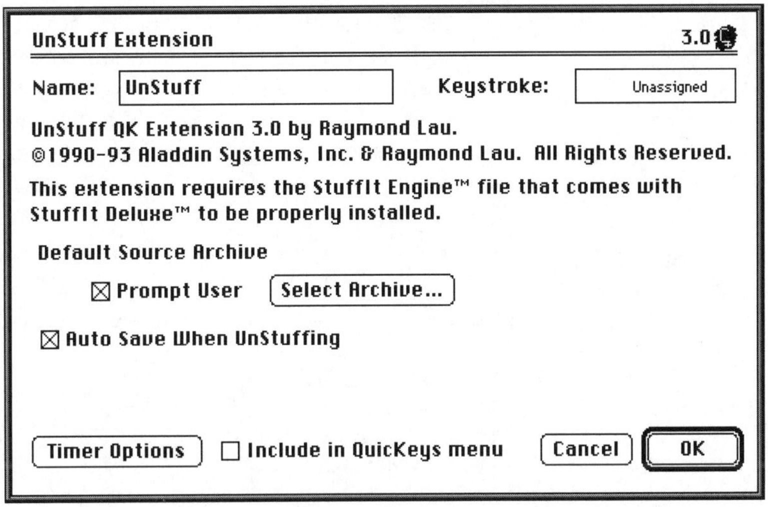

Prompt User checkbox. If the Prompt User checkbox is checked, you are asked to name the archive you want to uncompress when the UnStuff shortcut is activated. If the archive contains multiple files, you can then designate which you want to unstuff. Check the Prompt User checkbox if you want to make a generic Unstuff Anything shortcut.

Select Archive button. Pressing the Select Archive button elicits an Open dialog box in which you can choose a target archive from which this shortcut will unstuff.

Auto Save When UnStuffing checkbox. Checking the Auto Save When UnStuffing checkbox takes out some options when your UnStuff shortcut is invoked. With this box checked, once you choose the archive (either by preselecting it or, if the Prompt User checkbox is checked, selecting it at the prompt), it is immediately and completely uncompressed into its own folder. When you check this box, you are *not* prompted to enter the file names of multiple-file archives you wish to uncompress—they just uncompress.

Stuff Files Dialog Box

Sometimes when you use the Stuff shortcut, you'll confront the Stuff Files dialog box, from which you choose the file (or files) you want to compress. It's pretty spiffy (see Figure 5.10). It consists of two scrolling lists: the files available to stuff are on the left and the files you want to stuff are on the right. You select a file from the list on the left, and add it to the list on the right. At the top of the box on the right is an information line which tells you how many files you are allowed to stuff and how many are on the to-be-stuffed list. You can choose a file from the list on the left and then press the Add button, which adds the file name to the list on the right. There is no way to select multiple files from one list and add them all at once to the other list.

Figure 5.10
Stuff Files dialog box

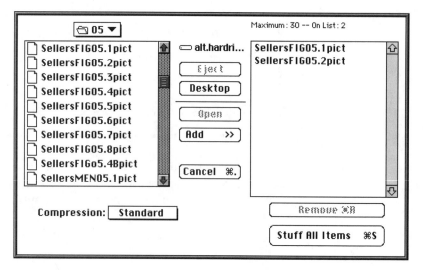

At the bottom of the list on the left is the Compression pop-up menu. You can use it to select the degree of sophistication of your compression. As sophistication increases, speed decreases, which accounts for the apples-and-oranges nature of the items listed. You can choose None if you wish to archive some files without compressing them. Even the most sophisticated compression level, Better (shouldn't it be Best?), is pretty darn quick.

You can remove any item from the list on the right by choosing it and pressing the Remove button. When you are ready to activate the stuffing mechanism, press the Stuff All Items button.

Stuff and UnStuff Considerations

The Stuff and UnStuff extensions were written by Raymond Lau, who knew more about computers when he was 12 years old than we will ever know. These shortcuts are pretty sublime, but they are a compromise. Their major asset is that they are quick—you don't have to open your StuffIt Deluxe application to get some of its benefits. But the accompanying drawback is that you don't get all the bells and whistles available through the mother application. Here are a couple of limitations.

No way to append an archive. StuffIt Deluxe lets you add files to an archive; you can't do that with the Stuff extension.

No way to automatically delete an archived file. StuffIt Deluxe gives you the option of erasing the source files that you have archived. You can't do that here.

Another consideration is that stuffing an open file may not work. We couldn't stuff open Microsoft Word files. So if you want to stuff active files, you must test the files of a particular application to see if they will stuff when they are active.

If for some reason your StuffIt shortcuts don't work, it could be that you are missing something from the StuffIt Deluxe program. One critical item is the StuffIt engine, which lives in the Extensions folder of your System folder.

Stuff and UnStuff Tactics

Use Stuff to quickly compress files through StuffIt Deluxe.
Use UnStuff to quickly uncompress StuffIt Deluxe archives.

We have a generic shortcut for each of these extensions, as part of our Universal set. But in special circumstances we could see having shortcuts that targeted specific files and archives. If we were constantly dealing with one large file and we were short of disk space, we might dedicate a Stuff shortcut and an UnStuff shortcut to it. But one warning in this situation: if you do have a StuffIt shortcut that targets a specific archive, it will always wipe out what that archive had in it before. You might be warned (depending on how you set your options), but it will be replaced. So you will usually only target the archive to save to in situations where you are repeatedly saving one constantly updated file to one target archive.

6 Shortcuts That Control Windows

This chapter covers a long list of shortcuts that control four objects: document windows, application windows, menus, and buttons. Shortcuts that control document windows constitute the lion's share of window-control shortcuts, but they're all functionally similar, so they're easy to remember and use. We employ almost all the shortcuts described in this chapter on a daily basis.

- Mousies
- Select Rear Window
- Select Second Window
- Menu Selection
- Pop-up Menu
- Buttons

Document Windows (the Mousies)

Document-window shortcuts adjust windows. All these shortcuts are found in the Mousies submenu of the QuicKeys Editor's Define menu, which makes good sense as most of them directly mimic mouse clicking in different control areas of a document's window. And a couple of these shortcuts give you control options not found on most applications' windows. Because all these shortcuts are functionally similar, we'll treat them as group, but discuss their individual peculiarities.

The edit dialog box is the same for all Mousies (see Figure 6.1).

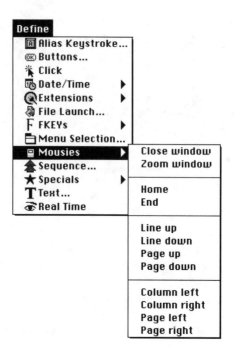

Figure 6.1
Mousie edit dialog
box

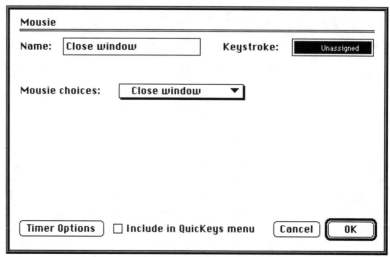

Although the dialog box displays the Mousie shortcut you chose
from the submenu, you can also click on the Mousies Choices pop-up
menu and select any others (see Figure 6.2).

Figure 6.2
Mousies Choices
pop-up menu

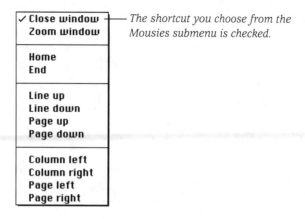

Figure 6.2
Mousies Choices
pop-up menu

The shortcut you choose from the Mousies submenu is checked.

Document Window Considerations

Most Mousies are stand-ins for clicking in a standard Mac document window (see Figure 6.3). Two additional Mousies, Home and End, move the scroll box within the vertical scroll bar to the top and bottom, respectively. Here are a few Mousie considerations.

Figure 6.3
Standard Mac
document window

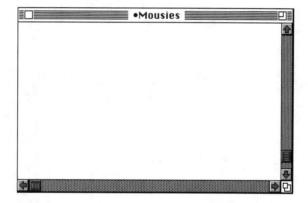

No box, no click. The window you are attempting to adjust with a Mousie must have the feature to be clicked present or the Mousie won't work. For example, the Close Window Mousie won't function if there is no close box on the active window. However, if the feature *is* included, the Mousie might be able to make it function even if you can't. For example, if you have a very large word-processing document, it is often impossible to click between the scroll box and the scroll arrow when the window is near the document's beginning or end. The Page up or Page down Mousie can.

Mutant windows. Mutant document windows (those that don't follow the Mac guidelines) can sometimes fool the Mousie into clicking where it shouldn't or not click at all. Some programs have double sets of arrows, some have weird scroll bars (see Figure 6.4), and some are just bizarre.

Figure 6.4
A different
document window

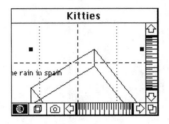

*Some Mousies don't work
with this creature.*

Sometimes Mousie shortcuts scroll work windows instead of the main document window. Aldus PageMaker is a good example. If the Colors Palette or Styles Palette is open and its scroll bar is visible, then Mousies will adjust them (see Figure 6.5). If these windows are closed or enlarged so that their scroll bars go white (that is, their entire contents are showing), then control goes back to the main document window. We asked Ole Kvern (who probably knows more about the convolutions of PageMaker than anyone) why. He said, "That's just the way it is."

Figure 6.5
PageMaker
windows

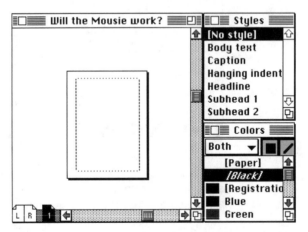

*The Styles Palette is
controlled preferen-
tially over the main
document.*

*The Colors Palette is
controlled preferen-
tially over the Styles
Palette.*

Insertion-point movement in word-processing programs. Many word-processing programs, especially Microsoft Word, have a quiver full of keyboard shortcuts that can make you really fly. Many of them use the keys on the extended keyboard, such as Home, End, Page up, and Page down, that are designed for these tasks. Just because these keys have names identical to certain Mousies doesn't mean that the application-dedicated functions they invoke are also identical. Sometimes it's close, but not the same; where the insertion point ends up often accounts for the difference. The Mousies don't move the insertion point, just the window. Many applications move the window and the insertion point together. Neither way is superior; they're just different, and you can take advantage of that.

Document Windows Tactics

Use document-window shortcuts (Mousies) to manipulate an individual document's window.

Mousies are generalists, so you don't need more than one copy of each. Because there are so many Mousies and because some of them aren't too useful in our daily work, we have standardized only six Mousies Mac-wide by putting them into our Universal set. Page up, Page down, Home, and End are dedicated to the keys of the same names on our extended keyboards. Because this pre-empts the built-in function of these keys in Microsoft Word, Don redesignated those functions (Command-Home, Command-End, and so on) using Word's Commands dialog box. This procedure overrides keystrokes from a couple of other Word shortcuts, but their functions are so obscure that Don didn't mind losing them.

The only other Mousies we use regularly are Zoom Window and Close Window. The keystrokes you use for them and for any additional Mousies you find valuable depend on your layout strategy (see Chapter 17, *Keystroke Strategies*).

Application Windows (Select Rear Window and Select Second Window)

The two application-window shortcuts move between open windows within an application.

In the Specials submenu are two shortcuts for flipping through windows, Select Rear Window and Select Second Window. The standard procedure for applications which lets you have more than one document open is to push the previously active window behind the newly opened one. So if you first open Document A and then B and then C and then D, their respective windows are layered as in Figure 6.6.

Select Rear Window will pull the window off the bottom and bring it to the top. Repeatedly invoking Select Rear Window will loop through all the open windows in an application. Select Second Window will bring the previously active window to the top. Repeatedly invoking Select Second Window will toggle between the two previously active windows.

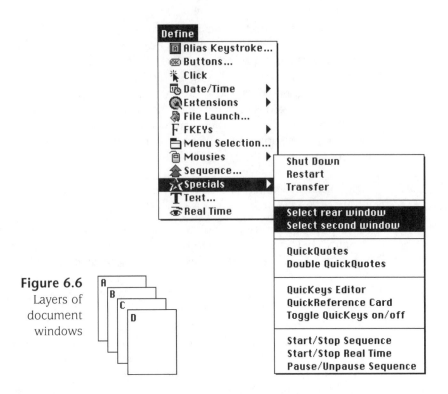

Figure 6.6
Layers of document windows

Application Window Considerations

To activate a window, it is usually quicker to trigger an application-window shortcut than to use the mouse to choose from a menu list of open documents within an application (which is how most applications are engineered). Sure, a menu item is more precise, but you can use QuicKeys to toggle through windows as fast as an IRS auditor can find an anomaly in your tax records (we're talking pretty quick).

One trick to speed the process is to make your windows as small as possible. The Mac waits until one window is drawn on the screen before it draws the next, and the Mac draws smaller windows faster. But unless you are punching your way through a zillion open windows, the speed gain is not worth the trouble of shrinking each one.

Application Window Tactics

Use application-window shortcuts to move to different open windows within an application.

Select Rear Window and Select Second Window are powerful shortcuts. They're generalists, so we include one of each in our Universal Sets. Don triggers Select Rear Window with Command-Option-Right arrow on his extended keyboard. He thinks of it as his application window's Show Me key because most of the time he has no idea on what layer different document windows exist (often he has little idea which docs he has open). He just jams through the windows until he finds the one he's looking for. Don uses the Select Second Window shortcut to toggle back and forth between two windows—for example, when he is doing a lot of cutting and pasting between two documents.

Menu Selection

The Menu Selection shortcut selects commands (or items) from a standard menu bar. This shortcut is powerful because it is precise, and QuicKeys gives you various controls to fine-tune the shortcut to your particular application and needs.

The first step in building a Menu Selection shortcut is to ensure you are in the application whose menu you intend to target. Also, it helps if the specific menu item is listed (many applications have menu items which change, depending on conditions).

A good, overall Menu Selection shortcut is one that chooses Save As from the File menu. Because this command is available but missing a keystroke shortcut in many applications, it is useful to make one for the Universal set that will trigger Save As from wherever you are. In this case, you can be in any application that has a Save As menu item.

Choosing Menu Selection from the Define menu, turns your cursor into a tiny Menu icon as a little instruction dialog box appears (see Figure 6.7).

Figure 6.7
Menu Selection
instruction dialog
box

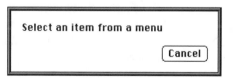

You can select Save As from the File menu, even if it is dimmed with the cursor, and a Menu Selection edit dialog box appears (see Figure 6.8) with many of the choices preselected by QuicKeys.

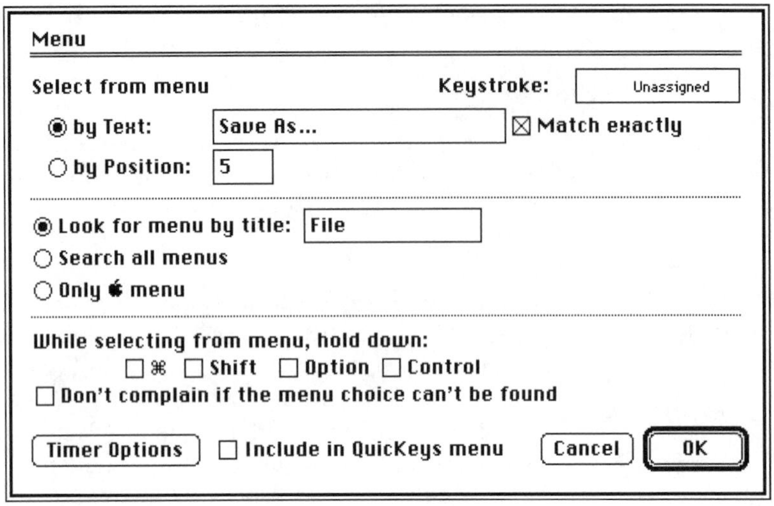

Figure 6.8
Menu Selection
edit dialog box

The Menu Selection edit dialog box has a number of controls that require a little explanation. These controls give you the power to work around *most* of these menu anomalies.

■ Some menu items' names change depending on recent events (Undo in Microsoft Word sometimes appears as Undo Typing, Redo Paste, and so forth).

■ Some menu items' names change depending on whether a modifier key is pressed. (Print changes to Fax when modifier keys are pressed when you open the File menu with certain fax-modem software installed.)

■ Some menu items toggle back and forth between two names (Show Ruler, Hide Ruler).

■ Some menu items have similar but not identical names in different applications (Word Count in Microsoft Word is the same as Statistics in Vantage).

■ Some identical menu items fall under different menus in different applications (Bold is on the Format menu in Word, but on the Type style submenu of the Type menu in PageMaker).

These menu-anomaly controls are grouped in three areas: Item-selection control, Menu-selection control, and Modifier-key control (see Figure 6.9).

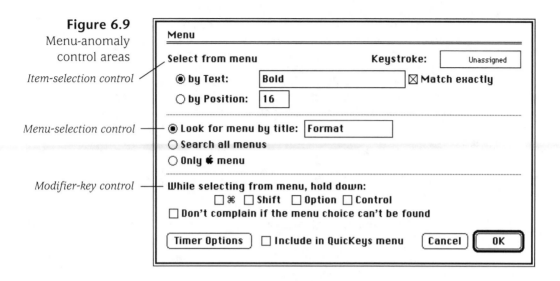

Figure 6.9
Menu-anomaly
control areas

Item-selection control

Menu-selection control

Modifier-key control

How you adjust these fine-tuning controls often depends on whether you are making a Universal shortcut (one that selects an identical or similar menu item in a variety of applications) or an application-specific shortcut. It also often depends on the extent to which the menu item changes.

Item-selection control (Select from Menu). By default, the By Text option is checked and the menu item you chose is listed by name.

■ **By Text.** Use when you are targeting a menu item whose name does not change much or at all.

■ **Match Exactly.** This means nearly what it says. It's not case sensitive, but it sure can tell the difference between three periods in a row and ellipses.

■ **By Position.** Use this option when the item name changes significantly (for example, Undo Typing becomes Redo Paste) or a non-text menu item (like a color palette). By Position is almost always application specific, because identical menu items are often in different positions in different applications.

Menu-selection control. This control area determines how QuicKeys looks for the menu on which your target item is located. Menu-selection control defaults to Look for Menu by Title and QuicKeys fills in the title of the menu you chose.

■ **Look for Menu by Title.** Use this default for most application-specific situations and in Universal Set shortcuts when you are sure that the target menus all have identical names in every possible application.

■ **Search All Menus.** Use this option when a Universal Set shortcut triggers a command located on menus that carry different names in different applications. It's also useful when shortcuts, for some reason or another, can't seem to find the menu item.

■ **Only Apple menu.** This is a holdover from the Menu/DA shortcut, and so won't usually come into play. However, if you use the Menu Selection shortcut to select an item from the Apple menu, selecting this option limits the search for your menu item to the Apple menu.

Modifier-key control. Some menu items change their form if a modifier key is pressed while the menu item is selected. These modifier-key control options tell QuicKeys which modifiers you want held down so the target menu item will appear.

When you construct a Menu Selection shortcut that needs a modifier, you can hold down the correct modifier key when you pick the menu item with the little menu cursor. For example, holding down Command-Option when you press on the File menu changes the Print item to Fax when you have STF fax software installed. To build a Menu Selection shortcut that accesses this Fax item, you can press the appropriate modifiers (in this case Command-Option) while making the menu selection. This causes QuicKeys to fill in the correct name of the target menu item and to check the appropriate modifier key boxes in this control area.

Menu Selection Considerations

You're usually best off using the automatic entries that QuicKeys makes in the Menu Selection edit dialog box. But sometimes you will have to change them, especially in situations where you want to select a menu item that has a name with an ending that varies somewhat from application to application (or within an application). If you enter a truncated version of the menu item name and *uncheck* Match Exactly, QuicKeys searches through the menu items top to bottom and left to right and selects the first match. For example, entering Undo in the text edit box and unchecking Match Exactly allows the shortcut to select Undo Typing or Undo Paste and so forth.

Checking Match Exactly sometimes leads to problems when you type the menu item name into the text edit box yourself. This is because the true menu item name often differs slightly from the version you entered. Check to see if spaces and special symbols are correct (don't worry about an initial space; QuicKeys ignores it). And the three dots you see in menu items which bring up a dialog box are almost always the ellipsis character (Option-;).

Certain applications employ menu designs that deviate from the Mac interface standards. Sometimes what appears to be a menu isn't generated by the program in a standard manner. Sometimes an application can think a menu has a different name than it displays. The QuicKeys automatic entries in a Menu Selection edit dialog box are occasionally frighteningly perspicacious in determining a workable suggestion. For example, Figure 6.10 shows a hierarchical menu item chosen in PageMaker.

Figure 6.10
PageMaker's Type
Style submenu

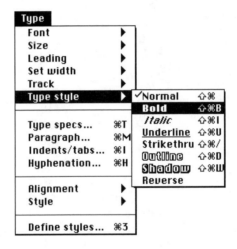

The menu title is Type and the submenu is Type Style, but the automatic entry that QuicKeys made in the Menu Selection edit dialog box has the submenu name Format. And, of course, it finds the menu item perfectly when it thinks it is looking in the Format menu (wherever *that* is—it's not on the Menu bar). However, if you try a similar procedure in QuarkXPress, QuicKeys doesn't deign to suggest what the menu title might be. The fix here, and a good one for similar problems, is to check Search All Menus. The menu item is selected, tickety-poo.

If your Mac beeps when you make the menu choice while constructing a Menu Selection shortcut, it's an indication that this is a non-standard menu and there probably is no way to use shortcuts to access it. Pop-up menus are accessible with Version 3 of QuicKeys (hallelujah!), but you have to use the Pop-up Menu extension discussed later in this chapter.

Menu Selection Tactics

Use Menu Selection shortcuts to select a menu item.

The most common use of Menu Selection shortcuts is to give an application's menu command a keystroke equivalent (for example, assigning keystrokes to the Clear and Define menu items in FileMaker Pro). This type of job can also be done (sometimes easily) with ResEdit, but some people don't want to mess with so powerful (and unforgiving) a utility program.

The More Universal Shortcuts set that comes with your QuicKeys package suggests seven universal Menu Selection shortcuts (see Figure 6.11).

Figure 6.11
More Universal
Shortcuts set

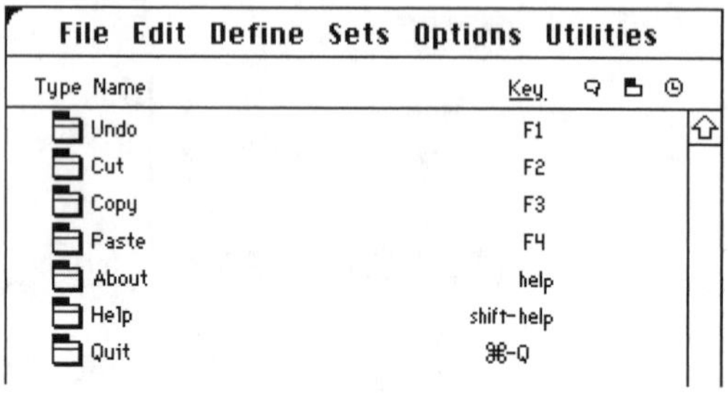

QuicKeys-suggested keystrokes.

Four Menu Selection shortcuts standardize the basic Edit menu commands and assign them to the function keys with the appropriate labels on the Mac extended keyboard (F1 through F4). This approach works for some folks, but we wonder why you should waste perfectly good function keys when these menu items already have standard keystroke activation in most applications. So we standardize them the old-fashioned way (see Figure 6.12).

Figure 6.12
Our Universal Set

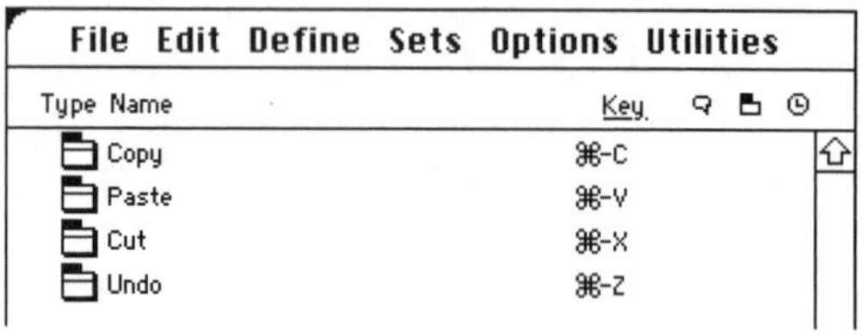

With the old-fashioned keystrokes

Pop-up Menu

Pop-up Menu is a long overdue new extension that selects items from pop-up menus. When we heard this extension was released we cheered, remembering the time a few years back we were asked to make a shortcut

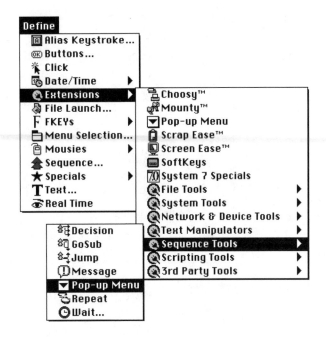

to perform the simple task of selecting a printer driver in QuarkXPress. The task *seemed* simple, except the driver options lived on a pop-up menu. We spent hours creating one of the great kludges of all time, a Sequence shortcut using Clicks and Real Time steps all cobbled together that sort of worked. All we needed was a Pop-up shortcut. Now we have one.

To create a Pop-up Menu shortcut, select the shortcut from the Extensions submenu of the QuicKeys Editor's Define menu. We've used Extension Manager (see Chapter 18, *QuicKeys Utilities*) to give this shortcut a place of honor over the extension categories on the submenu so we don't have to dig into the Sequence Tools submenu to access it. When Pop-up Menu is selected, the Pop-up Menu edit dialog box appears (see Figure 6.13).

Click the Select Pop-up Menu button. The QuicKeys Editor window closes and QuicKeys waits for you to select an item from a pop-up menu. Then the Pop-up Menu edit dialog box reappears containing data on your selection. The dialog box is an odd mix of the Menu Selection edit dialog box and the Click edit dialog box, providing some options to help QuicKeys find the right item on the pop-up menu. In most cases, you'll find that the way QuicKeys automatically configures this dialog box works fine. But sometimes you'll need to tweak.

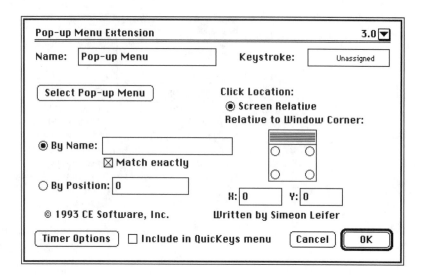

Figure 6.13
Pop-up Menu edit
dialog box

By Name. The By Name option lets you type in the name (or an approximation) of the pop-up menu item. If you check Match Exactly, the shortcut requires you to enter an exact name for it to match. Not checking this box causes the shortcut to select a partial match. Usually, QuicKeys automatically selects the By Name option and fills in the name of the pop-up menu item you chose. To ensure reliability, you may have to check the Match Exactly checkbox yourself if another menu item has a name that begins with the same item as you have chosen. For example, when we chose SuperMatch 20 from a pop-up menu in QuarkXPress, the shortcut chose another item—SuperMatch 20•T—until we checked Match Exactly.

By Position. The By Position option lets you fill in a number indicating the position of the item on the menu (counting down from the top of the menu to the item you want to select). Choosing this option may work when a number of pop-up menu items are similar or when QuicKeys just seems confounded by the names.

Click Location. QuicKeys locates a pop-up menu by screen location (it calls this the click location; you can usually see the cursor jump to a particular location when you trigger the Pop-up Menu shortcut). When you first select a pop-up menu item, the shortcut records the coordinates of your selection in the x = and y = text boxes of the Click Location area. The upper-left window corner is the default origin, or 0,0 point, but you can pick any other corner, just like with the Click edit dialog box (see Chapter 7, *Shortcuts That Mimic the Keyboard and Mouse*, for a more thorough description of how x- and y-coordinates are used to locate a point on the screen).

You also have the option of locating the pop-up relative to the entire screen. The Click Location option may have to be massaged quite a bit to get the shortcut to work properly.

Pop-up Menu Considerations

Pop-up menus seem to be growing by leaps and bounds in applications, especially in graphics and desktop publishing programs. Although the Pop-up Menu shortcut is a great advance, in some situations it just doesn't work right with the automatic entries. A number of programs have pop-ups that confound this shortcut.

However, in other cases when the Pop-up Menu shortcut doesn't initially function properly, it can often be tweaked to perform flawlessly. A good example of this is the Layout pop-up menu in the upper-left corner of FileMaker Pro. The automatic entries in the Pop-up Menu edit dialog box produce a shortcut that clicks about one-half inch to the right of the pop-up menu (we don't know why and we don't ask). Changing the Click Location option to Screen Relative fixes the problem, until you move the FileMaker Pro window somewhat, then the click goes in the same place relative to the screen, but the wrong place on the FileMaker Pro document.

The workaround is to use the Relative to Window Corner option for the upper-left corner and then change the x-coordinate of the click to account for the displacement (an x value of –40 worked for us). See Chapter 22, *QuicKeys and FileMaker Pro*, for more details.

You may find cases where the Pop-up Menu shortcut just doesn't function reliably, as is the case in the Control Palette in PageMaker 5.0. The workaround is to make the same selections from the PageMaker menus using Menu Selection shortcuts.

One other anomaly that we've encountered: Pop-up Menu shortcuts can sometimes select items from a pop-up menu *even if the command is grayed out*. In CompuServe Navigator, for instance, the Delete Message item is grayed out if you're reading a message from one person to another (the message wasn't sent to you, so you have no deletion rights). Our handy Pop-up Menu shortcut, however, happily selects the item. Go figure.

Pop-up Menu Tactics

Use Pop-up Menu shortcuts to access items in pop-up menus.

Pop-up Menu shortcuts can be very useful, and a few of them are standard equipment in some of our application sets. You can also use Pop-up Menu shortcuts as part of Sequences. Indeed, that is how CE thinks you will use them, which is why the shortcut is located on the Sequence Tools submenu of the Extensions menu. However, you cannot directly create a Pop-up Menu step in a Sequence, because it is just too difficult for QuicKeys to go through all the convolutions required. Instead, you must record it in the Sequence (easy enough) or create it first and copy and paste (or import) it into the Sequence (easy, too). See Chapter 14, *The Sequence*, for more details on how this works.

Buttons

Buttons shortcuts click a button or checkbox in a dialog box.

There's no mystery here; the Buttons shortcut has an obvious task and simple controls. Just choose Button from the Define menu, and the Button edit dialog box appears.

Buttons Edit Dialog Box

The Buttons edit dialog box is designed so that you enter into the Name text box the name of the button you want to click.

QuicKeys can choose the correct button even if you only type the first letter or few letters, as long as no other buttons in that dialog box start the same way (see Figure 6.14).

The options area of the Buttons edit dialog box was created to give you specialized control of checkboxes—but it can affect the clicking of buttons, so always choose the top option (Always Click Button) for buttons.

Unlike buttons, a checkbox toggles between two modes when it is clicked. Generally, you won't want to worry about whether the checkbox is already checked; you just want to change it to either checked or unchecked mode. That's what options two and three are for. If you choose the first

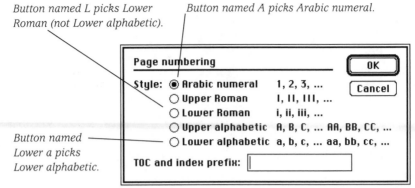

Figure 6.14
QuicKeys buttons
title discrimination

Button named L picks Lower Roman (not Lower alphabetic).

Button named A picks Arabic numeral.

Button named Lower a picks Lower alphabetic.

option, Always Click Button, for a checkbox, the shortcut will toggle the mode of the checkbox.

A Buttons shortcut will not display a notice if its target button is not available.

Button Tactics

Use Buttons shortcuts to click a button or a checkbox.

You'll probably use Buttons shortcuts in application-specific areas. Often, Sequences contain at least one Buttons shortcut.

Many times, applications have keystroke shortcuts to press buttons in dialog boxes. But you might find yourself in a situation where you must repeatedly press buttons that don't have these shortcuts built in. Application-specific Buttons shortcuts fill this role nicely.

If you find yourself in this situation only occasionally, you might just want to use the DialogKeys application which came in your QuicKeys package. This lets you tab through the buttons in a dialog box and click the one you want without using the mouse.

Don has a few Button shortcuts in his Universal Set, just because he doesn't use DialogKeys often (see Figure 6.15). Steve uses DialogKeys.

Figure 6.15
Don's Universal
Buttons shortcuts

Type Name	Key
OK Cancel	opt ctrl–F4
OK Yes	opt ctrl–F6
OK No	opt ctrl–F7
OK OK	opt ctrl–F8

File Edit Define Sets Options Utilities

7

Shortcuts That Mimic the Keyboard and Mouse

This chapter discusses two similar shortcut types: Alias Keystroke and Click. Both act as stand-ins for different parts of the Apple Desktop Bus (the keyboard and mouse), and both perform simple tasks. Although creating an Alias Keystroke shortcut is easy, making Click shortcuts function properly sometimes might seem like battling the controls of a crippled 747.

Alias Keystroke

Alias Keystroke shortcuts remap one keyboard key (and any modifiers) to another keyboard key (and any modifiers).

A good example of this type is an Alias Keystroke shortcut that Steve created to overcome a hardware/human interface glitch. The extended Apple keyboard has its Help key about one-half inch to the right of the Delete key. Sometimes, when Steve is burning up the keyboard trying to meet a deadline, his killer Delete index finger overshoots its intended touchdown on Delete and instead bounces off Help and back to Delete. This causes the Help feature of Microsoft Word to seize control of his machine, ponder a bit, and finally deliver a Help screen on deleting text and graphics. Steve fixed this using an Alias Keystroke shortcut (see Figure 7.1).

Steve's fix fools the Help key into thinking it is Delete. The Delete key still triggers the Delete function, but now Help does the same. In order to retain the Help function, Steve created a second Alias Keystroke

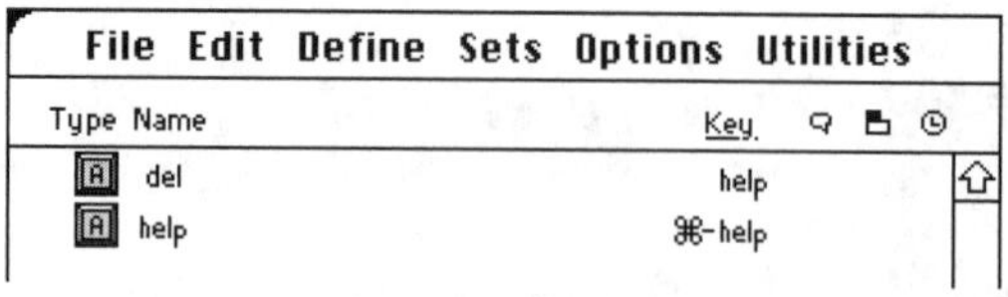

Figure 7.1
Steve's fix

File Edit Define Sets Options Utilities			
Type Name		Key	⊡ ▣ ◷
🅰 del		help	⇧
🅰 help		⌘-help	

shortcut to invoke it using Command-Help. This problem occurs in enough applications (word processors, desktop publishers, art programs, etc.) that Steve put the Alias Keystroke shortcut in his Universal Set.

This shortcut of Steve's does make his Mac somewhat less than user-friendly for novitiates (if they press the Help key, it deletes all their selected text) and also points out one of QuicKey's great strengths—the ability to play really nasty practical jokes on friends and co-workers. 'Nuf said.

Alias Keystroke Considerations

The Alias Keystroke shortcut is almost foolproof. The only hazard to worry about is inadvertently mapping over a function that you want to retain. Don't.

Alias Keystroke Tactics

Use Alias Keystroke shortcuts to make a keystroke combination invoke a different keystroke combination.

Except for situations like Steve's, where you want one key to do what another does, you probably won't find yourself using many Alias Key-stroke shortcuts as single units. However, Sequences (see Chapter 14, *The Sequence*) often employ an Alias Keystroke shortcut as a step.

PowerBook users and others who do not have an extended key-board also find Alias Keystrokes very useful for making keystrokes that aren't on their keyboards. QuicKeys gives you a number of sets that include Alias keys for different extended keyboard keystrokes that you can copy and paste into your Key sets. Look for them in the QuicKeys Example Sets folder in the QuicKeys Tools folder. See also Chapter 10, *Shortcuts for PowerBooks*.

Click

Click shortcuts mimic mouse clicking and movement.

The first steps in creating a Click shortcut are simple, and, if QuicKeys fills in selections for the Click edit dialog boxes that fit your situation (it usually does), the Click will give you no problem. However, if you have to tweak or edit your Click shortcut, you may find the multiple edit dia-log boxes fairly daunting. We'll show you what you have to worry about and what you don't.

Creating a Click shortcut involves a QuicKeys-aided process of recording. Some sights that you see during the process are very similar to those you see when you record a Sequence (see Chapter 14, *The Sequence*).

A useful example of this shortcut type is a shortcut that will shrink a document window to its smallest size. It's easiest to begin the process with a document that's open to a normal size. Then you can select Click from the Main Editor's Define menu (or choose Record One Shortcut from the QuicKeys submenu of the Apple menu). This causes a little microphone icon to flash over the Apple menu. Use the cursor to click and drag the bottom-right corner box (the size box) in your document window all the way to the top-left of the screen (the window will stop shrinking at some point but you can continue to drag all the way to the screen's top-left corner).

After you release the mouse button, a Click edit dialog box appears (see Figure 7.2). The center part of this dialog box contains three buttons (Click, Window, and Control Area). To the right of each button is a report on its settings. Under these buttons are two additional option control boxes. If you want multiple clicks on something, you need to fill in the appropriate number in the Click Time(s) box. If you want a modifier key held down while you click with the mouse, you can check the appropriate box in the Hold Down area.

Figure 7.2
Click edit dialog box

```
Click
─────────────────────────────────────────────────────────
Name:  [Click            ]        Keystroke:  [ Unassigned ]

          (    Click:    )   From:(560,424) from top-left corner
                             To:(-560,-464) from current location

          (   Window:   )    Window #1 from front

          ( Control area: )  None
─────────────────────────────────────────────────────────
          Click  [1]  time(s)
─────────────────────────────────────────────────────────
          Hold down:  □ ⌘  □ Shift  □ Option  □ Control  while clicking

          ( Timer Options )  □ Include in QuicKeys menu   ( Cancel )  ( OK )
```

The Click Location Edit Dialog Box

Clicking on the Click button invokes the Click Location edit dialog box. This edit dialog box is divided into a right and a left section (see Figure 7.3). Each section corresponds to a different location that the Click type records when you create a Click shortcut.

Figure 7.3
Click Location edit dialog box

The click control area—where you pressed down on the mouse button.

The drag control area—where you released the mouse button.

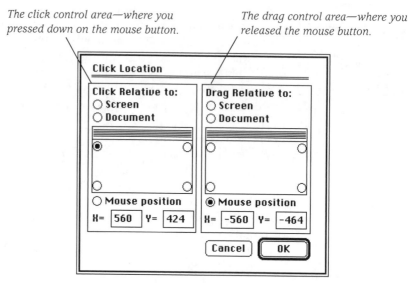

QuicKeys remembers two things:

■ It records where you pressed down on the mouse button (click-down). This location is displayed on the left section of the Click Location edit dialog box.

■ It records where you let go of the mouse button (click-up). This location is displayed on the right section of the dialog box.

These positions are also described on the bottom of the dialog box as x- and y-coordinates stated as x = and y = text entry boxes that you can manually edit.

Units of measurement. The numbers in the bottom coordinates boxes are measured in *pixels* (little dots that make up the image on your Mac's monitor). A pixel equals about $1/72$ inch on most Mac monitors, but has no exact size; the pixel array can be larger or smaller depending on the monitor you use. Each standard class of Mac monitor displays a set number of pixels (see Table 7.1).

Table 7.1	**Monitor Pixel Counts**

Monitor	Pixels
Mac 12-inch monochrome monitor	640 x 480
Mac 12-inch RGB monitor	512 x 384
AppleColor RGB monitor	640 x 480
16-inch color monitor	832 x 624
2-page monochrome or color monitor	1152 x 870
Apple Portrait monitor	640 x 870
Compact Mac displays	512 x 342

Original sin. Although each section of the Click Location edit dialog box only contains one location (specified by an x- and a y-coordinate), each possesses various other controls. These controls consist of options for locating where the x- and y-coordinates are measured from (which, as you might remember from your first geometry class, is called the *origin*).

QuicKeys automatically selects one of these options and fills in the x- and y-coordinates of your click location relative to that origin. If you choose a different option, QuicKeys automatically recalculates the coordinates. You will only need to fill in the coordinates yourself if you are tweaking the automatic entry.

You can select three different options areas (see Figure 7.3) on each section (click-down and click-up) of the Click Location edit dialog box.

- **Screen.** If this option is chosen, the coordinates are measured from the top-left corner of the entire screen. So the top-left corner pixel of Don's 15-inch color portrait monitor has the coordinates (0,0) and the bottom-right corner pixel has the coordinates (639,869). Use this option when you want to pick out something relative to the whole screen, like the Trash Can.

- **Document.** This gives you the option of measuring from any corner of a document window. The graphic within the Document section might be a little misleading. There are five buttons: Document and one for each of the four corners. The Document button is redundant with the top-left corner button in the window beneath it. The corner buttons measure from the extreme corners of the document window (outside the scroll bars, for instance), not from within the window as it appears in the graphic. Use this option when you want to click on something relative to the window, like the grow region in the lower-right corner of most document windows.

■ **Mouse Position.** This differs a little depending on which section of the dialog box it is in. In the left-hand section, this coordinate represents a point measured from where the mouse cursor was when you pressed its button down. So when this option is chosen, the coordinates displayed are always initially (0,0), since you always clicked where the mouse was when you recorded the shortcut. The option can then be used to tweak the click position by changing the coordinate entries.

In the right-hand section, the Mouse Position option represents the coordinate of the cursor's location when you let go of the mouse button (a click and drag) relative to where the button was pushed down. If you just make a Click shortcut without a drag, then the Mouse Position option is automatically checked in the click-up section and the coordinates (0,0) are filled in, to show that there was no movement between where the mouse was pressed down and where it was released.

You may notice in all these cases that the x-coordinates *increase going toward the right* of the screen and the y-coordinates *increase going toward the bottom* of the screen. This is different from the standard Cartesian coordinate system (where the x- and y-coordinates increase right and up) but makes perfect sense in the context of monitor and cursor behavior.

The Window Edit Dialog Box

The Window button on the main Click edit dialog box invokes the Window edit dialog box (see Figure 7.4). This dialog box selects the window in which the Click shortcut does the click.

This dialog box offers three options.

■ **Any.** Any is the automatic choice if the click is not within an application window. The click is made regardless of what shows on the screen.

Figure 7.4
Window edit
dialog box

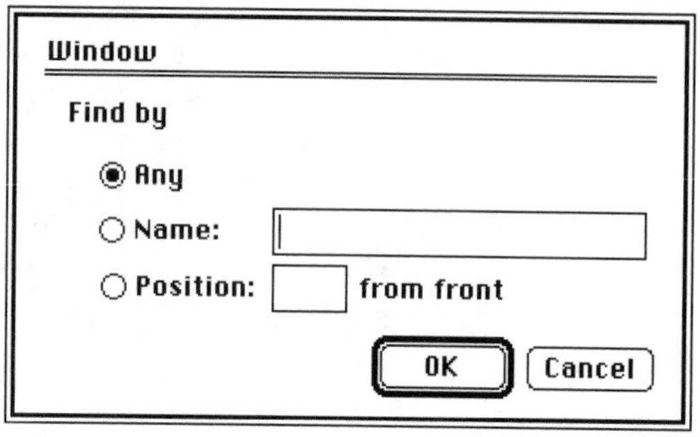

94

■ **Name.** This button and its text edit box choose the document to be clicked on by its name. If you choose this option, the click only happens if the active window has the same name that you entered in the text edit box. The text box of this option is automatically filled in with the name of the application document when you click on it. But, if you want this option, you need to select it yourself.

■ **Position.** If you click on an application window, the document's position is entered in the text edit box and the Position button is selected. If you choose this option, the click will occur in the window that is as many layers back from the front as you enter in the text edit box. This is particularly useful in applications like PageMaker where the Main window is rarely the top window.

The Control Area Edit Dialog Box

Pressing the Control Area button on the main Click edit dialog box invokes the Control Area edit dialog box (see Figure 7.5). This dialog box controls how the Click shortcut finds its target if the click occurs on a button or a scroll bar.

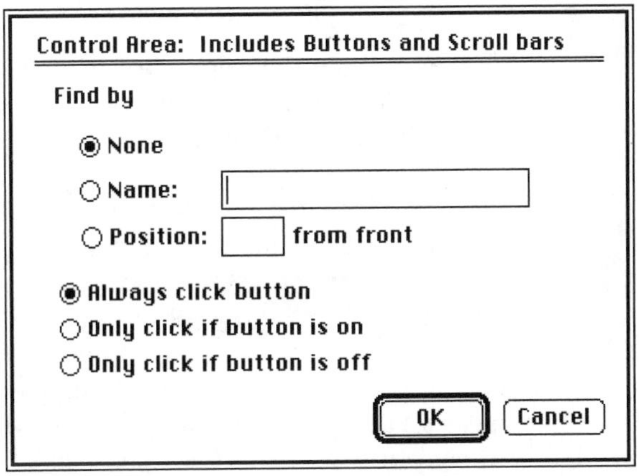

Figure 7.5
Control Area edit dialog box

If your Click shortcut was recorded by clicking in a scroll bar, checkbox, or button, then the name of that control area appears in the text edit box after the Name radio button in this edit dialog box. Also, the Position radio button will be turned on, with the position of the control area automatically filled in. You probably don't want to mess with the Control Area edit dialog box. If you want to click on a button, try using a Button shortcut instead. Use this option in the very unusual situation where the control area (button) doesn't have an apparent name.

- **None.** None will be on if you haven't clicked in a Control Area.

- **Name.** If you want the Click shortcut to target a control area by name, then click this radio button and fill in the name of the control area. (QuicKeys probably already filled in this area for you.)

- **Position.** Different control areas occupy different transparent layers that can be used to identify the particular area you want. QuicKeys often fills in the correct position for you.

- **Button click options.** Three options can be used to ensure that buttons are correctly pressed.

Click Considerations

The biggest tip regarding the Click shortcut is to use it only when no other type will do the trick. In certain circumstances, Button, Mousies, File Launch, Pop-up Menu, or Menu Selection might be a better choice than Click. Use Click as a last resort, because it is sometimes tricky to modify and isn't as adaptable to most changes in conditions (for instance, if a modal window moves, or if you move an icon you have clicked on after you set up the shortcut) as other shortcut types that are more specialized for a particular job.

Click coordinate manipulation. Occasionally you might want to change the coordinates that QuicKeys automatically enters in the $x =$ and $y =$ fields. This might happen if you set up the Click shortcut on some icon and then move the icon.

The things to remember here are that x-coordinates increase to the right and y-coordinates increase going down. These coordinates are approximately 72 to the inch, so use that as your benchmark. For example, replacing $x = 400$ and $y = 200$ with $x = 418$ and $y = 182$ moves the click point one-quarter inch to the right and one-quarter inch up. When you find your Click is missing the point you want it to hit, you can actually measure the screen with a ruler—from the transitory arrow that appears when you trigger the Click shortcut to the object you wish to target. Then work out the arithmetic and change the settings in the Click Location window appropriately.

Gunther Blaschek, the author of PopChar, has written a handy little freeware INIT called Corner that helps measure screen distances, so you can accurately determine how to tweak the $x =$ and $y =$ fields. It is available from many online services.

Click in Sequences. Sequences are important enough to have two chapters devoted to them (Chapter 14, *The Sequence*, and Chapter 15, *Sequence Shortcuts*), but the Click shortcut presents a special situation within the Sequence, so we want to mention it here. When you are constructing a Sequence, the Click shortcut is not made available to you from the Define menu. Instead, you must either use the Record More or Import buttons on the Sequence edit dialog box to create a Click shortcut or import an already-extant shortcut into your Sequence. For more, see "Import" in Chapter 14, *The Sequence*.

Click Tactics   *Use Click to click or drag something when other types can't be used.*

We often find ourselves using a Click shortcut when we tried to use another type, but it just didn't work. This sometimes occurs with programs that don't comply with the Apple guidelines for control areas. A button may not have a name, for instance, so we can't ask QuicKeys to click that button. So, when we try to use a Button shortcut to click what appears to be a button and it doesn't work, we resort to a Click shortcut.

Our few Click shortcuts tend to be in application-specific sets or within Sequence shortcuts. Don has two Click shortcuts he uses enough to keep in his permanent collection: Trash It and Close Zoom.

Trash It. This shortcut lives in the Universal set. It drags whatever icon the cursor is on to the Trash. Figure 7.6 shows the appropriate settings for Don's monitor; when you record the Click yourself, the To location that's correct for your set up will be filled in.

Figure 7.6
Trash It Click
shortcut

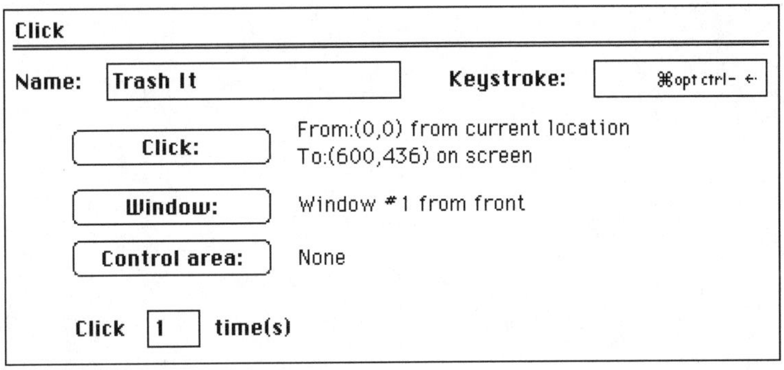

Close Zoom. This Click shortcut drags the image size box in the lower-right corner of the top application window up and to the left so that the window shrinks to its smallest size. Don keeps this shortcut in his Universal Set and its activating key is next to his Zoom Mousie shortcut (which essentially performs the opposite function). Figure 7.7 shows the settings for Close Zoom. Some applications (such as PageMaker) don't work well with this shortcut, because their Main window is never on the top layer.

Figure 7.7
Close Zoom Click
shortcut

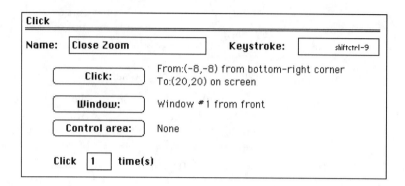

8 Shortcuts That Control the Mac System

System control shortcuts make high-level adjustments to your Mac; they automate the switches, levers, knobs, bells, and whistles of your Mac's interface. Some automate processes found on certain menus; others instantly change the settings on control panels. Many shortcuts in this chapter perform one job—they don't have multiple targets—so you usually need just one of each in your QuicKeys environment. This chapter describes how to use these tools.

- Shut Down
- Restart
- Screen Ease
- Speaker Changer
- System 7 Specials
- ProcessSwap
- FKEYs

Switches

Restart and Shut Down are the two "switches" for your Mac that are normally activated from the Finder's Special menu. You can make QuicKeys restart or shut down your Mac by using a Menu Selection shortcut to choose each option directly from this Special menu, but that only works when you're in the Finder. The Restart and Shut Down Specials shortcuts take a more direct route to these switches, no matter what program you are currently running.

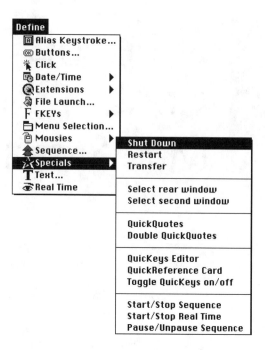

Choosing either Restart or Shut Down from the Specials submenu of the Main Editor's Define menu gives you the Special edit dialog box (see Figure 8.1); its operation is completely self-evident.

Figure 8.1
Special edit dialog
box

Choosing either Restart or Shut Down from the Specials submenu of the Main Editor's Define menu gives you the Special edit dialog box (see Figure 8.1); its operation is completely self-evident.

We both have Shut Down and Restart shortcuts as part of our per-manent Universal sets. Don uses Control-Option-Delete to activate Shut Down and Control-Option- = (the key adjacent to Delete on the Apple Extended Keyboard) to trigger Restart. Steve uses Control-Delete for Shut Down, and Control-Option-Delete for Restart, because they're far apart and hard to press by accident. Whatever keystroke strategy you use, you don't want to be able to trigger either of these shortcuts inad-vertently, so multiple modifiers accompanied by a long finger stretch help to create a fail-safe guard.

Switches Tactics   *Use Shut Down and Restart shortcuts instead of accessing these switch functions from the Finder's Special menu.*

Picture and Volume   Screen Ease and SpeakerChanger can adjust your monitor display and your speaker volume. For those who use System 7.5, some Apple Scripts may be available to launch from the Automated Tasks submenu of the Apple menu that perform some of the same functions as Screen Ease and SpeakerChanger. However, running these scripts is a slower and less elegant process to change settings than using the shortcuts.

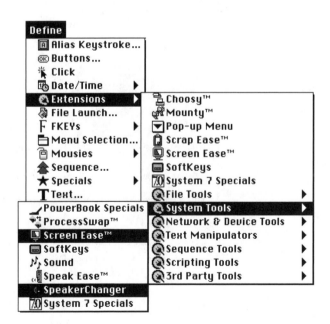

Screen Ease

The Screen Ease shortcut adjusts various controls located on the Monitors control panel: with it, you can choose how you display different colors and shades of gray. Additionally, Screen Ease can make the changes permanent (until you change them again) or temporary (until you restart your Mac).

You can make shortcuts that will select specific settings, or you can choose options that will vary settings in a particular direction. This shortcut is exceptionally useful for color monitors, where you can change the pixel depth depending on the requirements of your application programs (generally, high-end graphics and CAD programs require more definition and pixel precision than word processing and spreadsheet programs). It's also really useful on PowerBooks where running in color or grayscale slows down screen refreshing.

You can make a Screen Ease shortcut by choosing it from the System Tools submenu of the Extensions submenu of the Define menu. The Screen Ease edit dialog box appears (see Figure 8.2).

Figure 8.2
Screen Ease edit
dialog box

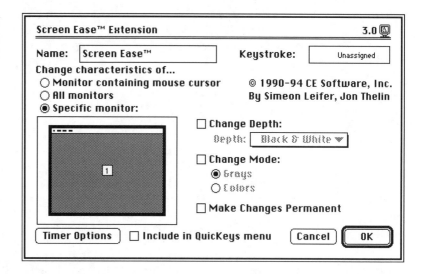

The left side of this dialog box gives you options for selecting the target monitor in multiple-monitor setups. The right side contains the adjustment options, including the Depth pop-up menu (see Figure 8.3).

By pressing on the pop-up menu, you can choose a level of color or gray-scale display. Those available on your Mac are outlined. At the bottom

Figure 8.3
Depth pop-up
menu

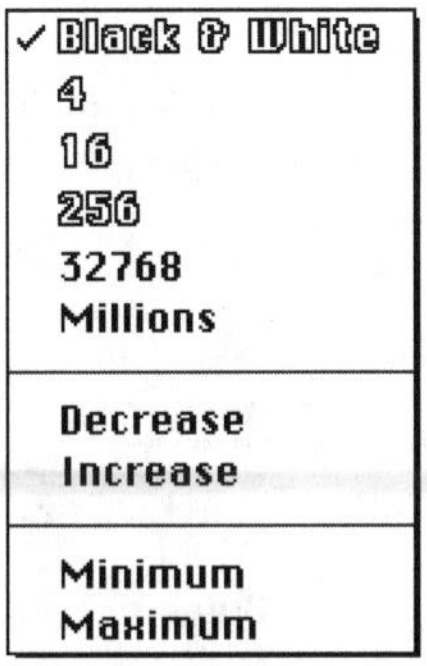

✓ Black & White
   4
   16
   256
   32768
   Millions

   Decrease
   Increase

   Minimum
   Maximum

of the menu are two option areas: Decrease/Increase and Minimum/ Maximum. Decrease/Increase adjusts the depth level in steps; Minimum/ Maximum takes you to the simplest or the most complex depth level available to you.

Screen Ease Tactics and Considerations

Use Screen Ease shortcuts to adjust your monitor settings.

How often and in what manner you use Screen Ease depends on your particular situation. If you need a Screen Ease shortcut, you probably will want to make more than one; you'll want one for your standard monitor settings and others for special situations.

There are two basic tactics for Screen Ease shortcuts.

■ **Targeted.** Make one Screen Ease shortcut for your standard setting and others for specialized applications. You can embed a Screen Ease shortcut in a Sequence that opens a sophisticated graphics application (like Photoshop) to make the screen change to a higher resolution level automatically.

■ **Toggled.** Make two Screen Ease shortcuts—either Decrease/Increase or Minimum/Maximum. Don uses a Decrease/Increase combination in his Universal set.

What if you don't know the level your monitor is rendering at the moment? A third-party extension can tell you—Bit Depth, written by Ed Ludwig of Vectre Systems. Bit Depth is a single-use shortcut that pops up a box containing the number of levels your monitor is currently displaying. See the Appendix, *Resources*.

SpeakerChanger

The SpeakerChanger shortcut sets the volume of your speaker. When it is chosen from the System Tools category of the Extensions submenu, the SpeakerChanger edit dialog box appears (see Figure 8.4). Any volume adjustments you make with the SpeakerChanger shortcut will disappear when you reboot; your volume level will revert to the Speaker Volume setting in your control panel.

Figure 8.4
SpeakerChanger
edit dialog box

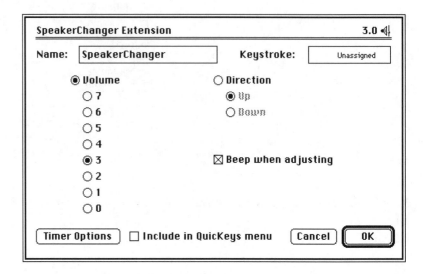

SpeakerChanger Considerations and Tactics

Use SpeakerChanger to adjust the volume of your Mac's speaker.

We have two SpeakerChanger shortcuts: one to increase the volume and one to decrease it. Every time we trigger one, we get a beep signifying the new volume level. Two beeps indicates that we have hit the maximum setting; the menu bar flashing without any beep indicates that we have reduced the setting to zero.

System 7 Specials

The System 7 Specials are shortcuts that allow you to access and control some enhancements to the Mac operating system first introduced with System 7, such as Balloon Help, the Application menu, and file sharing.

Open the System 7 Specials edit dialog box by choosing System 7 Specials from the Systems Tools category of the Extensions submenu of the Define menu. The System 7 Specials edit dialog box contains a pop-up menu selection of seven shortcuts (see Figure 8.5).

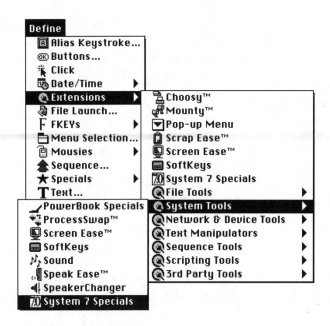

Figure 8.5
System 7 Specials
edit dialog box

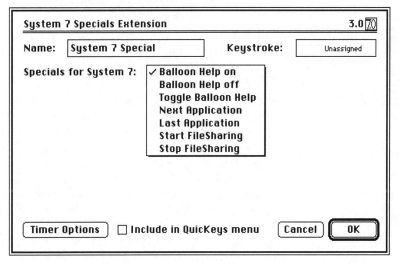

Balloon Help   Never let it be said that CE doesn't give you options. There's one shortcut to turn Balloon Help on, one to turn it off, and one to toggle it on
and off. What abundance! Unfortunately, we don't use any of them,

because we find Balloon Help more of a marketing gimmick than a real feature. We might turn it on someday when we are in a totally foreign program that is well supported by Balloon Help. But until then, we just remember that these tools exist.

Application Switching

One of System 7's best features is its ability to switch between applications. The System 7 Specials shortcut provides a limited type of multitasking support by letting you switch your active applications.

The two application-switching tools, Next Application and Last Application, let you march through all the applications you have open, in either direction. Applications are layered in the order in which they were opened, not in the order in which they appear on the alphabetical Application menu.

The ability to flip through your open applications in one direction is great; the ability to go in the other direction is sort of stupid. A shortcut that toggles back and forth between two applications would be very useful—like the Select Second Window shortcut, which is exactly what the Last Application ProcessSwap shortcut (discussed later in this chapter) does. So we find these System 7 Special application-switching shortcuts limited and use ProcessSwap instead.

File Sharing

The introduction of System 7 provided the powerful feature of file sharing. File sharing is a lot like Sitka's Tops, a networking package we used for a long time. Although it does have more features than Tops, it is also more complicated and less intuitive to use and entails opening myriad control panels and commands to initiate. File sharing is for networked computers, so if you are working out in the woods with only your fax machine and the sound of a rushing brook to keep you company, you can ignore this. But if you are networked with other computers, System 7 offers the ability to share files among them.

Two file-sharing shortcuts control the master switch for your file sharing. One starts it, and the other stops it. We haven't found these shortcuts too useful because we have file sharing activated constantly; we control access by exercising prudence when adjusting the settings when we select Sharing from the File menu.

However, you might want to use these shortcuts if you repeatedly turn file sharing on and off (as you must do if you want to eject a removable-media cartridge, such as a SyQuest). Note that the Stop FileSharing shortcut acts a little differently from clicking Stop in the Sharing Setup control panel. Clicking Stop in the control panel invokes a dialog box in which you enter a delay before file sharing actually ceases (see Figure 8.6).

Figure 8.6
Delay End File
Sharing edit
dialog box

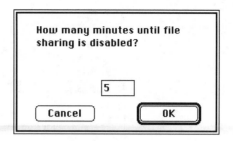

How many minutes until file
sharing is disabled?

5

Cancel   OK

This gives people who are sharing your files a chance to save what they are working on. The Stop FileSharing shortcut shuts down file sharing immediately.

Stop FileSharing can also be useful when the system gets confused and thinks you are still using a shared volume when you aren't, so it won't let you shut down.

System 7 Specials Tactics and Considerations

Use System 7 Specials shortcuts to enhance your use of Balloon Help, application switching, and file sharing.

If you use System 7 Specials shortcuts, you probably will want to access them from any application, so these shortcuts belong in your Universal set. A good keystroke for the Balloon Help shortcuts would be various modifiers with the Help key. File-sharing control keystrokes depend on your own setup (see Chapter 17, *Keystroke Strategies*). But because of the immediate effect of Stop FileSharing, you might want its keystroke to be difficult to enter as a fail-safe. We don't use the application switchers, preferring ProcessSwap instead.

ProcessSwap

As mentioned earlier, the truly elegant way to move between applications on your Mac is not to use the System 7 Specials' application switching shortcuts, but rather the ProcessSwap shortcut. ProcessSwap lets you move between applications with a keystroke, rather than use the mouse to pull down the Application menu to select another application. You can create ProcessSwap shortcuts to switch to particular applications, to move through all open applications in succession, or to switch back and forth between two open applications.

What's a process? A Mac running System 7 provides a *cooperative multitasking environment*. This means that you can have more than one application running at one time (although only one is really active at a time), and the Mac manages who gets access to the computer and

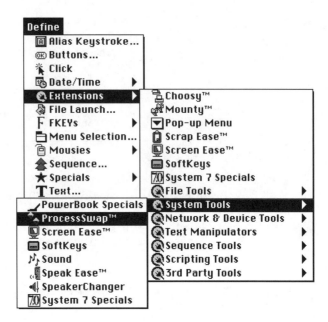

when. In addition, you can switch between open applications, selecting which one gets computer time.

A *process* is an open application, the object managed by the Mac in the multitasking environment. The Mac has a Process Manager to mange the status, memory use, and processing timing of your processes. So now that you know that process equals open application, you won't be intimidated when first viewing the ProcessSwap edit dialog box (see Figure 8.7) that is displayed when you choose ProcessSwap from the System Tools category of the Extensions submenu of the Define menu.

The ProcessSwap edit dialog box provides a number of options. Pull down the Operation pop-up menu to select how you want to move between applications.

- **Switch To.** Selecting Switch To moves you to the specific application that you choose in the Process pop-up menu.

- **Switch Back.** Selecting Switch Back moves you from your currently active application to whichever application you last switched to using ProcessSwap.

- **Switch To (From List).** This operation tells the ProcessSwap extension to display a list of open processes from which you can select the application to move to.

Figure 8.7
ProcessSwap edit
dialog box

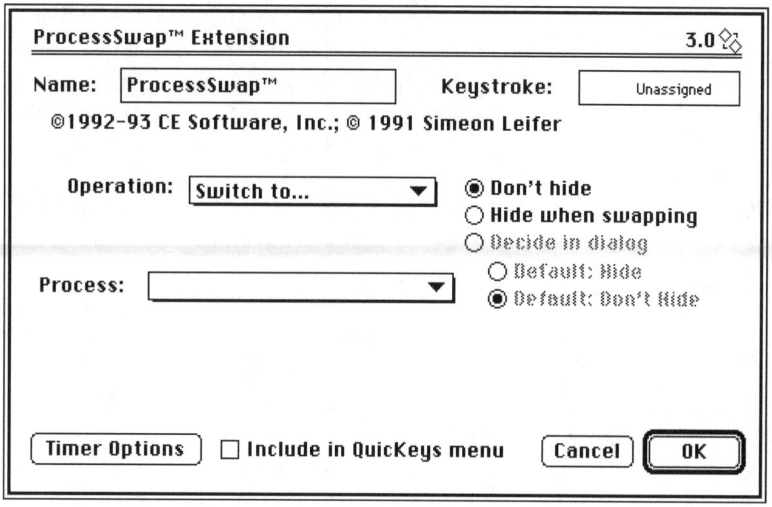

- **Previous Application.** Selecting this operation makes ProcessSwap switch to the previous application in the Application menu.

- **Next Application.** Selecting this operation makes ProcessSwap switch to the next application in the Application menu.

The ProcessSwap edit dialog box also provides the option of hiding other windows when you toggle to a new application.

ProcessSwap Tactics and Considerations

Use a ProcessSwap shortcut to switch between open applications without using the Application menu.

ProcessSwap is a powerful tool for moving around your desktop. Since we all have a tendency to open as many applications as we have memory for and don't close them until we are warned of low memory (or crash), the usefulness of ProcessSwap is the ability to manage moving between these open applications effortlessly.

Don uses his Next Application ProcessSwap shortcut all the time. He set it up with the Hide When Swapping option because most of the time he just wants to see the active application. Switching to the next application seems natural to Don using Option-Control-Right arrow, but many people like to use Command-Tab because it mimics the well-implemented method of switching between open applications in Windows. He also has Previous Application and Switch To (From List) ProcessSwap shortcuts resident in his Universal set for the occasions when he wants to toggle between different applications.

If you switch back and forth between two or three open applications, you may want to create targeted Switch To ProcessSwap shortcuts for each. Remember that you have to open these applications before creating or invoking a targeted ProcessSwap shortcut.

FKEYS

FKEY shortcuts give you the power to invoke FKEYs with your own keystroke combination. You must have the FKEY resident in your system for it to function.

Many folks who aren't too familiar with the Mac get confused about FKEYs. They *aren't* the function keys (F1, F2, F3, and so forth) on an extended keyboard. They *are* little utility programs that come inside your system that you can invoke from your keyboard. You can also get third-party FKEYs and install them using a program like Suitcase or MasterJuggler.

The FKEYs tool is available straight from the main Define menu, perhaps too prominent a position for such a seldom-used commodity. When you press on the FKEY menu item, a submenu of all your available FKEYs appears. However, we have some FKEYs in our system (like Command-Shift-1, which ejects the floppy in the internal drive) that don't show on this list, because the system handles them in a non-standard manner. You can use an Alias Keystroke shortcut to access them.

Choosing one of your FKEYs from the submenu invokes the FKEY edit dialog box (see Figure 8.8). All the FKEYs that QuicKeys can access

Figure 8.8
FKEY edit
dialog box

*FKEY choices
pop-up menu.*

FKEY

Name: 3-Screen to paint   Keystroke: Unassigned

FKEY choices: 3-Screen to paint ▼

Timer Options   ☐ Include in QuicKeys menu   Cancel   OK

are listed in the FKEY choices pop-up menu. Choose the FKEY you want, enter your keystroke combination, and you're ready to go.

FKEYs Considerations and Tactics

Use FKEY shortcuts to access FKEYs with your own keystrokes.

Many folks believe that FKEYs belong on that great big pile of unrecyclable paraphernalia (you know that pile—the one that's full of vinyl records, reasonable prices, entertaining television shows, and honorable political advertising). It is true that most FKEY functions can also be performed by system extensions and control panels. But a number of spiffy third-party FKEYs are available from online services like CompuServe (see Appendix, *Resources*). Some are free, and some are shareware. Here's a sampling.

- FKEY Icon Maker by Kevin Collier. This FKEY grabs graphic images and saves them as ICN# resources.

- Applause FKEY by Tony Karp, TLC Systems. Press the FKEY combination (Command-Shift-5), and you'll get a heartwarming round of applause.

- Mickey 1.0 FKEY by Tony Karp, TLC Systems. Mickey 1.0 is an FKEY that lets you change mouse tracking (sensitivity) without going through the control panel.

- Large cursor FKEY by Andy Hertzfeld. This program installs an FKEY 8 resource, which implements a large (32 x 32-pixel) cursor, in your System file.

- Toggle Key 1.51 by Lofty Becker. Toggle Key 1.51 changes the < and > on the keyboard to , and . and back again. Convenient for touch typists.

- Screen Dump FKEY. The Screen Dump FKEY provides color and black-and-white dumps of the screen or top window, and saves the result in a PICT file with a name you choose.

Shortcuts for Networks and Devices

Previous versions of QuicKeys offered two network support shortcuts, Choosy and Mounty, both promising yet not fully realized management vehicles. QuicKeys 3 builds on these earlier network shortcuts, adding more versatility to Choosy and Mounty, as well as increasing the power of QuicKeys through two new extensions: NetModemChoosy and Phone Dialer. Together, these shortcuts assist you in switching printers, mounting peripheral devices and modems on your network, and saving your fingers from the hazardous duty of dialing your phone. This chapter describes these shortcuts.

- Choosy

- Mounty

- NetModemChoosy

- Phone Dialer

Choosy

You can switch between various printers with the Choosy shortcut. Selecting Choosy from the Network & Device Tools category of the Extensions submenu of the Define menu invokes the Choosy edit dialog box (see Figure 9.1).

Pull down the Change Printer To pop-up menu to reveal the printer drivers on your system. After you make your selection, the dialog box changes depending on whether the driver is for a serial or network printer and the options available for that driver. If you are printing over a network, click the Choose Printer button to display a dialog box where you can select a specific printer and zone (see Figure 9.2).

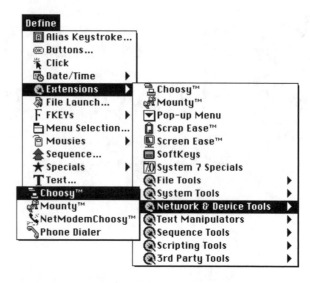

Figure 9.1
Choosy edit dialog box

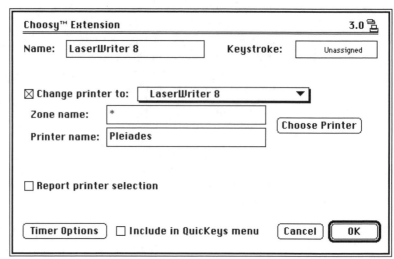

If you only have one network available, QuicKeys enters an asterisk in the Zone Name text edit box, which means current zone in AppleTalk-ese. Networks in big companies can get pretty huge and therefore contain many zones. One local company has a network so extensive that an employee can choose to print a document on any printer in any of its offices—national or international. So one could create a Choosy short-cut that would select the LaserWriter IINTX in the Tokyo office.

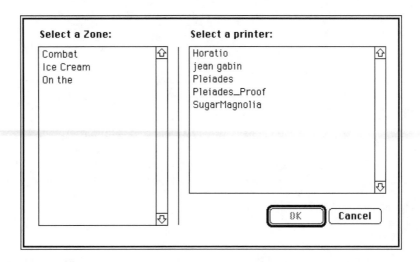

Figure 9.2
Selecting a zone
and a printer for a
Choosy shortcut

**Choosy Tactics
and
Considerations**

Use Choosy to switch printers.

If you have trouble with the Choosy shortcut type, it may be that your Chooser device name is not entered *exactly* as it is listed in the Chooser; choose a printer using the Choose Printer button so you're sure you've got it right.

One old Choosy problem (or feature, depending on your point of view) was that Choosy wouldn't let you know if the printer you chose was actually chosen, because it made the selection in the background. This was great for many folks because it was fast, but some people like to be notified that something has actually happened. The new Choosy feature notifies you when the printer changes. Click on the Report Printer Selection checkbox to use this feature.

The corollary to this new feature is that if you check the Report Printer Selection checkbox and don't check the Change Printer To checkbox, you have a shortcut that just notifies you of the currently selected printer, but doesn't change anything.

At this writing Choosy doesn't display a background printing option for the Laserwriter 8.x driver. We regret this deficiency (which is due to Apple changing things in its update), because with the previous Laserwriter driver we made two shortcuts for some of our printers: one with background printing on and one with it off. We can only hope this will be fixed quickly. For now, we have built a File Launch shortcut that targets the Chooser so we can access the Chooser directly.

Steve likes to put his Choosy shortcuts on the QuicKeys menu (which he accesses as a pop-up using Control-Option-click) because he has so many that it's tough to assign a mnemonic keystroke to each. Don uses modified function keys.

Mounty

QuicKeys 3 comes with an updated Mounty shortcut, a more robust and useful way to mount and dismount AppleShare volumes. With Mounty, you can speed up the process of accessing a file server because the shortcut can automatically enter the network and/or volume password as well as your user name. Mounty now also dismounts volumes, incorporating the features of the defunct Dismounty shortcut.

This increased functionality provides an efficient way to access needed volumes without going through numerous screens and dialog box queries. You can choose Mounty from the Network & Device Tools category of the Extensions submenu of the Define menu. The Mounty edit dialog box appears (see Figure 9.3).

Figure 9.3
Mounty edit
dialog box

Mounty™ Extension   3.0

Name: Mounty™   Keystroke: Unassigned

Zone: _____

Server: _____   Choose Server...

Volume: _____

User: Phoenix

Password: _____   Volume Password: _____

When Connecting:
☐ Ask user and password
☐ Ask password
☐ Connect as Guest

Type of Shortcut:
◉ Toggle Mount/Dismount
○ Mount Only
○ Dismount Only

Timer Options   ☐ Include in QuicKeys menu   Cancel   OK

If you use AppleShare or AppleShare Pro, then you are no doubt familiar with its terminology, so the different controls and text edit boxes are fairly straightforward. You can either fill in the names of the zone and the server manually (be sure to enter their names exactly; AppleShare is case-sensitive), or you can press the Choose Server button and the Choose Server dialog box appears (see Figure 9.4). You do still need to know (and type) the *exact* name of the volume you want to mount, because the Choose Server dialog box offers server and zone names only (too bad; we'd like to be able to choose the volume name from a list when we create the shortcut, similar to Choosy).

Figure 9.4

Choose Server dialog box

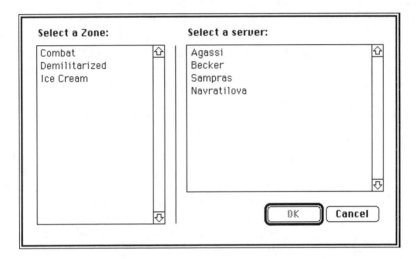

You can select the zone and server in the Choose Server dialog box and click on OK—they will be entered in the Mounty edit dialog box automatically. After choosing a server, enter the volume name exactly as it appears. Be sure it's properly spelled and capitalized. If it's wrong, you have to quit Mounty, search the Chooser for the volume name, and restart the shortcut building process, so note the volume name before starting your construction effort.

When Connecting checkboxes. In the new version of Mounty you can either enter your password in the Password text box, or, if you prefer not to keep it so accessible, you can check either the Ask Password option or the Ask User and Password option in the When Connecting section. Checking the other option here, you can elect to log on to the mounted volume as a guest by checking the Connect as Guest checkbox.

Of course, for the connection to be made, the volumes must be configured to accept the entries.

Type of Shortcut checkboxes. Because Mounty assumes the duties of DisMounty, the Mounty edit dialog box has an additional section, called Type of Shortcut, that lets you select if you want to toggle between mounting and dismounting a volume, Mount Only, or Dismount Only a volume by clicking on the appropriate radio button. Toggling between mounting and dismounting a volume causes the shortcut to switch roles each time it is triggered.

Mounty Considerations

Unlike the new version of Choosy, Mounty does not inform you that it has actually done anything when you trigger it but the volume does appear in the Finder. Even if you choose the When Connecting: Ask Password option: the dialog box that asks for your password doesn't tell you which server you are mounting. This can be annoying if you access many servers using many passwords.

Mounty Tactics

Use Mounty to mount or dismount an AppleShare volume.

We generally use the Toggle Mount/Dismount option for our Mounty shortcuts. But if you opt for the Mount Only or Dismount Only options, it is logical to use function keys with a fairly obscure modifier combination (like Shift-Control-Command) with the mount and dismount functions tagged in pairs (for example, F1 mounts Connors, F2 dismounts Connors). You might need to use a visual reminder (see Chapter 17, *Keystroke Strategies*) to remember which keys go with which servers—but it's easy to remember that odd-numbered keys mount and even-numbered keys dismount.

It's also useful to build your Mounty shortcuts into Sequences with Message shortcuts, so you're reminded what server you're mounting or dismounting.

As with Choosy shortcuts, Steve likes to put Mounty shortcuts on the menu so he doesn't have to remember the keystrokes. Don likes to live more dangerously, electing for the speed, while cluttering up his mind with keystrokes.

NetModem-Choosy

NetModemChoosy is a new highly specific shortcut that you need only if you use Shiva Corporation's NetModem to communicate with the outside world from your network. This shortcut type switches between

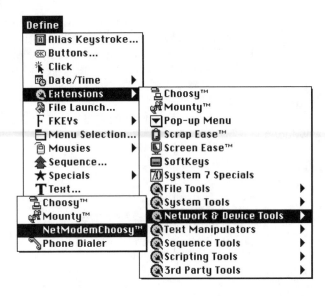

NetModems on your network. It works just like Choosy, letting you select the NetModem and its zone on your network.

Selecting NetModemChoosy from the Network & Device Tools category of the Extensions submenu of the Define menu invokes the NetModemChoosy edit dialog box (see Figure 9.5).

Figure 9.5
NetModemChoosy
edit dialog box

Enter the zone and NetModem names in the text edit boxes for the specific NetModem and zone. Click on the Choose NetModem button to display a dialog box where you can select a specific modem and zone from a list of all available modems and zones (see Figure 9.6).

Figure 9.6
Selecting a zone and a NetModem for a NetModemChoosy shortcut

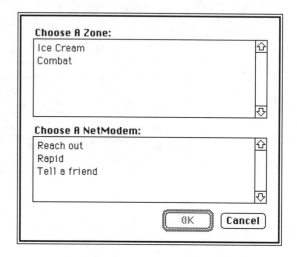

As in Choosy, if you only have one network available, QuicKeys enters an asterisk in the Choose a Zone text edit box, which means current zone in AppleTalk-ese.

NetModem-Choosy Tactics and Considerations

Use NetModemChoosy to switch Shiva NetModems.

Like the other shortcuts that access devices on networks, if you have trouble with the NetModemChoosy shortcut, it may be that your NetModem name is not entered *exactly* as it is listed in the Chooser. So to make sure you've got it right, use the Choose NetModem button to choose a NetModem. Remember to select a serial port (either Modem or Printer) from the Port radio buttons to allow NetModem to communicate properly with your Mac from the network.

Like the new Choosy, NetModemChoosy includes a Report Selection checkbox. When selected, NetModemChoosy lets you know which net modem it has just chosen.

Phone Dialer

The Phone Dialer shortcut was on the QuicKeys users' wish list for years before it finally arrived. Unfortunately, its initial version wasn't worth the wait, but now most of the bugs are worked out. The new Phone

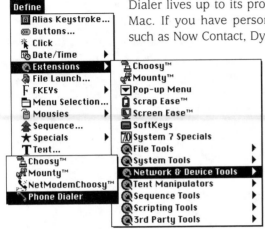

Dialer lives up to its promise to let you dial your telephone from your Mac. If you have personal information management (PIM) software, such as Now Contact, Dynodex, InTouch, or TouchBase, you may already have the Mac do your dialing, but Phone Dialer has some handy features that make us prefer it to our PIM in certain situations. For example, with Phone Dialer you can dial a number using any text file (such as an electronic mail message) just by copying the phone number to the Clipboard.

Phone Dialer edit dialog box. Selecting Phone Dialer from the Network and Devices category of the Extensions submenu of the Define menu invokes the Phone Dialer edit dialog box (see Figure 9.7).

Figure 9.7
Phone Dialer edit
dialog box

```
┌────────────────────────────────────────────────────┐
│ Phone Dialer Extension                     3.0.1 ✎  │
│                                                      │
│ Name: │Phone Dialer      │   Keystroke: │Unassigned│ │
│                                                      │
│ Get number from:  ◉ Clipboard                        │
│                   ○ Last number dialed               │
│                   ○ Other: │              │          │
│ ⊠ Confirm/enter number before dialing                │
│                                                      │
│            ┌ Configure Dialer... ┐                   │
│                                                      │
│ ┌Timer Options┐  □ Include in QuicKeys menu ┌Cancel┐┌ OK ┐│
└────────────────────────────────────────────────────┘
```

The Phone Dialer edit dialog box has three radio button options for the phone number to be dialed.

■ **Clipboard.** Whatever is on the Clipboard. When you cut or copy something it usually goes on the Mac Clipboard.

■ **Last Number Dialed.** Whatever number was last dialed using Phone Dialer.

■ **Other.** Select this option and enter a number in the text field for a Phone Dialer shortcut dedicated to dialing a particular phone number.

Below these three options is the Confirm/Enter Number Before Dialing checkbox. This can be used in conjunction with any of the three options just described. With this checkbox selected, Phone Dialer will display a dialog box containing the phone number it intends to dial so you can verify it. This feature provides a fourth way of giving Phone Dialer a phone number. If you choose the Other option and check this checkbox, on triggering the shortcut, Phone Dialer displays a dialog box with a blank Phone-number-to-dial text edit box. Fill in the box with the phone number you want and click the Dial button.

Configure Dialer edit dialog box. To bring up the Configure dialer box, click on the Configure Dialer button (see Figure 9.8).

Figure 9.8
Configure Dialer
edit dialog box

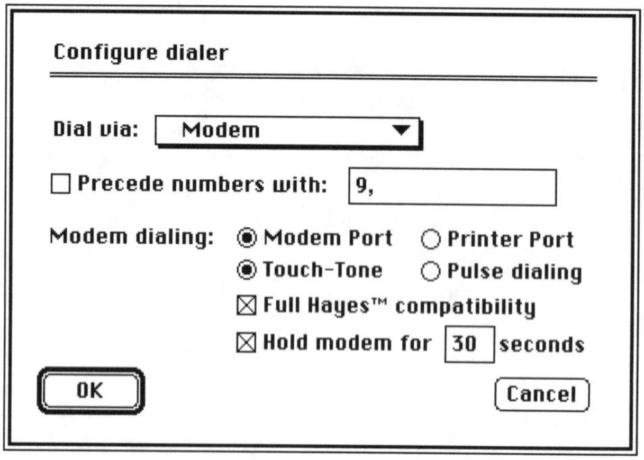

The Dial Via pop-up menu has three options for how your telephone is dialed: through the Mac speaker (you can hold your handset up to it), Modem, or Desktop Dialer (a third-party black box that enables you to dial your phone from the Mac).

The other options are fairly self explanatory, except perhaps the bottom two. Configure Dialer wants to know if you have a Hayes modem or not. Check this box if you know that your modem supports all Hayes telecommunications protocols (meaning the AT command set). Luckily, today most modems can be set to be Hayes-compatible. By checking the Hold Modem for checkbox and entering a figure in its text entry box, you can set the number of seconds that Phone Dialer will keep the phone off hook before hanging up the modem or dialer.

Phone Dialer Tactics and Considerations

Use Phone Dialer to dial modems or telephones from applications.

Phone Dialer is pretty smart. It knows how to use commas for delays in dialing, so enter commas between digits where you need the dialer to pause. Also, the dialer will ignore hyphens and parentheses, which is what you'd expect, but it's nice to know the shortcut is well implemented. But it will interpret letters as numbers (don't ask us how or why), so Don uses the Confirm/Enter Number Before Dialing option to ensure that he is really dialing the telephone number he thinks he is. Steve lives dangerously.

For us, Phone Dialer's ability to dial the phone using what's on the Clipboard makes the shortcut worthwhile. It even is able to dial what's on Microsoft Word's private Clipboard. When people send us messages electronically that include their phone numbers, it is a simple task to select the number, copy it to the Clipboard, and trigger our Phone Dialer shortcut. Steve has his Dialer shortcut built into a two-step Sequence, which copies whatever's selected and then dials the Clipboard.

We have other means of dialing our often-used phone numbers, but many users will find themselves making many Phone Dialer shortcuts for their most frequently called numbers. Keep your Phone Dialer shortcuts in your Universal set, because you will want to trigger them from just about anywhere.

10 Shortcuts for PowerBooks

Because QuicKeys bursts with so much power and provides such a broad range of functions, users constantly expect it to do everything, to replace all the utilities on their Macs—and CE Software keeps trying to deliver. QuicKeys 3 provides a slew of shortcuts for PowerBook users that manage battery life, memory, screen brightness, cursor presence, and a number of other items that make laptop life easier. This chapter describes the PowerBook shortcuts and the prepackaged sets you can use to make QuicKeys enhance your PowerBook's performance.

PowerBook Specials

QuicKeys 3 includes an extension called PowerBook Specials that offers 14 shortcuts to make life easier for PowerBook users. You can create PowerBook Specials shortcuts by selecting PowerBook Specials from the System Tools category of the Extensions submenu of the Define menu on your QuicKeys Editor window. When the PowerBook Specials edit dialog box is displayed (see Figure 10.1), select the shortcut type you want to create from the Specials for PowerBook pop-up menu.

The Specials for PowerBook pop-up menu is divided into four areas. The top area contains a grab bag of different shortcuts. The next three sections contain shortcuts for features that can be toggled on and off.

Most PowerBook Specials concern themselves with saving energy, because once you use a PowerBook away from an AC outlet, battery life becomes your biggest headache. The PowerBook Specials extension offers shortcuts that spin down your hard drive, adjust your backlighting, dim your screen, disable/enable processor rest, or put your PowerBook to

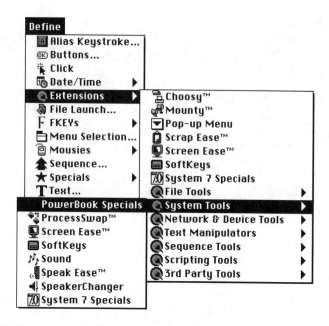

Figure 10.1
PowerBook
Specials edit
dialog box

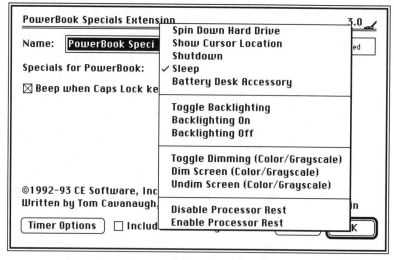

sleep; all of which help increase the life of your battery. In addition, a PowerBook shortcut can shut the PowerBook down and help locate the cursor.

These PowerBook shortcuts are similar to some tools found in PowerBook utility programs sold by third-party vendors, such as Connectix,

Symantec, and Claris. But the power of PowerBook Specials can be enhanced by using them within Sequences until they almost reach the robustness of these dedicated products.

Miscellaneous PowerBook Shortcuts

The top section of the Specials for PowerBook pop-up menu contains five useful shortcuts for managing your PowerBook. In addition, the Beep when Caps Lock Key is Pressed checkbox provides an additional pseudo-shortcut.

Spin Down Hard Drive. Triggering a Spin Down Hard Drive shortcut turns off your PowerBook's hard drive when it is not in use. Keeping the hard drive spinning consumes power, so spinning it down when not in use conserves battery life. The hard drive automatically turns itself back on when the PowerBook senses it is required.

Show Cursor Location. Some PowerBook displays—especially the passive color matrix of the 165c—cause the cursor to submarine or ghost when it's moved around the screen. Because the display can't repaint the screen as fast as the cursor moves, you can lose track of where the cursor's gone. This shortcut places a flashing circle around the cursor for a few seconds, helping you to pinpoint its location as you move it around the screen.

Shutdown. This shortcut turns off the PowerBook in the same manner that the Shutdown shortcut turns off your desktop Mac.

Sleep. A Sleep shortcut is the same as selecting the Sleep command from the Special menu in the Finder, except you don't get the dialog box warning. The PowerBook goes to sleep immediately. This can be a problem if you are connected to a network and have files or applications from a network volume open.

Battery Desk Accessory. The Battery Desk Accessory shortcut (which is actually the Battery menu item in System 7) automatically displays the Battery menu item's dialog box, letting you check your power reserves without having to mouse around in the Apple menu and Control Panels folder.

Beep when Caps Lock Key is Pressed. Okay, okay, this is a checkbox in the PowerBook Specials edit dialog box and not on the pop-up menu, but we include it here because we can't figure out why it is separate. It is an option that tells the PowerBook to generate an audible click (it doesn't beep, it clicks) whenever Caps Lock is depressed. (Remember that the Caps Lock key on a PowerBook doesn't lock into place.)

Toggling PowerBook Shortcuts

The PowerBook Specials extension supplies three other groups of short-cuts that control backlighting, screen dimming, and the processor rest state.

Toggle Backlighting. All PowerBooks use an auxiliary lighting system to enhance their screen's visibility in different lighting environments. You can create one of three shortcuts to either turn backlighting on, off, or toggle on/off, depending on your external light source and backlight-ing needs.

Toggle Dimming. On some PowerBooks, you can use a switch on the front of the screen to modulate the brightness of the screen's image. On some PowerBooks, you can use a control panel to set the screen display's brightness. If you own a PowerBook that can control the screen through a control panel, use these shortcuts to either dim or brighten the screen, or to toggle between the two settings with a single keystroke.

Disable Processor Rest. Processor Rest is a special mode that PowerBooks' CPUs can be set to. This mode turns the CPU's speed down to 1MHz; most CPUs normally run at 16 to 33MHz. The CPU drains a fair amount of power, so Processor Rest mode reduces overall power requirements without totally disabling the computer as Sleep mode does.

PowerBook Specials Tactics and Considerations

Use the PowerBook Specials to save battery power or perform standard housekeeping chores on your PowerBook.

Most of the 14 PowerBook Specials shortcuts perform activities already available on your laptop through some combination of menu commands, control panels, or manual activities. Others provide helpful aids in working on the run. One function of the PowerBook Specials (Sleep) can also be done with a Finder Event shortcut.

We don't regularly use PowerBooks, but our officemate Glenn carries one hither and yon. He suggests preserving battery power by keeping the backlighting turned down to its lowest usable setting and keeping the hard drive spun down as much as possible. QuicKeys' PowerBook Specials shortcuts handle these tasks with the flick of a keystroke. And the Show Cursor Location shortcut can cause a submerged cursor on a passive-matrix screen to surface.

If you are into using Apple Events, you can send an Apple Event to the Finder to put a PowerBook to sleep rather than use the PowerBook Specials shortcut. The simplest way to do this is to use the Finder Event extension and select the Sleep option.

The QuicKeys installer won't put the PowerBook shortcuts on a non-PowerBook, which is just as well. For example, invoking the Enable Processor Rest shortcut on a Mac II gave a nice bomb—which was to be expected. However, Don likes to use the Beep when Caps Lock Key is Pressed shortcut on his desk Mac, even though its implementation is rather bizarre. Unlike most shortcuts, which are triggered by pressing a key combination or at a certain preset time, the Caps Lock beep is found in a checkbox and can only be turned on and off by selecting PowerBook Specials and checking or unchecking it. Why did CE do this? Only the software engineers know for sure.

Sets for PowerBooks

When you perform a full installation of QuicKeys, a number of sets are installed in the QuicKeys Example Sets folder that may be of use with the PowerBook. One set provides keystrokes that are unavailable on the small PowerBook keyboard. Two other sets, located in the PowerBook Sets folder, are designed specifically for use with PowerBooks.

Extended Keyboard Alias Set

QuicKeys installs the Extended Keyboard Alias set in the QuicKeys Example Sets folder to provide extended keyboard keystrokes to folks who don't have them (PowerBooks and the older standard Mac keyboards). Being able to generate these keystrokes comes in handy in particular applications where a feature can be triggered with an extended keyboard keystroke.

To put these keystrokes into your repertoire, just open the Alias Keystroke set, copy the shortcuts for the modifier-keystroke combinations you want, paste them into your Universal set, and give them your own triggers.

Of course, if you are working in an application like Microsoft Word, where you can reassign the application's keystroke triggers, consider reconfiguring the application rather than building a shortcut to do the same job (it's cleaner and will probably work faster). The Extended Keyboard Alias set just includes unmodified and single-modifier combinations of the extended keyboard keystrokes, which is probably all you will need. But if for some reason you want multiple modifier combinations with these extended keyboard keys, consider plugging an extended keyboard into your PowerBook or create the shortcuts on a desktop Mac and transfer them to your PowerBook.

PowerBook Sets

QuicKeys installs two sample sets for use with PowerBooks in the QuicKeys Example Sets folder. The PowerBook Universal Set contains a number of shortcuts preselected and configured to help make life with your

PowerBook more productive. Eighteen of these shortcuts make up a virtual keypad.

PowerBook Universal Set. The PowerBook Universal Set contains a thoughtful sampling of useful PowerBook shortcuts. Many PowerBook Specials shortcuts are available, as are a number of System 7 Specials to control system functions such as file sharing and Balloon Help. The set provides a preconfigured SoftKeys Palette to trigger many other shortcuts. Finally, a group of 18 Alias Keystroke shortcuts are included. They make up the virtual keypad of keypad keystrokes that are mapped to a section of the PowerBook keyboard. The Calculator set contains just these virtual keypad keys.

Most shortcuts that aren't part of the virtual keypad don't have triggering keystrokes, which is just as well. The PowerBook's abbreviated keyboard limits the strategies you can use as triggering keystroke combinations, so you will probably want to assign keystrokes based on your own well-considered layout scheme.

Calculator set. The Calculator set contains just the virtual keypad shortcuts from the PowerBook Universal set. These shortcuts enable you to use the virtual keypad with an Apple menu item calculator. To install these shortcuts, launch your favorite calculator desk accessory, and then open the QuicKeys Editor window. Open the Calculator set using the Open Set command from the File menu (the path is QuicKeys Tools:QuicKeys Example Sets:PowerBook Sets). Select all the shortcuts, copy them, and paste them into your calculator's set. Then your PowerBook's virtual keypad switches on only when your calculator is active.

11 Shortcuts for Sight and Sound

Sight and Sound shortcuts can play sounds, speak words, and run QuickTime movies. Sound shortcuts are most often used within Sequences. The more sophisticated Speak Ease and QT Movie shortcuts require Apple's PlainTalk and Quick Time system extensions, respectively, to function.

Sound

The Sound shortcut selects and plays sound resources from your System file. When you choose Sound from the System Tools category of the

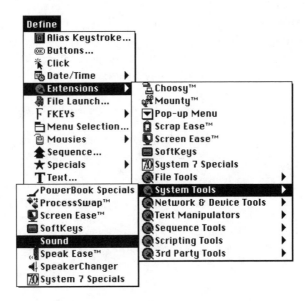

Extensions submenu of the Define menu, the Sound edit dialog box appears (see Figure 11.1). If you press on the Play Sound pop-up menu, the available sounds are displayed. Choose the sound you want to play.

Figure 11.1
Sound edit
dialog box

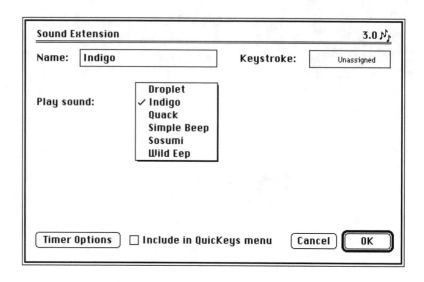

Sound Considerations and Tactics

Use Sound shortcuts to select sounds you want your Mac to play for System activities.

Depending upon how frivolous you are with your Mac's memory resources, you can install thousands of sounds available both commercially and online. Your Mac can sound like a symphony, Monty Python, Star Trek, or Barney. If you can't remember what a sound sounds like, Sound plays the sound when you select it from its menu.

Sounds are often used within Sequences, to inform you when the Sequence passes a certain step or to prompt you that a user action is required. See Chapter 14, *The Sequences*, for information on how to include shortcut steps in a sequence.

You can make a stand-alone Sound shortcut, triggered by the timer, that plays a sound every hour—just like all those watches did in movie theaters, before they drove everyone away. Don (Mr. Ergonomics) has a Sound shortcut on a timer that goes off every fifteen minutes letting him know it is time to look up from the monitor and stare into the distance for 10 seconds to rest his eyes. If you adopt this beneficial practice, do not get in the easy habit of ignoring the reminder sound.

Speak Ease

The new Speak Ease shortcut provides support for the speech features of Apple's new multimedia Macs. To use Speak Ease, you need to install a new System extension called PlainTalk that is available on the new Macs and with System 7.5. PlainTalk is an outgrowth of the technology that created an old shareware product called MacInTalk that used to come with Talking Moose. This new extension works the same way to let the Mac speak certain words. Basically, you teach the Mac how to recognize words by either typing or pasting them into a text block. Then, when you trigger Speak Ease, the Mac talks to you. The shortcut can also speak the contents of the Clipboard.

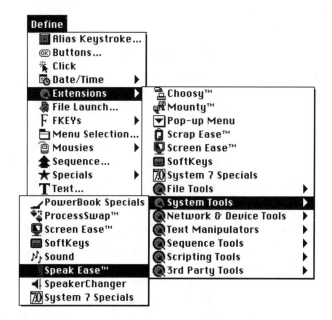

To create a Speak Ease shortcut, select Speak Ease from the System Tools category of the Extensions submenu on the QuicKeys Editor's Define menu. QuicKeys displays the Speak Ease edit dialog box (see Figure 11.2).

Use the Voice pop-up menu to select the PlainTalk voice you want to use. Enter the text to be spoken in the Speak Text text box (or leave the text box empty if you choose the Speak Clipboard option).

Like Talking Moose, PlainTalk speaks in several different voices. One new feature of PlainTalk is the ability to designate how the Mac will

Figure 11.2
Speak Ease edit
dialog box

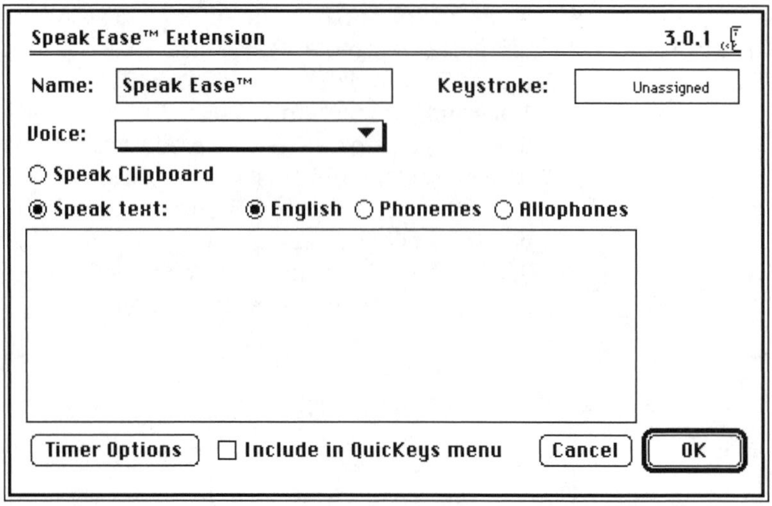

Speak Ease™ Extension		3.0.1
Name: `Speak Ease™`	Keystroke:	`Unassigned`

Voice: `▼`

○ **Speak Clipboard**

◉ **Speak text:**   ◉ **English** ○ **Phonemes** ○ **Allophones**

(Timer Options) ☐ Include in QuicKeys menu (Cancel) (OK)

interpret the pronunciation of your text. You can select straight English (which may become garbled if the Mac has to interpret foreign-sounding words), standard linguistic phonemes (which breaks your text down into syllables and spells them as they sound), and a new ability called allophones (which produce very high quality speech by further breaking down the words into smaller pronounceable units).

Speak Ease Tactics and Considerations

Use a Speak Ease shortcut to amuse your friends.

We guess that Speak Ease is the beginning of Apple's knowledge navigator dream, in which you perform work by giving your Mac tasks, such as "Find me the Jones file and call Jim for an appointment." Your Mac would use the metaphor of a person's face to tell you the status of the search and modem work. This virtual person would speak to you in colloquial sentences while performing its artificial intelligence projects. Right around the corner, right? For now, Speak Ease lets the Mac talk to you, as long as you tell it what to say.

Just because we don't use this shortcut doesn't mean you won't. You might want to include Speak Ease steps in Sequences to ask you (or another user for whom you've designed the shortcut) for input when it's needed. Or Speak Ease might be useful in creating a more friendly Mac environment for the visually impaired. CE used to do a cool demo of Speak Ease reading QuickMail messages. It can be a powerful tool.

QuickTime Movie

QuickTime is an add-on package that lets you play moving pictures within applications that support multimedia, or by itself. Because QuicKeys has something for everyone, there's an extension for running these movies, called QT Movie.

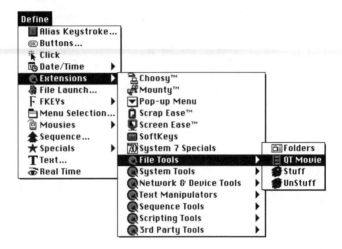

To create a QT Movie shortcut, choose QT Movie from the File Tools category of the Extensions submenu. The QT Movie edit dialog box appears (see Figure 11.3). Clicking on the Select button makes a standard

Figure 11.3
QT Movie edit
dialog box

Open dialog box appear, from which you can select the clip you want to play. If you check the Show Controller checkbox, the movie will appear within a window that includes playback controls. The Play Sound If Available option will do just that.

QT Movie Tactics and Considerations

Use QT Movie to run a QuickTime movie anywhere on your Mac.

You can only use this extension if you have QuickTime installed on your Mac. We can't think up a good use for this shortcut, unless you want to play a clip of your mother telling you to clean up your office every 10 minutes (we've found this does no good). But if you have QuickTime movies you want to see, this is a handy way of displaying them.

12 Shortcuts That Manipulate Text and Graphics

This chapter discusses shortcuts for working with text and graphics. Most of the are five shortcut types in this category manipulate text.

- **Text.** These shortcuts simply type text.

- **Scrap Ease.** The new Scrap Ease shortcut replaces the Grab Ease, Type Ease, and Paste Ease shortcuts, and lets you create files in which to store text and graphics, and then copy and paste them (even in places where normal Cut, Copy, and Paste functions don't work).

- **Date/Time.** If you want to insert the date or time in a text stream, use a Date/Time shortcut.

- **Quotes.** Use QuickQuotes and Double QuickQuotes to type curly quotation marks and apostrophes.

- **Display Text.** The Display Text shortcut is actually a mini word processor for working with text files.

The following sections explore each shortcut type.

Text

Text shortcuts are simple. When you trigger them, they type text. To create a Text shortcut, select Text from the Define menu in the QuicKeys Editor window. The Text edit dialog box appears (see Figure 12.1). You can assign a name and an invoking keystroke and enter up to 255 characters in the Text to Type box. You can cut, copy, and paste text in this box, using the standard Macintosh Command-X, Command-C, and Command-V keyboard shortcuts.

The characters you type in the Text to Type box can include carriage returns (what you get when you press the Return key), tab characters (they appear as little triangles), and all the special characters you get when you press Option and Shift together with various keys. The text is probably displayed in Chicago (the Macintosh default font), so the special characters you type may not be the ones you get when you've applied a different font in your application.

Figure 12.1
Text edit dialog box

Text

Name: FutureMedia   Keystroke: Unassigned

Text to type:

FutureMedia△The Corporation
141593 Decimal Drive
Present Tense, CA 91233

Timer Options   ☐ Include in QuicKeys menu   Cancel   OK

Text Tactics

Use Text shortcuts to type text.

The primary use for Text shortcuts is to store boilerplate text for use in various applications. They're great for dropping your online signature at the end of all your electronic mail messages or for putting your closing and full name at the end of letters, bracketing your signature. If you have a standard disclaimer or series of formulas, you can store each of these in a Text shortcut.

You can also use Text shortcuts within Sequence shortcuts. A string of letters in a Text shortcut plays out more slowly than a string of Alias shortcut steps, so it often works (the application can keep up with it) where the Alias steps don't.

Text Considerations

The main point to consider when you're planning to use a Text shortcut is how long your text is and whether it includes any formatting. If your text contains more than 255 characters, you'll either have to use multiple Text shortcuts or use Scrap Ease instead.

Unbelievably, while working in Microsoft Word you still can't paste text copied in Word into the Text to Type box in the Text edit dialog box. We hoped that this deficiency, caused by Word's private Clipboard, would have been worked around long ago. The solution is to copy the text in Word, then switch into another application (like the Finder) before you launch QuicKeys. Word will dump the contents of its private Clipboard into the Mac Clipboard so it can be pasted.

Scrap Ease

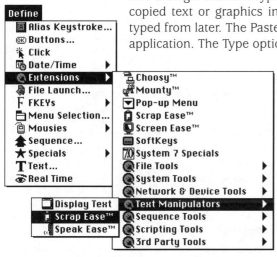

A spiffy streamlining in QuicKeys 3 is the consolidation of the copying, pasting, and typing functions of Grab Ease, Paste Ease, and Type Ease into a single shortcut type, called Scrap Ease. The Copy option saves copied text or graphics in a file (called a clip) that can be pasted or typed from later. The Paste option pastes one of these saved clips in an application. The Type option types a clip into dialog boxes and applications, such as some telecommunications programs, that do not have a Paste command. Scrap Ease has nothing to do with the similarly named Screen Ease, except that they're both QuicKeys extensions.

Using Copy Action. To paste or type something using Scrap Ease, you must have a saved clip. And to save a clip, you need to first build a copier Scrap Ease shortcut by choosing Scrap Ease from the Text Manipulators category of the Extensions submenu of the Define menu. The Scrap Ease edit dialog box appears (see Figure 12.2). Select Copy from the pop-up Action menu and (optionally) assign a name and keystroke to the shortcut.

Next, select some text or a graphic in your favorite application, and trigger your Scrap Ease Copy action shortcut. The Save New Clip As dialog box appears (see Figure 12.3). Type in the name of the clip in

Figure 12.2
Scrap Ease Copy
edit dialog box

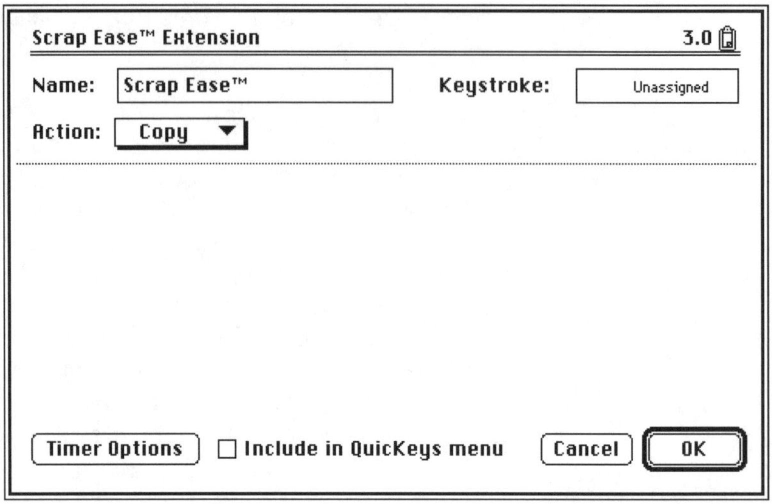

Scrap Ease™ Extension   3.0 📋

Name: |Scrap Ease™ | Keystroke: | Unassigned |

Action: | Copy ▼ |

[Timer Options]   ☐ Include in QuicKeys menu   [Cancel] [OK]

Figure 12.3
Save New Clip As
dialog box

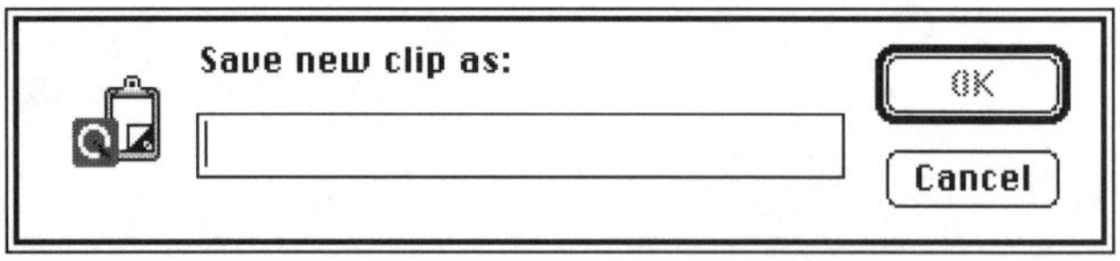

Save new clip as: [OK]

| | [Cancel]

which you want to save the information. Scrap Ease saves the item as a clip, stored in the Clipboards folder within the QuicKeys folder.

Pasting or typing your clip. Now that you have some information stored in a clip, you can insert it somewhere using either Paste or Type actions. You use the same actions to create either a pasting or typing Scrap Ease shortcut, so we will use just the pasting option as an example for both. First, open the Scrap Ease edit dialog box and select Paste from the Action pop-up menu. Clicking the Things to Paste pop-up menu will display a list of all the clips stored, plus the Ask When Playing Shortcut option (see Figure 12.4).

Figure 12.4
Things to Paste
pop-up menu

✓ **Ask when playing shortcut**

Altbier
Bitter
India Pale Ale
Lager
Lambic
Stout

Select a specific clip to paste or choose the Ask When Playing Shortcut option to have the shortcut ask you which clip to paste from when you trigger it. If you use the Ask When Pasting option, you'll see the dialog box in Figure 12.5 when you trigger the shortcut.

Figure 12.5
Ask When Pasting
edit dialog box

Select a clip, choose either Paste or Type, and click on OK to complete the process.

Type action shortcuts work exactly the same way, except that they act as if they're typing the information, rather than pasting it, so you can use them in certain dialog boxes and other places where pasting doesn't work. Obviously, Type only works with text; you can't type graphics with it (we tried).

Scrap Ease Tactics and Considerations

Use Scrap Ease to build your own library of text and graphic elements and paste them (just about) anywhere.

Don triggers his Copy Action Scrap Ease shortcut with Command-Option-Control-C, a keystroke that feels like power copy to him.

We have a small number of targeted pasting Scrap Ease shortcuts with our names and addresses. We don't need the typing action because all the applications we use regularly have a Paste function (even our terminal emulators are smart enough to paste). (The Type action is faster than the Paste action in many cases, but paste is fast enough not to be a bother.) We also have one untargeted Paste Action Scrap Ease that gives us the opportunity to paste any clip we may have. All these Scrap Ease shortcuts live in our Universal set.

You might find yourself using a number of clips for a project. And when the project is finished you want to get rid of the clips. The way to do this using QuicKeys is to open the Scrap Ease edit dialog box, choose the clip from the Things to Paste pop-up menu, and then press the Delete This Clip button. Or, just trash the clip files you don't want from the Clipboards folder in the QuicKeys folder.

■ ■ ■ ■ ■

Date/Time

Date/Time shortcuts do exactly what you'd expect: they type in the current date or time, in the format you choose. When you choose one of the Date/Time formats from the Date/Time submenu of the Define menu, you see the Date/Time edit dialog box (see Figure 12.6).

No matter which format you chose, you can change your mind here and switch to another format. Then apply an activating keystroke, and you're done.

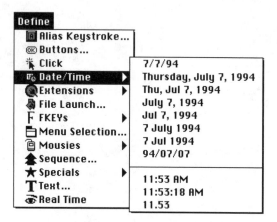

Figure 12.6
Date/Time edit
dialog box

Date/Time		
Name:	Monday, July 4, 1994	Keystroke: Unassigned

Date/Time choices: Monday, July 4, ... ▼

(Timer Options) ☐ Include in QuicKeys menu (Cancel) (OK)

Date/Time Tactics and Considerations

Use a Date/Time shortcut to type the date or time.

The main characteristics to remember about Date/Time shortcuts are that they insert the *current* time and that inserted time doesn't change. If you want a date or time stamp that continuously updates, you'll have to use the one in your word processor, spreadsheet, or page-layout program.

Quotes

If you've read *The Mac is not a typewriter*, you know that ugly old type-writer-style straight quotes are anathema to even moderately skilled Mac users. If you want to use curly quotes and apostrophes (', ', ", and ") instead of straight quotes and apostrophes (' and "), these shortcuts can help you.

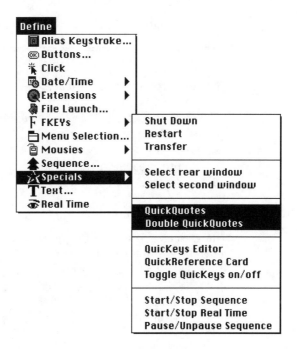

To create a Quotes shortcut, select either QuickQuotes or Double QuickQuotes from the Specials submenu of the Define menu. The Special edit dialog box appears, with the appropriate Quote options selected in the pop-up menu (see Figure 12.7).

The normal technique for using the Quotes keys is to trigger QuickQuotes with the apostrophe (') and Double QuickQuotes with the

Figure 12.7
Special edit dialog
box

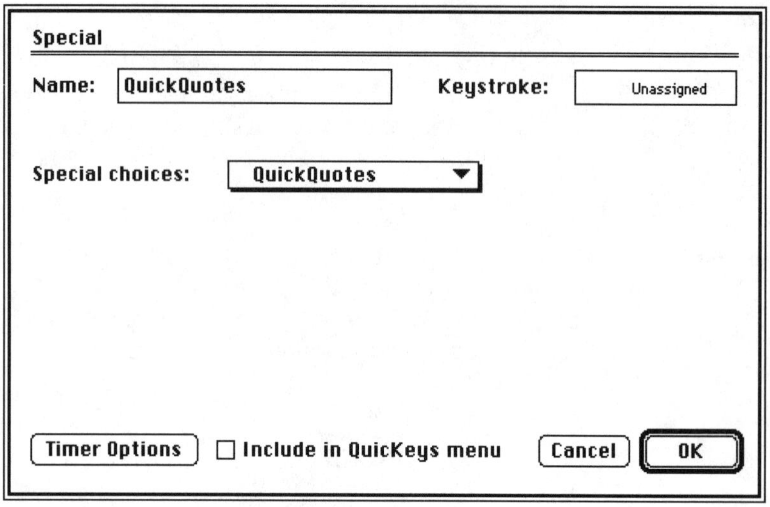

Special

Name: | QuickQuotes   Keystroke: | Unassigned

Special choices: | QuickQuotes   ▼ |

(Timer Options)   ☐ Include in QuicKeys menu   (Cancel) (OK)

Shift-Apostrophe (") key. That way every time you type ', you get ' or ',
and when you type ", you get " or ".

But how does QuicKeys know whether to give you an open or close
quote? It's based (not terribly intelligently) on your last action before
using the Quote shortcut. As explained in the manual, if it's a {, (, [, <,
", ', Return, Space, Tab, or mouse click, you get a left quote. In any
other situation, you get a right quote.

Quotes Tactics

Use Quotes shortcuts to type single and double curly quotes.

The Quotes shortcuts aren't super smart, so you might want to take
advantage of the smart-quotes capability in your application software,
if it exists (Word's is excellent, as are QuarkXPress' and PageMaker's).
If you're working in some other application, check out Quote Init, a
shareware control panel that handles smart quotes on the fly as you
type, in addition to ligatures, em dashes, and double spaces.

**Quotes
Considerations**

No matter what method you use to generate smart quotes, be aware
that in some cases—notably when you're sending electronic mail—you
want straight quotes instead of curly ones. When you send a message
with curly quotes, they tend to come out as little Qs and such.

There are a few ways to turn off your Quotes shortcuts after you've
set them up. Choose the one that's best for your circumstances.

■ Turn off QuicKeys. Steve uses Command-Option-Control-. (period) for that task, so if he wants to type a straight apostrophe, he presses that keystroke, then the Apostrophe key, then his QuicKeys toggle again. Both Microsoft Word and Quote Init give you keystrokes to toggle smart quotes on and off.

■ Make an Alias Keystroke shortcut for your straight apostrophe. Since your unmodified apostrophe key is tied to QuickQuotes, just give yourself another keystroke that types a straight apostrophe—Command-' (apostrophe) might do.

■ Make an Alias Keystroke shortcut in specific application sets that override the Quotes shortcuts in your Universal set. You would only do this if your setup would be enhanced by having Quotes active in most applications, but inactive in one.

Display Text

Who would have thought it? A QuicKeys shortcut that's a word processor! Well, it's not a full-blown word processor but a little editor that lets you view, edit, format, and print text files. That's the Display Text shortcut.

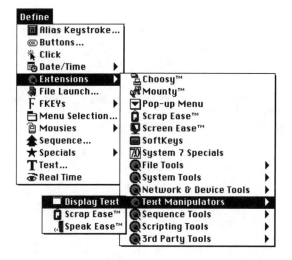

To create a Display Text shortcut, select Display Text from the Text Manipulators category of the Extensions submenu of the Define menu. You'll be rewarded with the Display Text edit dialog box (see Figure 12.8). Assign a triggering keystroke to the shortcut, and if you want to, click the Change button to select a text file for this Display Text shortcut

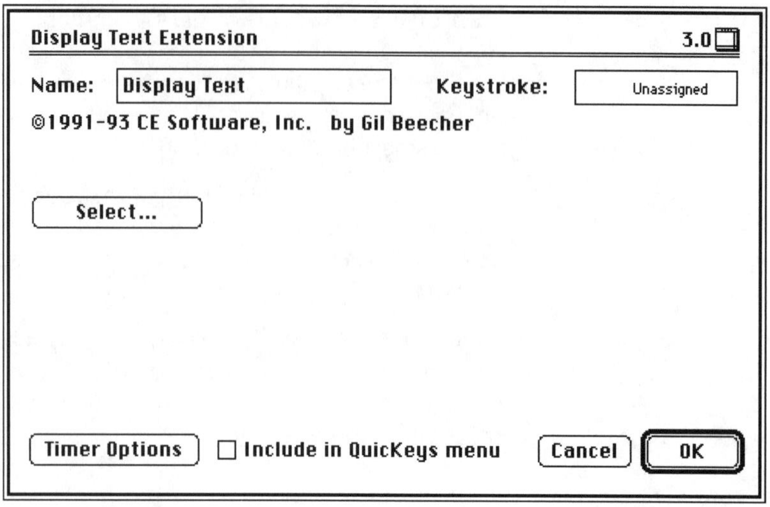

Figure 12.8
Display Text edit
dialog box

Display Text Extension   3.0

Name: Display Text   Keystroke: Unassigned

©1991-93 CE Software, Inc.   by Gil Beecher

Select...

Timer Options   □ Include in QuicKeys menu   Cancel   OK

to open. If you don't select a file, when you use the shortcut you'll get a
standard Open dialog box asking which file you want to open.

In either case, Display Text comes up as a stand-alone word-processing window (see Figure 12.9) in which you can manipulate text.
You can edit text in the normal ways, change the font, size, type style,
and color of any group of characters, search for a text string, save the
file, and print (a new feature in QuicKeys 3). That's it.

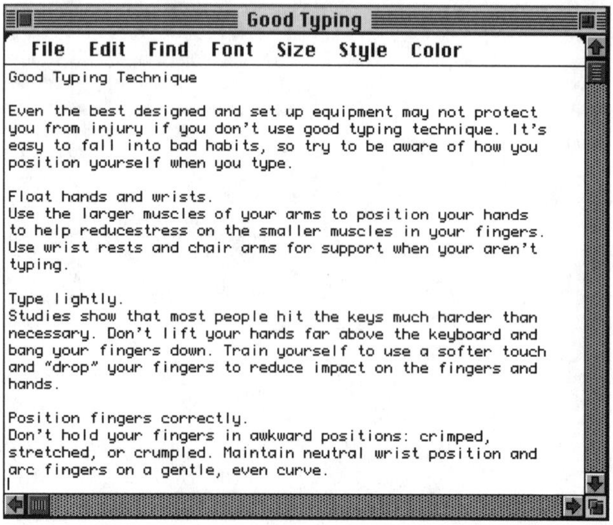

Figure 12.9
Display Text's
word processing
window

Good Typing

File   Edit   Find   Font   Size   Style   Color

Good Typing Technique

Even the best designed and set up equipment may not protect
you from injury if you don't use good typing technique. It's
easy to fall into bad habits, so try to be aware of how you
position yourself when you type.

Float hands and wrists.
Use the larger muscles of your arms to position your hands
to help reducestress on the smaller muscles in your fingers.
Use wrist rests and chair arms for support when your aren't
typing.

Type lightly.
Studies show that most people hit the keys much harder than
necessary. Don't lift your hands far above the keyboard and
bang your fingers down. Train yourself to use a softer touch
and "drop" your fingers to reduce impact on the fingers and
hands.

Position fingers correctly.
Don't hold your fingers in awkward positions: crimped,
stretched, or crumpled. Maintain neutral wrist position and
arc fingers on a gentle, even curve.

Display Text Tactics and Considerations

Use Display Text shortcuts to view and edit text files.

There are better tiny text editors in the world than Display Text (the shareware McSink comes to mind), but few can bring up a designated file so quickly and easily. Display Text shortcuts are great for maintaining text files like your to-do list, Rolodex file, or other commonly accessed text file. One keystroke, and it's up and ready for you. Another keystroke and you're searching.

When you apply formatting to a text file with Display Text, it performs a little bit of magic. It formats the text, so the next time you open the file with Display Text, all your formatting will be there. But it doesn't change the nature of the straight text file by inserting formatting information. You can open the file with any other word processor or text editor, and it opens right up as an unformatted text file.

For those who care, Display Text manages this magic by adding a couple of new resources to the text file. The data stays the same, so other programs can read them, but Display Text also looks at the new resources for the formatting information.

One more word of caution: like most QuicKeys file-using shortcuts (for example Speak Ease and AppleScript), Display Text files are limited to 32K size. Don can use Display Text to maintain his diary, because his life is so boring, but South-of-France Steve needs more.

13 Shortcuts That Control QuicKeys

QuicKeys controllers are the shortcuts that give you power over various QuicKeys functions. Some QuicKeys controllers are trivial, some are indispensable, and some are redundant with items in the QuicKeys menu. QuicKeys controllers break down into three groups.

- Those that access parts of the QuicKeys program

- Those that can be used to trigger shortcuts from a list

- Those that start and stop shortcut recording

Most QuicKeys controllers appear on the Specials submenu of the Define menu.

QuicKeys Access Shortcuts

Two shortcuts give you access to different parts of the QuicKeys program. One of them, QuicKeys Editor, invokes the QuicKeys Editor window. We use the QuicKeys Editor more often than any other shortcut. Another QuicKeys controller, Toggle QuicKeys On/Off, is arguably the most powerful of all shortcuts. Toggle QuicKeys On/Off puts QuicKeys to sleep; it deactivates all shortcuts except one (itself)—so even though you can turn QuicKeys off, one shortcut is left active to turn the program back on again.

Each of these shortcuts has only one target or purpose, so you only need one of each in your Universal set. When you create one, the only entry you need to make in the edit dialog box is your activating keystroke combination.

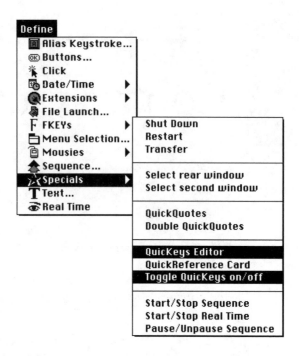

The QuicKeys Editor Shortcut

What could be simpler? Trigger the QuicKeys Editor shortcut, and the QuicKeys Editor window appears. Of course, you can always get the QuicKeys Editor window by choosing QuicKeys from the QuicKeys menu, but why go menu-pulling when you have a utility program that does what you want with only a keystroke?

QuicKeys Editor Tactics and Considerations

Use the QuicKeys Editor shortcut to bring up the QuicKeys Editor window.

We could not live without the QuicKeys Editor shortcut, because we are constantly building new shortcuts (or modifying old ones). Invoking the QuicKeys Editor window is the first step in this process (most of the time—see "Recording Switches" later in this chapter). Don uses Control-Option-Q to trigger QuicKeys; Steve uses Command-Option-Return (and Don ridicules him because it's so un-mnemonic, but Steve says, "Hey—it's the default").

Interesting to note is that the More Universal Set, included in your QuicKeys package as a starter set of universal shortcuts, does not include this—the most useful shortcut. However, when you first install QuicKeys, the Universal set automatically created for you does contain this shortcut (among others).

Toggle QuicKeys On/ Off

Power. Toggle QuicKeys On/Off gives you the ultimate power over QuicKeys. If for some reason you want QuicKeys off—for example, if it's overriding a keystroke shortcut in a particular application—you can stun it with this keystroke, and it seems to go to sleep. However, invoking Toggle QuicKeys On/Off a second time wakes QuicKeys up again.

Power requires control, and you have to watch out for a couple of silly situations you can get into with Toggle QuicKeys On/Off. First, it is possible to create a Toggle QuicKeys On/Off shortcut without assigning it an invoking keystroke combination; for example, you could just check the Include in QuicKeys menu option in the edit dialog box.

If you do so and choose this shortcut from the QuicKeys menu, QuicKeys deactivates itself—and the Toggle QuicKeys On/Off menu item disappears. There is no apparent way to turn QuicKeys on again without rebooting! But there is a fail-safe On button lurking in the QuicKeys control panel.

A similar situation can occur if you just create one Toggle QuicKeys On/Off shortcut, and make it part of a Sequence. When you trigger the Sequence, as soon as it gets to the Toggle QuicKeys On/Off step, QuicKeys goes dormant. You can't use the same Sequence to turn QuicKeys back on, because the dormant QuicKeys will only recognize *one* shortcut— Toggle QuicKeys On/Off. QuicKeys will not recognize any Sequences, even those containing the Toggle QuicKeys On/Off shortcut.

Toggle QuicKeys On/Off Tactics and Considerations

Use the Toggle QuicKeys On/Off shortcut to play God over shortcuts.

The insurance is to *always* have a pure Toggle QuicKeys On/Off shortcut as part of your Universal set. The More Universal Set has one, with the keystroke combination Command-Option-. (period). CE Software suggests that you don't change that keystroke (so everybody who uses the machine knows how to toggle QuicKeys on and off), but Don doesn't like it much—it doesn't fit his keystroke strategy (see Chapter 17, *Keystroke Strategies*). Don uses Control-Option-Command-Q as his QuicKeys toggler.

Shortcuts That Trigger Shortcuts

Two shortcuts, QuickReference Card and SoftKeys Palettes, display listings of shortcuts that can be clicked and played. QuickReference Card can display a list of shortcuts in both the Universal set and the current application set. SoftKeys Palettes displays up to 10 prechosen shortcuts.

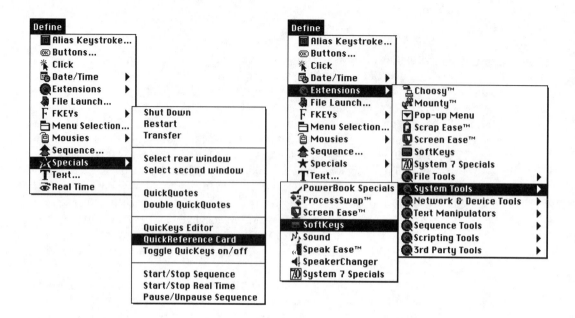

QuickReference Card

The QuickReference Card shortcut gives you access to the QuickReference Card, a display of your active shortcuts. It is usually set up to display the shortcuts in two sets, the Universal set and the set of your active application (see "Configuring the QuickReference Card" next). Like the QuicKeys Editor window, the QuickReference Card is also accessible from the QuicKeys menu (see Figure 13.1).

The QuickReference Card looks and acts a lot like the Shortcuts window in the QuicKeys Editor window but has some important and useful differences (see Figure 13.2).

Figure 13.1
QuickReference Card on the menu

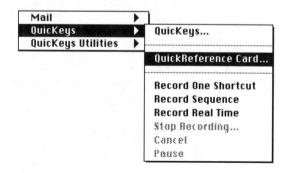

Figure 13.2
QuickReference
Card

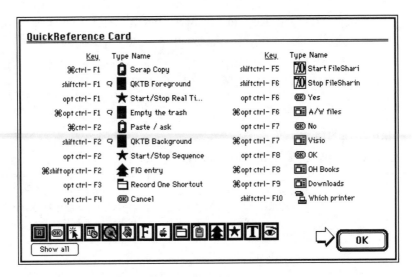

First, let's look at the similarities.

■ **Display sorting.** You can change how the display is sorted by clicking on the column headers (Key, Type, or Name).

■ **Filter bar.** You can reduce the number of shortcuts displayed by clicking on the appropriate shortcut icon in the Filter bar. Multiple selections can be made by holding down Shift when clicking on an icon.

Here are some of the differences between the QuicKeys Editor Shortcuts window and the QuickReference Card.

■ **Two sets.** Instead of displaying one set, the QuickReference Card can show two: the Universal set and the set of your active application. Names of shortcuts in the active application set are displayed in bold type.

■ **Pages versus scrolling window.** Instead of a scrolling window, the QuickReference Card is displayed in a page format. Turn pages by clicking on the left and right arrows next to the OK button or by pressing your keyboard arrows.

■ **Hot key.** Pressing anywhere on the display of a single shortcut in the QuickReference Card returns you to the application you were in and plays that shortcut.

■ **No edit or keystroke change.** You can't edit or change a shortcut's activating keystroke from the QuickReference Card.

■ **Comment.** In the QuickReference Card, you can press on a shortcut listing to display its comment (if it has one). In the Shortcuts window, you can view (and edit) a comment by clicking in the Comment column.

Configuring the QuickReference Card

On the Options menu of the QuicKeys Editor window is a menu item called Configure QuickReference Card (see Figure 13.3).

Choose this item to display the QuickReference Card Options dialog box (see Figure 13.4). Two adjustments (Sort By and Display These Shortcuts) can also be changed within the QuickReference Card itself. The other two (List and Expand to Fill Screen) can only be set here. We generally want to list both sets and have the card expand to fill the screen.

Figure 13.3
Configure
QuickReference
Card on the
Options menu

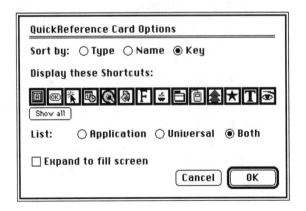

Figure 13.4
QuickReference
Card Options edit
dialog box

QuickReference Card Tactics and Considerations

Use the QuickReference Card shortcut to invoke the QuickReference Card

We don't often find it helpful to invoke the QuickReference Card. Steve doesn't even have a shortcut for it; he just chooses it from the QuicKeys menu when he wants it. Nevertheless, for many people it's a valuable mnemonic aid to go along with keystrokes and placement of shortcuts on the QuicKeys menu.

One thing you could do if you hate keystrokes is name your 40 favorite shortcuts so that they are all at the beginning of the alphabet list and set this option on the QuickReference Card display. Then it could act as a super SoftKeys Palette (discussed next). Some shortcuts don't give you the option of changing their names, however, so this has limited utility.

SoftKeys Palettes

We sure are grouches. CE Software keeps coming up with creative improvements to QuicKeys, and we generally find some fault with them. The SoftKeys Palette shortcut was created to help overcome the annoying problem of remembering what shortcuts you have and how to trigger them. The idea is good: make an easy-to-display palette listing 10 shortcuts that can be easily triggered. Unfortunately, the theory works a bit better than the practice.

To create a SoftKeys Palette shortcut, select SoftKeys from the System Tools category of the Extensions submenu. The SoftKeys edit dialog box appears (see Figure 13.5).

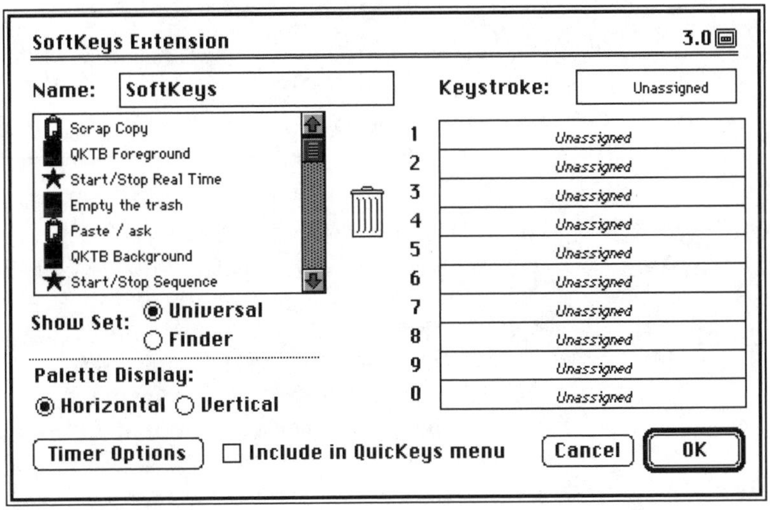

Figure 13.5
SoftKeys edit dialog box

You can choose shortcuts to put on your palette from either of the two active sets. Select the set whose shortcuts you want to use using the Show Set option. Then drag shortcuts from the scrolling window list on the left and drop them into the palette list on the right. Shortcuts can be rearranged in the palette list by dragging and dropping.

If you want to remove a shortcut from the palette list, drag it to the Trash Can; it will reappear in the scrolling set list on the left. Choose whether you want the palette oriented vertically or horizontally from the Palette Display options. Enter a triggering keystroke, and you're all set.

When you trigger your SoftKeys Palette shortcut, a palette appears on your screen (see Figure 13.6). You can trigger a shortcut on the palette by clicking its numbered button or by pressing the corresponding number key (at the top of the keyboard or from the numeric keypad, *not* the function key).

Figure 13.6
A SoftKeys Palette
in action

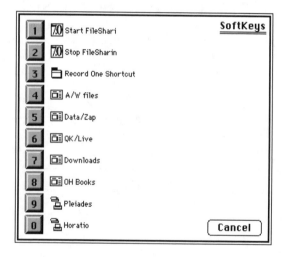

SoftKeys Palettes Tactics and Considerations

So what's wrong with SoftKeys Palettes? First, they are *ugly*. Second, they take up a lot of room. Third, they don't float above your applications; you have to trigger the palette to display and then make your shortcut choice, making the shortcut trigger a two-step process.

However, even with these shortcomings, some people might find them the answer to lost shortcuts. If you put many of your shortcuts on palettes, you can reduce the keystrokes to remember to just those that trigger palettes. This is anathema to us, because we want to speed at all times, but it may work for you. To use SoftKeys Palette shortcuts effectively, you must give the shortcuts they contain descriptive names, so you can easily choose the shortcut you want.

We've been told we're way off base with our disdain of SoftKeys Palettes. Here's a synopsis of what a CE insider had to say:

> "We got a *lot* of feedback from people who wanted better ways to organize their shortcuts because they just couldn't remember keystrokes for all the shortcuts they created. Many beginning users felt the same way.
>
> "Our user testing of SoftKeys Palettes showed that when users grouped their shortcuts in palettes, they were able to easily remember the triggering keystrokes to get to a category of shortcuts. So their most common choices in the palettes became a simple two stroke combination (SoftKey trigger + number). The repeated process of using the palette formed a 'habit' and allowed them to remember more. While not for everyone, this did make QuicKeys more accessible for some and helped others get more out of the product."

A clever strategy that CE Software promotes is to have a parent SoftKeys Palette that contains shortcuts to trigger 10 child SoftKeys Palettes containing your shortcuts. You can use the Instant QuicKeys utility (see Chapter 18, *QuicKeys Utilities*) to create this hierarchy, with the 10 child palettes holding shortcuts for different functions (for example, Go To Folders, Control Panels, and so forth). Pretty clever.

Recording Switches

Like Superman and Bizarro Superman, these two shortcuts sort of look the same, but one is a distorted and contemptible mockery of the other. Start/Stop Sequence is a fine instrument that unlocks all the power and finesse that shortcuts are capable of. Start/Stop Real Time is a crowbar to beat things with, when all else fails. The former leads you nearer to QuicKeys nirvana, the latter to QuicKeys hell.

Well, *maybe* we are overstating the case a bit, because both these shortcuts can be useful in the appropriate situations. But don't confuse the two. They both start and stop the recording of actions, but one does it intelligently, the other like a clod. Both shortcuts produce a Recording Palette that gives you finer control over recording actions, including Pause, Stop, Cancel, and Insert.

A Real Time or a Sequence shortcut recording can be initiated in one of three ways.

■ Choose Record Sequence or Record Real Time from the QuicKeys menu.

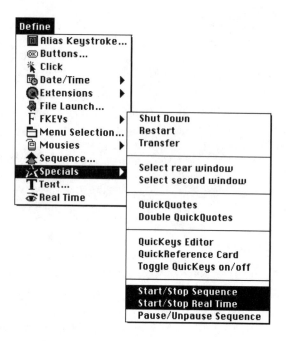

- Choose either the Sequence or the Real Time option from the Define menu of the QuicKeys Editor window.

- Trigger either a Start/Stop Real Time shortcut or a Start/Stop Sequence shortcut.

A Real Time or Sequence shortcut recording can be terminated in one of three ways.

- Click the Stop button on the Recording Palette that automatically appears whenever you're recording a Sequence or Real Time shortcut.

- Choose Stop Recording from the QuicKeys menu.

- Trigger either a Start/Stop Real Time shortcut or a Start/Stop Sequence shortcut.

Start/Stop Real Time

Start/Stop Real Time records the mouse movements, clicks, and keystrokes you make and plays them back as quickly (or as slowly) as you made them. Real Time recordings are played back blind: they don't know what applications they are in or what menu items they are choosing. They can remember mouse movements by screen position only.

If you want to be able to initiate a Real Time recording with a keystroke, you need to include a Start/Stop Real Time shortcut in one of your sets (the Universal set is the most logical). Choose Start/Stop Real Time from the Specials submenu of the Define menu on the QuicKeys Editor window, enter a keystroke combination, and you are ready to make Real Time recordings. If you intend to record Real Time shortcuts often, it is a good idea to make an easy-to-trigger one-handed keystroke for Start/Stop Real Time. This allows you to create shortcuts as efficiently as possible.

Real Time is a good name for this kind of recording. Real Long Time might be more descriptive, because you can't reduce a Real Time recording to its essential components. Real Time recordings *can't be edited* and have limited usefulness.

You might find a use for a Real Time recording as a demonstration device: you can record cursor movements, menu pull-downs, and such, so that it looks like an invisible operator is in charge of your Mac (the potential for practical jokes has not escaped us). We do create a Real Time recording every so often when an application has a nonstandard interface—for example, if the way the application builds menus is so screwy that a Menu Selection shortcut doesn't work with it. A Real Time shortcut might just do the trick. We occasionally used Real Time shortcuts for pop-up menus before the Pop-up Menu shortcut delivered us from that ugly workaround.

Making a Real Time recording starts with invoking your Start/Stop Real Time shortcut (or using one of the other three methods listed earlier). A Recording Palette is displayed (see Figure 13.7). Use the Recording Palette to cancel, record, insert shortcuts, or pause a recording task.

Then you do your thing, and Real Time will record and record and record (you can make very lengthy recordings this way) until you tell it to stop. The easiest way to stop recording a Real Time shortcut is to invoke Start/Stop Real Time again or push the Stop button on the Recording Palette. In either case, the straightforward Real Time edit dialog box appears; the only option unique to it is the Record More button, which lets you do just that.

Figure 13.7
Recording Palette

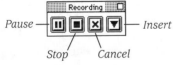

Pause — Stop Cancel — Insert

Use Real Time shortcuts when nothing else works.

Real Time Tactics and Considerations

The key to recording a Real Time shortcut is speed. Set up everything in advance, so you can start creating the shortcut as quickly as possible after you start recording. In some situations you may even want someone else to work in tandem with you, in order to make things as efficient as possible. This may sound like overkill, but a sluggish Real Time shortcut will quickly drive you nuts.

When you trigger a Real Time shortcut, you are giving QuicKeys control of your computer. There is just a slight chance that a Real Time recording can get you into trouble—really big trouble. In the last version of this book we described how inadvertently triggering a Real Time short-cut made for QuarkXPress could erase your hard disk when you were in the Finder. Okay, okay, it was a *very* far-fetched scenario, but tell that to people who operate nuclear power plants.

The key point is this: clicking the mouse button stops a recording playback, and presents the Playback Palette with which you can terminate the playback altogether. This gives you some control over rogue Real Time shortcuts—if your fingers are fast enough.

Don Brown, the author of QuicKeys, thinks we are too hard on this shortcut. Maybe that's true, and maybe you'll discover all sorts of spiffy uses for it. At any rate, we don't use Real Time recordings enough to have a Start/Stop Real Time shortcut in our permanent repertoire. If we want to create a Real Time shortcut, we record it using the controls in the QuicKeys menu.

Start/Stop Sequence

Start/Stop Sequence initiates the recording of a QuicKeys Sequence. Sequences are analyzed exhaustively in the next two chapters (see Chapter 14, *The Sequence*, and Chapter 15, *Sequence Shortcuts*). Start/Stop Sequence is one switch to turn the recording of a Sequence shortcut on and off. It too now uses the Recording Palette to control its processes. To create this shortcut, choose Start/Stop Sequence from the Specials submenu of the Define menu on the QuicKeys Editor window.

Start/Stop Sequence Tactics and Considerations

Use the Start/Stop Sequence shortcut to record Sequences.

Don keeps a Start/Stop Sequence shortcut as part of his Universal set. He uses Control-Option-Command-F8 to trigger it; the F8 key is arbitrary, but the Control-Option-Command modifier combination denotes it as a powerful shortcut, not to be triggered lightly. Steve, always more daring, uses F14 (because it's right next to F15, his Pause keystroke, which he also uses a lot with Sequences).

Record One Shortcut

It's true. Record One Shortcut is not an option on QuicKeys' Define menu. It's a command on the QuicKeys menu. Nevertheless, it's so useful that we've created a menu shortcut to invoke it, and we're covering it here as if it were on the Define menu.

The fastest, easiest way to create a single-step shortcut is with this command. Steve uses Control-F14 to invoke his Menu shortcut, because F14 is his sequence record shortcut. Trigger the shortcut, perform any single action (click the mouse, press a key, whatever), and you've created a shortcut.

QuicKeys doesn't always create the type of shortcut you want with this technique (if you click on a pop-up menu, for instance, it creates a Pop-up Menu shortcut, when you might have wanted a Click shortcut), but it usually does a good job.

14 The Sequence

This chapter gives the ultimate answer. You've now arrived at the well where QuicKeys comes to drink, the true source of QuicKeys power: the Sequence. Sequence shortcuts give you the capability to incorporate individual shortcuts into a series of steps that together function as one distinct shortcut unit. The potential uses are only limited by your skill, imagination, and goals.

Creating Sequences

Just think of a Sequence as many strung-together shortcut functions. For example, if you want a shortcut that will first choose a menu item, then type something in a text edit box, and then press a button, you can create this composite shortcut by making a Sequence with Menu Selection, Text, and Button shortcuts as steps. Some shortcuts are designed to work *only* as steps in a Sequence; we discuss these in the Sequence Control shortcuts section in the next chapter.

There are two main ways to create a Sequence. First, you can record a Sequence (don't confuse this with Real Time recording—it's different); second, you can build a Sequence with the Sequence edit dialog box (a.k.a. the Sequence Editor). Which way to go depends on what your Sequence is like.

Recording Sequences

You record a Sequence by starting a Sequence recorder, performing the actions you want to record, and then stopping the Sequence recorder. QuicKeys provides a handy Recording Palette, much like the one you use to record Real Time shortcuts (see Figure 14.1).

Figure 14.1
Recording Palette

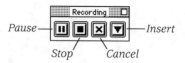

Use the Recording Palette to perform these functions.

- **Pause.** Clicking this button temporarily halts the recording of the Sequence. Clicking it again causes recording to resume. Since the Recording Palette records your every action, you need a way to halt the recording without disrupting your work. Using Pause lets you stop the action while you perform some other function, such as finding files or thinking through your Sequence's steps, without losing your place in the Sequence.

- **Stop.** Does just that. Stop retains the steps you have recorded, but ends the session and returns you to the Sequence Editor. You can also cancel or stop recording while paused.

- **Cancel.** The Terminator. Ends the recording session and does not save your recording.

- **Insert.** Clicking this button lets you insert shortcuts from a displayed list of options.

When you press the Stop button to end recording, QuicKeys displays the Sequence Editor with a list of the editor's *interpretation* of the steps you made.

A Sequence Example

Here's an example. We constantly find ourselves using the Word Count feature in Microsoft Word. Word Count is a menu item on the Tools menu that has its own keystroke shortcut in Word (Option-F15). But after you choose Word Count, you get a dialog box in which you always have to click the Count button to operate the Word Count feature. Let's record a Sequence shortcut to do both steps at once.

First, make sure you are in the correct application (with the correct document, if that matters). Then you can start recording a Sequence in any one of three ways.

- Trigger your Start/Stop Sequence shortcut (see Chapter 13, *Shortcuts That Control QuicKeys*).

- Choose Record Sequence from the QuicKeys menu.

- Select Sequence from the Define menu of the QuicKeys Editor window, and click the Record More button.

Next, choose Word Count from the Tools menu, and click on the Count button. Then stop the recording in one of three ways.

■ Press the Stop button on the Recording Palette.

■ Invoke your Start/Stop Sequence shortcut again.

■ Select Stop Recording from the QuicKeys menu.

QuicKeys then displays the Sequence Editor, with its interpretation of your actions (see Figure 14.2).

Figure 14.2
Sequence Editor

Editing control buttons

Sequence window

Insert arrow

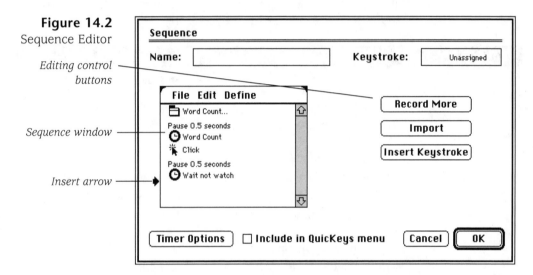

The Sequence window displays the recorder's interpretation of your Sequence's steps of choosing an item from a menu and clicking on a button. If you now assign a keystroke combination to this Sequence and activate it, you find that it works satisfactorily.

But what are all these steps? The two actions you performed, choosing Word Count from the Tools menu and clicking the Count button, are represented by the first and fourth steps, a Menu Selection shortcut and a Click shortcut, respectively. The Sequence recorder has also inserted four Pause and Wait steps to regulate the timing of when the action steps occur.

Ignoring the Pause and Wait steps for the moment (see "Editing Sequences" later in this chapter), notice that still all is not in QuicKeys harmony. The Sequence recorder interpreted your second action, clicking the Count button, as a Click shortcut rather than a Button shortcut. Yes, it works, but it isn't the best shortcut for the job—if circumstances change slightly the Click step could fail to act properly (it might not find the button), whereas a Button step would continue to function. The Sequence recorder does not always choose the perfect shortcut step.

Sequence Recorder Strengths and Weaknesses

The Sequence recorder can only make the correct interpretation (determine the most appropriate shortcut) for *some* of your actions. For example, if you type some text, the Sequence recorder will correctly interpret that as a Text shortcut; if you click on a Close box, the Sequence recorder will attribute that action to a Close window shortcut (Mousie). Table 14.1 shows actions which are *correctly* interpreted by the Sequence recorder.

Table 14.1	Actions and Sequence recorder interpretations
Your action	**Shortcut type recorded**
Typing text	Text
Typing a modifier-keystroke shortcut in an application	Alias Keystroke
Clicking in a window	Click
Clicking on a Close box	Close window (Mousie)
Clicking on a Zoom box	Zoom window (Mousie)
Choosing an item from a pop-up menu	Pop-up menu
Selecting an item from a menu	Menu selection
Typing the triggering keystroke for one of your shortcuts	Appropriate shortcut
Two or more actions	Pause and Wait between Sequence steps

But the Sequence recorder interprets many actions incorrectly or insufficiently. If you open the control panel and set the speaker level to three, the Sequence recorder interprets this as a Menu Selection shortcut and a Click shortcut, not as a SpeakerChanger shortcut. If you type the date, it will be interpreted as a Text shortcut, not as a Date/Time shortcut. Of course, creating a perfect Sequence Editor would be nearly impossible (it would have to read your mind). As it is, it's a good compromise between complexity and function. You can help the Sequence recorder create the most appropriate shortcut steps for your actions by following these guidelines.

■ Avoid simply clicking to select an item when recording a Sequence. For example, use menu commands or their keystroke equivalents to perform tasks such as opening or closing files or folders.

■ Type a document's name to select it from a list rather than selecting it with your mouse.

■ Use the Application menu rather than clicking on a window to change the active application.

■ When you know the Sequence recorder won't interpret your action with the best shortcut step, use the Insert button to place the proper shortcut step, instead.

One function the Sequence recorder does well is to put already extant shortcuts in a Sequence, if you type their invoking keystroke combinations. For example, if you already have a shortcut that sets the speaker level to three, invoking it while the Sequence recorder is running will place that SpeakerChanger shortcut into your Sequence.

Don't overlook the power of the Insert feature to help you overcome some of the Sequence recorder's inherent failings in interpreting an action with the correct shortcut step. When you are recording a Sequence and know your next action will be inadequately interpreted (see Table 14.1), then you may want to click the triangular Insert button on the Recorder Palette instead. A scrolling list of shortcut types appears from which you may be able to choose the shortcut step you want. Although this list of shortcuts is extensive, it isn't comprehensive, so the step you want may have to be inserted later during editing. Nonetheless, this Insert feature makes the process of recording a Sequence much more robust than with previous versions of QuicKeys.

Sequence Recorder Tactics

Earlier versions of the Sequence recorder often produced Sequences that got ahead of the applications they were working with and therefore failed to function properly. To remedy this, the new Sequence recorder puts Pause and Wait steps between virtually every action it records, increasing reliability significantly. Unfortunately, this reliability has been bought at the price of speed, because many of these Pause and Wait steps prove superfluous. They can be edited out, if necessary.

Don often uses the Sequence recorder when he builds a Sequence, but he always checks the resulting Sequence critically and often edits it substantially. The limitations of the Sequence recorder demand that you test and review Sequences it creates to determine if it is appropriate for your needs. If you only need a Sequence recorder-created shortcut temporarily and it functions well enough, you might want to use it as is, even though it may contain some inappropriate shortcut steps. But if you want to make it part of a permanent set, we strongly suggest you edit it to make it as good as possible. For that, you use the Sequence Editor.

Editing Sequences

Editing Sequences is easy because the Sequence Editor has some functions analogous to something you already know—the QuicKeys Editor window. In either one, you can invoke shortcut edit dialog boxes to create and modify different shortcuts. In the QuicKeys Editor window, they are individual shortcuts; in the Sequence Editor, they are shortcut steps in a Sequence. The Sequence Editor also contains Sequence-specific controls.

The Sequence window displays the different shortcut steps in your Sequence. Within the Sequence Editor, you can cut, copy, paste, and modify these individual shortcut steps; and you can add steps to the Sequence. Each shortcut step shown in the window is hot. Clicking once highlights it and allows you to copy or cut it; double-clicking invokes its edit dialog box.

The Sequence window contains three menus: File, Edit, and Define. They are based on the menus in the QuicKeys Editor window, but in many cases, items are dimmed because they have no function in this context.

File

New Set...	
Open Set...	⌘O
Close Set	⌘W
Save Set	⌘S
Save a Copy...	
Save Selection...	
Make Icon...	⌘I
Page Setup...	
Print...	⌘P
Quit	⌘Q

File. Most features of the File menu in the Sequence window are dimmed. The only items active are Page Setup and Print. By choosing Print you can print a list of the Sequence. This command is very useful for archiving and (especially) for debugging long Sequences. Here's a printing tip: if you normally have background printing chosen in the Chooser, you have to close the QuicKeys Editor window to print the sequence. However, if you turn off background printing you can print the sequence without even quitting the Sequence Editor.

Edit

Cut	⌘X
Copy	⌘C
Paste	⌘V
Clear	
Delete	
Undefine	
Modify...	⌘M
Select All	⌘A

Edit. When a shortcut step is highlighted in the Sequence window, the Edit menu is completely active. The other items are what you'd expect. Clear and Delete are functionally identical. Undefine removes the keystroke trigger. Modify produces the same result as double-clicking the shortcut step—it invokes its edit dialog box.

Define. The Define menu has an extra item: User/ Timed Pause at the bottom of the list of shortcut types. The Define menu functions as a source of shortcut

types that you can add to your Sequence. When you choose a shortcut type from the Define menu, its edit dialog box appears (without the keystroke box, because there is no need for it here). You can modify the shortcut as necessary, and then click OK. The new shortcut is inserted into your Sequence at the spot the Insert arrow points to.

Note that three shortcut types are dimmed on this Define menu. Click, Sequence, and Real Time shortcuts cannot be added to a Sequence from this menu. However, Click, Real Time, and Sequence shortcuts can be imported using the Import button (one of the editing-control buttons) or copying and pasting them from the QuicKeys Editor window.

Editing-Control Buttons

All three editing-control buttons are used to add shortcut steps to a Sequence (see Figure 14.3).

Record More. Clicking Record More pops you back into the Sequence recorder. Just add to the Sequence as you wish. You can then turn off the recorder (see Recording Sequences, earlier) and return to the Sequence Editor, which displays the Sequence with the new steps added.

Figure 14.3
Editing-control buttons

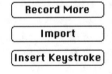

Record More is dimmed unless the Insert arrow points after the last step in your Sequence. Remember that you can always record more shortcuts at the end of a Sequence, then move the shortcuts up in the Sequence with Copy and Paste.

Import. The Import button, nestled between Record More and Insert Keystroke, seems innocuous enough, but it packs a lot of wallop. Import allows you to insert any existing shortcut (including Click, Sequence, and Real Time shortcuts) into a Sequence. You can click on the Import button and the Sequence Editor undergoes metamorphosis: its right side becomes a scrolling window that displays the shortcuts contained in the set showing in the Set pop-up menu below it (see Figure 14.4).

Click on any shortcut in the right-hand scrolling window, click the Copy button, and the shortcut is inserted into your Sequence in the position indicated by the Insert arrow (double-clicking achieves the same result). Note that after you have imported a shortcut (including a whole other sequence), changes you make to the original are *not* reflected in its copied version in the Sequence—there is no hot link.

Figure 14.4
Sequence Editor after an import-induced metamorphosis

Scrolling shortcuts window

Set pop-up menu

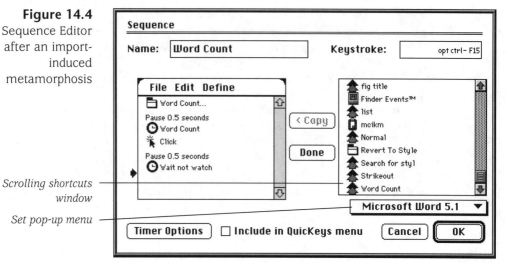

If you press on the Set pop-up menu at the bottom of the window, you see the sets for all your open applications listed (see Figure 14.5). Choosing any of them results in their shortcuts being displayed in the right-hand scrolling window, available for you to import into your Sequence.

Choosing Other from the Sets pop-up menu invokes an Open dialog box. With it, you can choose any one of your other sets, which will display

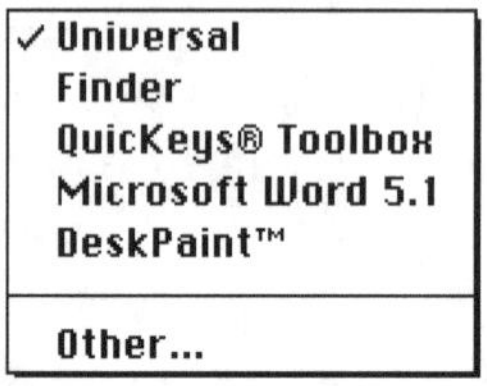

Figure 14.5
Sequence Editor Set pop-up menu

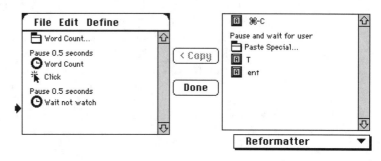

its shortcuts in the Import window. But you can also use it to open your Sequences folder, which stores your Sequence shortcuts. If you choose your Sequences folder, all your Sequences are displayed in the scrolling window of the open dialog box. Choosing one Sequence (or double-clicking on it) returns you to the Sequence Editor, with the steps of your chosen Sequence displayed in the Import window (see Figure 14.6).

Figure 14.6
Sequence steps in the Import window

You can now copy any step from the Import window to the Sequence window, or you can copy multiple steps by pressing Shift and clicking or dragging through a number of steps. By pressing Shift and dragging through the whole window (it automatically scrolls, if necessary), you can select and import all the steps in the Sequence. To get back to the Sequence Editor, click the Done button.

Insert Keystroke. The Insert Keystroke button is a useful shortcut to add an Alias Keystroke step to your Sequence. In our Word Count Sequence, we can replace the Menu Selection shortcut (which chooses Word Count) with an Alias Keystroke shortcut which enters Option-F15 (the Microsoft Word keystroke combination that invokes the Word Count function).

As before, the first step is to highlight the unnecessary step and cut it. Now, with the Insert arrow above the remaining steps, you can click on the Insert Keystroke button, and a prompt appears asking you to press a key. Press Option-F15, and you will return to the Sequence Editor with an Alias Keystroke key inserted and defined (see Figure 14.7). The same result can be obtained by choosing Alias Keystroke from the Define menu, but that's more complicated. Think of the Insert Keystroke button as an instant Alias Keystroke maker.

A note of caution on the Insert Keystroke button: you cannot make an existing shortcut a step in a Sequence by clicking the Insert Keystroke button and then typing the invoking shortcut keystroke. For example, let's say you have a Menu Selection shortcut with the keystroke Option-Command-S that you want to include in a Sequence. You *cannot* click the Insert Keystroke button and type Option-Command-S and have that step function correctly. You *can* import the shortcut into the Sequence. You can also *record* the shortcut into the Sequence *by typing the same invoking keystroke that didn't work with the Insert Keystroke button*. In this case, the Sequence recorder realizes what's happening and puts the correct shortcut step (in this example, a Menus Selection shortcut) in your Sequence.

Figure 14.7
Sequence window
after pressing
Insert Keystroke
Option-F15

Alias Keystroke step

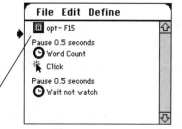

Editing an Example

Let's edit the Sequence we made to count words in the Microsoft Word document. Double-clicking on the shortcut in the QuicKeys Editor window makes its Sequence Editor appear.

We want to replace the Click shortcut with a Button shortcut. To obliterate the Click shortcut, you can click on it in the Edit window and then choose Cut, Clear, or Delete from the Edit menu (or press Command-X for Cut). The Click shortcut disappears into the alternate universe.

To add a new step to the Sequence, you must first ensure that the Insert arrow is in the correct spot. When the Sequence Editor opens, by default the Insert arrow is always after the last shortcut step, so if you want to add a step somewhere else, you must move the arrow by dragging it or by clicking above or below it (see Figure 14.8). Watch out for this when you are dealing with long Sequences.

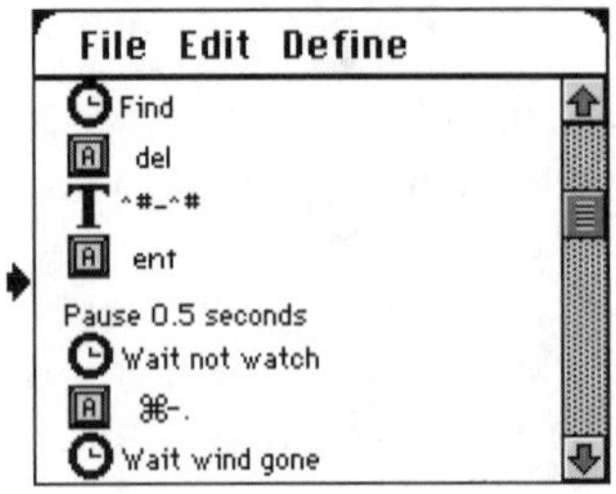

Figure 14.8

Insert arrow in a long Sequence

You can drag it up or down.

Click anywhere above or below to move the arrow to that point.

You can now add the Button shortcut by choosing Button from the Define menu. The Button edit dialog box appears. You can enter the name of the button (Count) and ensure the correct click option is selected (the Always Click option) and then click OK. The shortcut Button step appears in the Sequence window (see Figure 14.9).

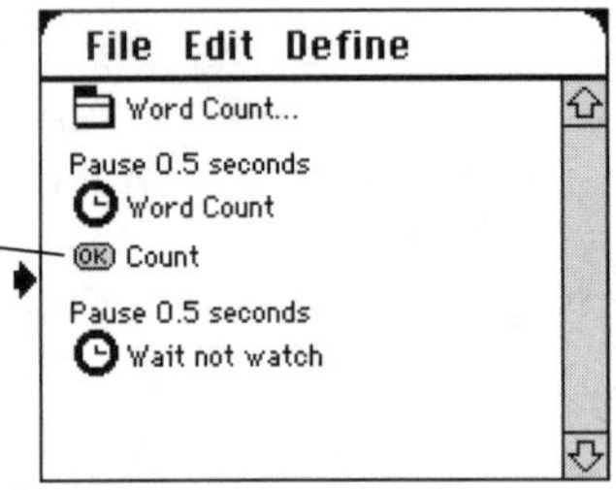

Figure 14.9

Word Count Sequence

Added Button step

Now how about those Pause and Wait steps? We could leave them where they are—the Sequence is short and works quickly, so why fix something if it ain't broke? Most of the time you won't need to edit out the Pause and Wait steps, especially if it takes more time to edit the Sequence than the stripped-down, optimized-for-speed version saves. But Don doesn't like to sully his sets with substandard shortcuts, so he savagely slices superfluous steps.

First, he deletes trailing Pause and Wait steps (after the Button step) because they don't add function to the Sequence—they occur after the last action step. Next, he deletes the other Pause and Wait, clicks OK in the Sequence Editor to return to the QuicKeys Editor window, and clicks OK there to return to Word. The stripped-down Sequence works faster.

■ ■ ■ ■ ■

Building Sequences

All the basic steps we used to edit Sequences can also be employed to build a Sequence from scratch. You can give yourself a *tabula rasa* Sequence window by choosing Sequence from the Define menu in the QuicKeys Editor window. Then, you can add steps by choosing shortcuts from the Sequence Editor's Define menu or by pressing the editing control buttons.

We build Sequences from scratch in situations that the Sequence recorder can't adequately handle. Sometimes we record the simple body of the Sequence with the Sequence recorder and then add some Sequence control shortcuts (see the next chapter, *Shortcuts for Sequences*) to the Sequence to enhance it.

Sophisticated Sequences

Sequences are often the solution to the knottier problems that QuicKeys can handle. In the next chapter, *Shortcuts for Sequences*, we introduce shortcuts intended to work just within Sequences and illuminate some finer points of advanced Sequence technique.

15 Shortcuts for Sequences

This chapter introduces and discusses the shortcuts designed to work within Sequences. The first three Sequence shortcuts, Wait, Decision, and Jump can modify how the Sequence proceeds based on testing the current condition of the Mac environment, like the name of the active document or whether a particular button is available—all three use the same tests. We call these conditional Sequence shortcuts. The remaining shortcuts for Sequences don't perform conditional tests, but can add powerful control to Sequences, such as repeating part of a Sequence a set number of times or asking the user for input that the Sequence can act on. We call these single-purpose Sequence shortcuts. At the end of the chapter, we offer a potpourri of Sequence tips and tricks. These shortcuts are discussed in this chapter.

- Wait
- Decision
- Jump
- Pause
- Repeat
- Gosub
- Message

Conditional Sequence Controls

We like to think of three shortcuts, Wait, Decision, and Jump, as conditional because they react to your Mac's condition. They test for certain conditions that you define and perform certain actions based on the outcome of the tests. You can nest several levels of decisions, resulting in very complex shortcuts. QuicKeys 3 introduces two redesigned extensions, Wait and Decision, which incorporate the functions of five older extensions. The Jump shortcut is totally new. Here's how the three conditional shortcuts work.

- **Wait.** The Wait shortcut halts the action of a Sequence until the particular condition occurs.

- **Decision.** The Decision shortcut can branch to another shortcut based upon one or more conditions.

- **Jump.** The Jump shortcut can jump over steps in a Sequence based upon the outcome of its logical testing of conditions.

But before we discuss the shortcuts, we need to explain the logical tests that all three of the shortcuts share.

Logical Tests

All three shortcuts modify the flow of control in your Sequences through the use of the same logical tests. Logical tests look at the Mac environment and, based upon the condition of the subject of the tests, cause the three extensions to act or not act. In fact, that is why we call the logical tests *conditionals*: they test for a true or false condition.

Whether you use a Wait, Decision, or Jump shortcut, the way you choose a logical test is the same: you choose the test from the pop-up menu near the top of their edit dialog boxes (see Figure 15.1). We call this the Test Category pop-up menu because from it you can choose the category of conditions you will test for. Each of the three shortcut edit dialog boxes labels the pop-up differently, but the choices are identical.

Figure 15.1
Test Category
pop-up menu

| Button Action |
| Cursor Action |
| Menu Action |
| Other Action |
| Window Action |

The Test Category pop-up menu gives you five choices.

- **Button Actions.** Button Action tests check for the presence of a specific button and if this button has been selected or is available.

- **Cursor Actions.** Cursor Action tests look at the shape of the cursor, which can indicate the status of the computer. For example, testing to see if the cursor is a watch indicates whether or not the Mac is busy.

- **Menu Actions.** Menu Action tests look to see if a specific menu is available on the screen and if that menu contains a specific command you need. It then can check if that command is available or selected.

■ **Other Actions.** Other Action tests perform several other logical tests on your Mac, such as testing the state of the system clock, the contents of the Clipboard, and the status of your application (is your application running and is it the active window?).

■ **Window Actions.** Window Action tests look at the status of your application's active window (the one on top). These tests can search for such conditions as whether or not the current window is a dialog box or whether or not the window's name includes a particular word.

Within each category you can test for one or more conditions. Thus, a window action test can act based on whether a certain window is in front *and* if it also has a certain name. If you test for two criteria, both have to be true for the test outcome to be true; one needs to be false for a false result (or both conditions have to be false for a false result).

Button Action

The Button Action logical test category controls the way a Sequence proceeds depending on whether a button exists, is enabled, or is selected. When you select the Button Action logical test, an edit dialog box with the Button Action options is displayed (see Figure 15.2). What you see will differ slightly from our generic Conditional Shortcut edit dialog box pictured here, depending on which of the three conditional shortcuts you use, but the logical tests options are the same.

Figure 15.2
Edit dialog box with Button Action tests

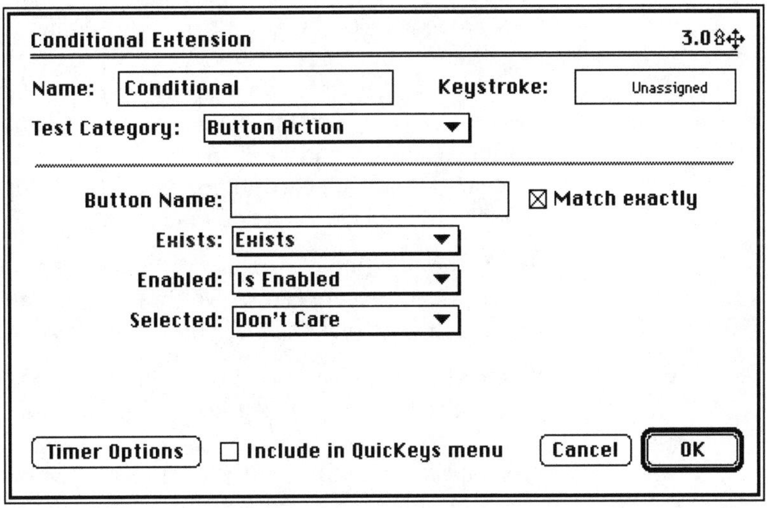

The Button Action tests contain four options. In the first, Button Name, you must enter the name of the button to be tested. The remaining three options comprise very straightforward tests.

- **Button Name.** To make any Button Action test, you need to enter a button's name. If you want to identify a particular button precisely, choose the Match Exactly checkbox, and be sure to spell the button name exactly, and use ellipses in the place of three periods, when necessary.

- **Exists.** You can test to see if a button exists not by choosing the option from the pop-up menu.

- **Enabled.** You can test to see if a button is enabled (available for selection) or not. If you don't want this condition tested, you can choose the Don't Care option.

- **Selected.** The extension checks to see if a button is selected or not, or if you don't want this condition tested. Use the pop-up menu to select one of three choices: Is, Is Not, or Don't Care. This pop-up menu is handy to use to check the status of radio buttons and checkboxes that modify command behavior, but do not really matter in the long run.

Cursor Action

The Cursor Action logical tests determine how a Sequence proceeds based on whether or not the cursor (pointer) conforms to a particular shape. The Cursor Action logical tests are simpler than the other logical test categories because Cursor Action looks for only two conditions: whether the cursor *is* or *is not* a specified cursor type.

You can create a Cursor Action test by selecting Cursor Action from the Test Category pop-up menu. An edit dialog box with the Cursor Action options is displayed (see Figure 15.3).

The Cursor Action options include two pop-up menus (one with a cursor display box), and two checkboxes.

- **Is.** The first pop-up menu provides the first part of the test. You can choose either the Is or Is Not option, testing to see if the cursor is or isn't the same as the one you choose from the Cursor pop-up menu.

- **Cursor.** The second pop-up menu provides a list of standard cursor shapes that is displayed in the little window to the right of the pop-up menu. Select the arrow, ball, watch, or other option to test for the shape of that cursor. If you choose Other from the Cursor pop-up menu, the Select Cursor window appears, which gives you a palette

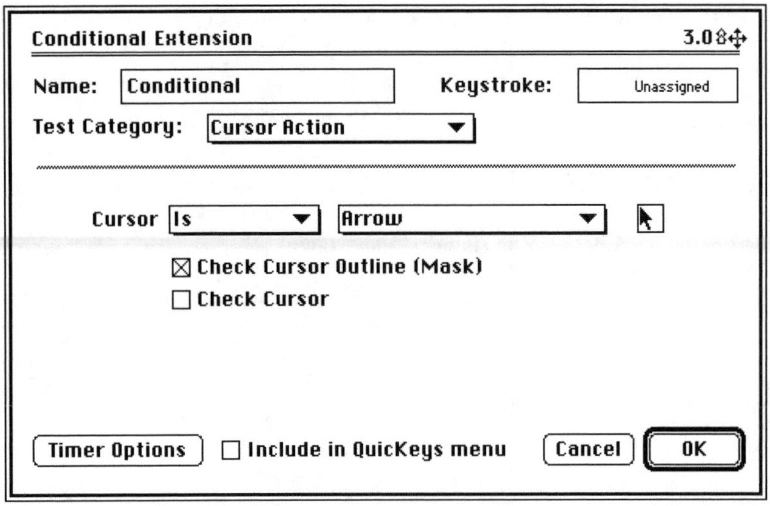
Conditional Extension
3.0
Name:
Conditional
Keystroke:
Unassigned
Test Category:
Cursor Action
Cursor
Is
Arrow
Check Cursor Outline (Mask)
Check Cursor
Timer Options
Include in QuicKeys menu
Cancel
OK

Figure 15.3 Cursor Action edit dialog box

of additional cursor choices from the active application and the system (see Figure 15.4).

- **Check Cursor Outline.** Select the Check Cursor Outline (Mask) checkbox when you are testing the existence of an animated cursor (such as a spinning ball or spinning watch hands) where the cursor changes but the outline remains the same. Also, different programs sometimes use slightly different graphic depictions of seemingly identical cursors, and by selecting the Cursor Outline (Mask) checkbox you may be able to test for these slightly varying cursors as a class.
- **Check Cursor.** The Check Cursor option does just that. Check the Check Cursor box when you are looking for a static cursor such as an arrow or hairline.

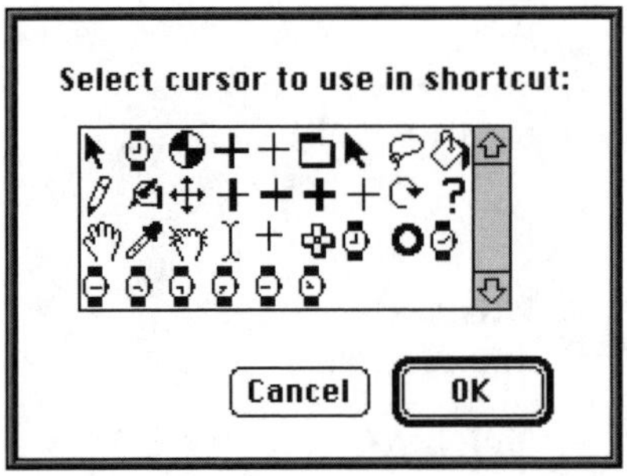
Select cursor to use in shortcut:
Cancel
OK

Figure 15.4 Select Cursor window

Menu Action

The Menu Action test category is similar to Button Action.

After selecting the Menu Action category from the Test Category pop-up menu, an edit dialog box appears with the Menu Action options displayed (see Figure 15.5).

Figure 15.5
Edit dialog box
with Menu
Action tests

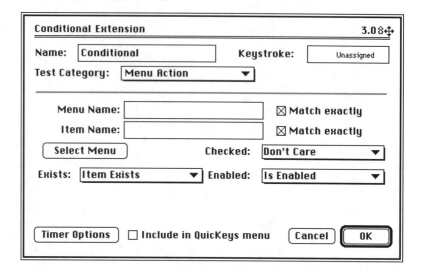

Like the Button Action test category, with Menu Action you enter the name of the item you are testing for and then choose from three test conditions by choosing options from pop-up menus. You can test each of the three conditions at the same time. The result is true if all three conditions are true and false if any prove to be false. Note that this makes the Don't Care selection crucial when you want to exclude a test. The Menu Action tests include these options.

- **Menu and Item Name.** To make a Menu Action test, you must enter a menu name and, optionally, a menu item name in their respective text edit boxes. The easiest way to do this is to click the Select Menu button and then choose the menu or item upon which you want to base the test. Note that even if a menu item is grayed out you can still select it as a criteria for the tests. After you have chosen a menu item, the Menu Name and Item Name fields are filled in.

- **Exists.** The extension will check to see if a menu item exists or does not exist, or if you don't care.

- **Match Exactly.** Select the Match Exactly checkboxes if you want to test for the menu or item by its exact name. One reason not to select this box is if you are working with a menu name that changes based on your actions, such as Undo in Word whose name changes to Undo Typing when you are entering text. In this case, uncheck the Match Exactly checkbox and use Undo for the item to make the shortcut function even with such a dynamic menu item.

■ **Checked.** The extension checks to see if a menu item is selected (a check mark appears next to its name on the menu) or not selected, or if you care about this test.

■ **Enabled.** The extension will check to see if a menu item is available for selection (enabled) or is not enabled, or if you care about this test. Use the pop-up menu to select one of three choices: Is, Is Not, or Don't Care.

Other Action

Okay, we lied to you. We said that the three conditional shortcuts share the same five categories of logical tests. That's true...except in the case of Other Action. For all three conditional shortcuts the Other Action test category contains a number of unrelated test areas that include the activity of the Mac's system clock, the status of an application, and the status and nature of data on the Clipboard. But the Wait shortcut adds two more: tests based on user actions and system beeps. Selecting Other Action from the Test Categories pop-up menu makes the Other Action options appear (see Figure 15.6).

Figure 15.6
Edit dialog box with Other Action options

You won't see these with a Decision or Jump shortcut.

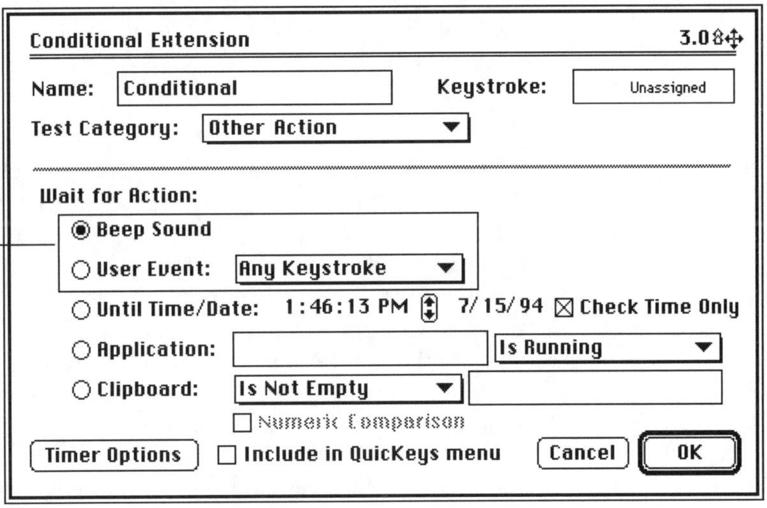

The Other Action options test three different areas (or five, with a Wait shortcut) of the condition of your Mac. Because these test areas are exclusive, you can only test in one area with any Other Action test.

- **Beep Sound.** Click the Beep Sound radio button to test for a System beep. This can only be used with a Wait step in a Sequence, so using this test will cause the Sequence to pause until the System beeps.

- **User Event.** Click the User Event radio button to test for a user's keystroke or click (choose one of the options from the associated pop-up menu). Like Beep Sound, this option is only available on Wait steps within Sequences. Using this test will cause the Sequence to pause until the chosen user event occurs.

- **Until Time/Date.** Click the Until Time/Date radio button to test for the System clock's status. Change the time or date you want to test for by double clicking the appropriate item and then clicking the Up and Down arrows. You can click the Check Time Only checkbox if you want the test to ignore the date.

- **Application.** Click the Application radio button to test if a specified application is running, not running, or front most (active). Enter the name of the application in the text box.

- **Clipboard.** Click on the Clipboard radio button to make tests based on the contents of the Clipboard. The pop-up menu offers a wide range of test choices. Where appropriate, you can enter a number or text in the associated text edit box that will be tested against the contents of the Clipboard. This comparison is based on the assumption that the contents are ASCII text unless you select the Numeric Comparison checkbox.

Wow! A staggering number of Clipboard tests are available in the pop-up menu. You can test if the contents of the Clipboard are ASCII text (such as a TeachText file) or another data type (such as a graphic file or a spreadsheet file). You specify the specific data type to test for by entering its four-letter name, such as PICT or EPSF, in the text box. You can even test to see if the data meets specific numeric criteria by selecting the appropriate Boolean logic from the pop-up menu (for example, Equals, Does Not Equal, Is Greater Than, or Is Less Than) and entering the data to check against in the text box.

Window Action

The Window Action option makes the shortcut evaluate a window's location, name, or type.

Selecting the Window Action test from the Test Category pop-up menu causes an edit dialog box with Window Action options to appear (see Figure 15.7).

Figure 15.7
Edit dialog box
with Window
Action options

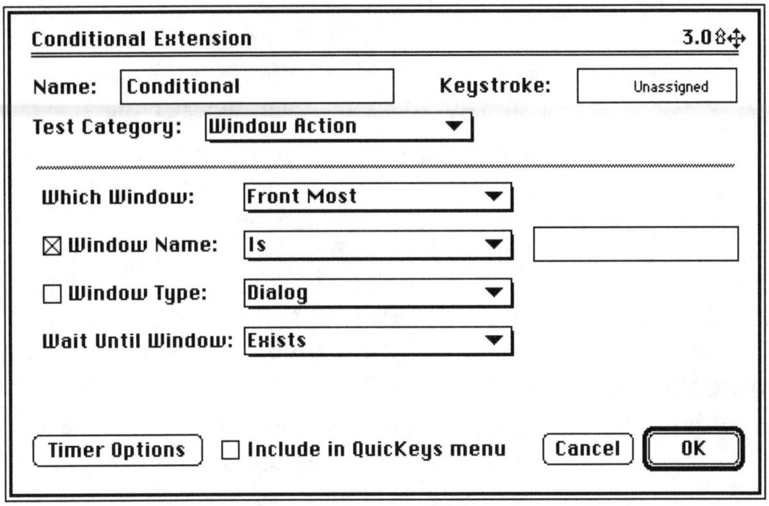

The edit dialog box contains three pop-up menus (one for window, one for name, and one for type). There is also a text edit box to the right of the Window Name pop-up menu, in which you enter text that's considered by the criteria chosen. You can use these options to refine your Window Action test.

- **Which Window.** You can select the window you want to test from the Which Window pop-up menu. You have two choices: Front Most or Any Window. Note that the two choices apply only to your *active* or top-most application. If you have other applications running, this test will not apply to their windows.

- **Window Name.** The Window Name pop-up menu and the accompanying text edit box comprise the Window Name tests. The four pop-up menu tests are straightforward. Choose one, and enter the text upon which it acts in the text edit box. Be sure to select the accompanying checkbox if you want to make a Window Name test.

- **Window Type.** Click the Window Type checkbox if you want to test for a certain window type. Then click the Window Type pop-up menu to choose the condition you want to be met.

Three window types can be tested for with the Window Type option.

■ **Dialog.** You've seen a zillion dialog windows—for example, the Finder's directory dialog boxes for opening or saving a document, Word's Style dialog box, and so forth. This category also includes alert boxes that the application displays.

■ **System.** System windows (emanating from your system) show up rarely. This category includes control panel windows.

■ **Document (formerly called User).** Document windows comprise all windows that aren't dialog or System windows—for example, windows of documents of other open applications, such as Excel or FileMaker, that you can access via the Application menu.

Conditional Shortcuts Strategies and Considerations

Certain generic rules of thumb apply to each of the five logical test categories. Here we describe how each type of condition can be used to its full advantage to test the status of your Mac.

Button Action. Button Action tests function in a similar manner to Menu Action tests (discussed later) even down to an occasional mis-cue because an application does not use standard Mac buttons (even though they look like them). Button Action tests can be used to ensure that the application you are in has displayed a dialog box that you want your Sequence to proceed with. When a particular button is active, you know the dialog box is up and ready. Also, some applications highlight a button when a process is complete.

Cursor Action. Cursor Action logical tests search for a specific type of cursor resource (such as the use of a Globe icon for indicating the operation of a process or Arrow icon for pointing and selecting) within the open document. If the application you are in does not treat cursors in this standard manner, it may be impossible to get the logical test to work correctly. Most popular programs use the cursors supported by this conditional test, but some games imported from the DOS world may not.

A good use of the Cursor Action test is with the Is Not Watch option chosen. These conditionals can be used to look for a time when an application is not waiting (an animated wrist watch is showing), say in a Wait extension in a Sequence that pauses but lets you know it is still alive by displaying a wristwatch. This starts up the Sequence again after the application finishes crunching (when the wristwatch disappears).

Menu Action. Some applications seem to have their own way of generating menus that may look like menus, act like menus, and smell like menus—but actually don't follow all the Apple guidelines for true menu-ness. So before incorporating a Menu Action test into your extension as an integral part of a long Sequence, check your particular application to see if the menu action test works the way it is supposed to. One test is to try a Menu Selection shortcut. If that works, the Menu Action will work.

Whether a menu item is able to be checked depends on the application. Many applications do not have any (or many) menu items that can be checked. Most menu items can be disabled (dimmed) under certain conditions, so you will probably use the Enabled conditionals much more often than the Checked conditionals.

Sometimes a menu is enabled or disabled for a reason unrelated to what you're trying to do, but nevertheless signals that an event has occurred that *is* important to what you're doing. The Menu Action logical test lets you create workarounds that you couldn't create otherwise.

Other Action. The Other Action conditionals test for several useful situations. You can use an If After Time/Date option to test a criteria for a specific time and then perform the extension's action. Using the Wait extension, for instance, you can pause the Sequence based on whether a specific application is available or the current (front-most) window. Often you want to save memory by purging the Clipboard. There is a conditional that tests to see if the Clipboard is Empty or Not Empty. Another lets you selectively paste or copy into the Clipboard based on a comparison of its contents to a numerical or textual criteria. Be sure to check the Numerical Comparison box to compare of numbers.

Window Name. The Window Name test has four name-matching criteria, giving you a lot of dexterity in dealing with potential window names. Here's the lowdown.

- **Is.** Matches the name of the window exactly as you've entered it in the Window Name text edit box. Use this when you want to pause, decide, or jump the Sequence when a specific window becomes active. For example, if you want the Sequence to wait for a window named Spelling to become active before proceeding, or decide to do something else based upon the window named Spelling becoming active, or jump to another shortcut when the Spelling window becomes active, choose this option.

- **Is Not.** The Sequence performs the extension based on a situation where the active window is any window but the window you have named exactly in the Window Name text edit box. For example, if you want to act based on the fact that the active window is not the Find window, this is the option to choose.

■ **Contains.** The Sequence performs the extension if the name of the active window contains text you enter in the Window Name text edit box. Use this when you want to test whether the active window has a generic quality—for example, if you want to wait until the window has a name containing the word Untitled. Untitled 1, Untitled 2, and so on all fulfill this condition.

■ **Does Not Contain.** The Sequence performs the extension if the name of the active window *doesn't* contain text you enter in the Window Name text edit box. An example similar to the one above might be what you're after: you want to wait until the window *doesn't have* a name containing the word Untitled. With this option chosen, Untitled 1 or Untitled 2 makes the Sequence wait. Any name without the word Untitled allows it to proceed.

You may have noticed that you can choose the Window Name option and the Window Type option simultaneously; they are not mutually exclusive criteria. If you do so, the extension looks for *both* conditions to be met. For example, if you are testing for a Wait situation, if you ask it to wait until the window name is Find and the window type is Document, the Sequence will wait until a user window named Find is active; it *will not* proceed only on a dialog window named Find.

Sometimes window types are not obvious, so you might want to test the type to be sure you have it right. An easy way to do this is to create a two-step Sequence. The first step is your Wait Extension with the correct criteria chosen. The second step is a Message Extension or a Sound Extension that confirms that the Wait step preceded it. Invoke your test Sequence with the questionable window active. If you get a confirmation, you know that Wait's criteria were met.

Now that we have reviewed how the five logical tests operate, let's see how the three extensions, Wait, Decision, and Jump, use these conditional tests to create useful Sequence tools.

Wait

The Wait shortcut halts a Sequence until a particular condition (that you select from one of the five test categories) occurs. The newly redesigned Wait extension incorporates the functions of the WindowWait, MenuWait, and CursorWait extensions into a single extension with the other logical tests described above.

You can add a Wait step to a Sequence by choosing Wait from the Sequence Tools category of the Extensions submenu of the Sequence editor's Define menu. The Wait edit dialog box appears (see Figure 15.8).

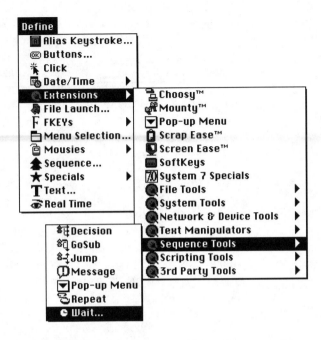

Figure 15.8
Wait edit dialog
box

Select one of the five test categories (for example, Menu Action, Button Action, and so forth) from the Wait Until pop-up menu (see Figure 15.9).

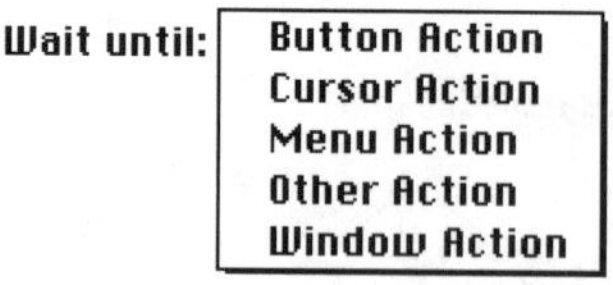

Figure 15.9
Wait Until pop-up
menu

Wait until:
| Button Action |
| Cursor Action |
| Menu Action |
| Other Action |
| Window Action |

When a Wait step occurs in a Sequence, the Sequence pauses until the outcome of the test you specify (for instance, the existence or absence of a specific dialog box, button, cursor shape, or menu item) is met. Then the Sequence proceeds with the next step.

Wait Considerations

Like the other conditional shortcuts, Wait is only aware of windows that exist within the application that's active when the Wait step occurs in the Sequence. If you manually flip to another application while Wait has paused your Sequence, QuicKeys does not pick up the change in windows, or the change in any windows in that subsequent application.

You can use the Window Action test of the Wait extension to pause a Sequence that is copying paragraphs from a number of documents and pasting them into just one. If you set up Wait to pause while the application is switching to the target document, you can ensure that your pasting is done correctly.

When Wait pauses the Sequence, it does so by activating the QuicKeys Pause function—so you can get the Sequence restarted (bypass the Wait conditional) by choosing Pause from the QuicKeys submenu, clicking the Pause button on the Recording Palette again if you are recording a Sequence, or invoking your Unpause shortcut. Here's a warning: just like Pause (described later), this mechanism can be confounded if you invoke a shortcut while Wait has suspended a Sequence. Do so at your own risk.

Wait Tactics

Use Wait to suspend a Sequence and restart it when the status of the Mac and/or your application changes.

Wait pauses a Sequence and then resumes it based on its tests for the existence and status of specific windows, menus, buttons, cursor shapes, applications, Clipboard contents, and so forth. Here's a good example of a Wait step. Steve works on long documents in PageMaker and often re-indexes them, using the Create Index feature, which displays a dialog box while it is working. Steve then flows the index into a page, using the loaded text gun that's displayed when the indexing is finished. In long documents indexing can take a long time, so he tried to make a shortcut which would choose Create index from the Options menu, click on OK, and then click in the space where he wanted the index to flow (see Figure 15.10). However, it didn't work because the Click step occurred while indexing was taking place.

■ ■

Figure 15.10

Failed attempt at an Indexing and Flowing Sequence

Figure 15.11

Wait steps to fix the Indexing and Flowing Sequence

So he placed a Wait for Window to Change step in the Sequence (see Figure 15.11), and it worked perfectly. Wait Until Dialog is Gone and Wait Until Window is Gone also work for this step.

Another example: Steve uses CIM's (CompuServe Information Manager's) Send and Receive All Mail command to check his CompuServe mail. That command won't disconnect from CompuServe when it's finished, but it does beep. So he has a sequence that invokes the command, waits for a beep, and disconnects. It is imperfect because mail errors can cause beeps, but he hasn't found another conditional that works.

When you use the Record Palette to record a Sequence, you will see many Wait steps in the result. Waits let the Sequence stay on track with the speed of your Mac to ensure that clicks and other cursor activities actually work. When you manually create Sequences, consider using Waits for the same reason—to make sure that your clicks and other selections actually do what you want. But only use them where necessary. With recorded Sequences, you can remove the excess Waits while troubleshooting.

Decision

The Decision shortcut incorporates the functions of two older extensions—WindowDecision and MenuDecision, plus the other logical tests described above. Decision is a branching shortcut, directing how the Sequence proceeds based upon the outcome of its logical tests. Decision can pass Sequence execution along to the next step after the Decision or branch to another shortcut step. After that shortcut step is finished, Sequence execution branches back to the next step after the Decision.

If you choose Decision from the Sequence Tools category of the Extensions submenu of the Define menu in the Sequence editor (whoosh!), the Decision edit dialog box appears (see Figure 15.12).

Decision redirects the Sequence to one of two other shortcuts, depending on whether its conditions have been met. You can enter the names of the shortcuts you want Decision to play in one of two text boxes: the If Condition is True Trigger Shortcut box or the If Condition is False Trigger

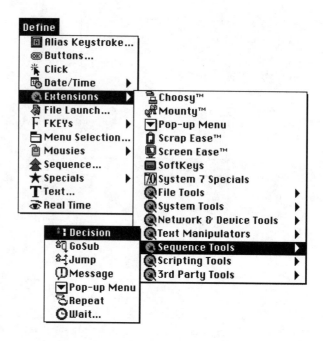

Shortcut box. If you leave one of the text edit boxes blank, the Sequence will proceed with its next step if that condition is met.

For example, if you choose a Window Action test to see if the active window is a dialog box, Decision plays the True shortcut if a dialog box

Figure 15.12
Decision edit
dialog box

Decision Extension   3.0

Name: Decision

Decision:

If Condition Is True Trigger Shortcut:

If Condition Is False Trigger Shortcut:

Cancel   OK

is active when the Decision step occurs. If a dialog box is not active, Decision plays the False shortcut. After either of the True/False short-cuts is played, the Sequence resumes with its next step.

Here's an example of a Sequence—an Automatic-save shortcut—created with a Decision step using the Window Action logical test (see Figure 15.13). It's a variation of an example given by Simeon Leifer, Decision's creator. It looks deceptively simple, but quite a bit of function lurks beneath. It resides in the Simple Text set and is activated by the timer every 10 minutes. Using Decision with Window Action selected as the logical test in the Decision pop-up menu, the Sequence determines whether your active window has previously been saved or not; it then displays one of two messages. The message boxes allow you to either cancel the subsequent Save step or continue and save the active document.

Figure 15.13
Save Sequence in the Simple Text set

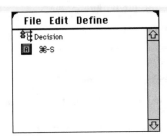

This Automatic-save Sequence has two steps: a Decision and an Alias Keystroke shortcut that invokes the Save command. The Decision step (Figure 15.14) asks if the document that's active contains Untitled—this checks whether the document has been previously saved. If the title includes Untitled, the conditional test has been met, so the Sequence is directed to the True shortcut, a shortcut we've named Save Query. If the title doesn't include Untitled, the Sequence is directed to the False short-cut, Save Warning.

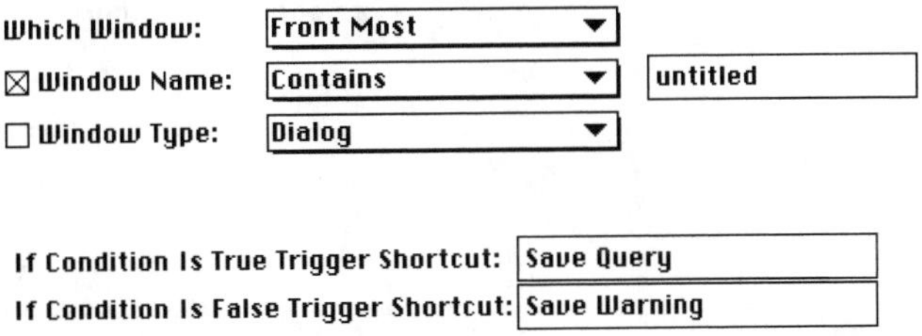

Figure 15.14
Decision Window Action conditionals and True/False shortcuts

Which Window:	Front Most ▼	
☒ Window Name:	Contains ▼	untitled
☐ Window Type:	Dialog ▼	

If Condition Is True Trigger Shortcut: `Save Query`
If Condition Is False Trigger Shortcut: `Save Warning`

Save Query is a Message shortcut (Figure 15.15) that states that the active document has never been saved. It gives the options of clicking Cancel to stop the Sequence or OK to continue the Sequence. If you click OK, the original Sequence picks up after the WindowDecision step and invokes Command-S.

Save Warning (Figure 15.16) is just like Save Query, except its mes-sage differs slightly.

Figure 15.15
Save Query
Message edit
dialog box and
resulting message

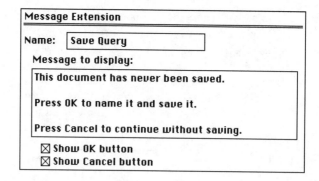

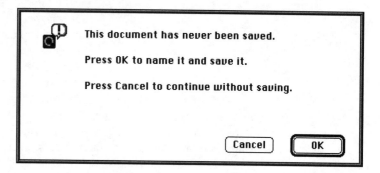

Figure 15.16
Save Warning
Message

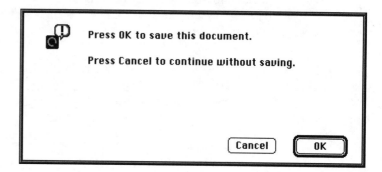

Decision Considerations

The shortcut names you enter in the True or False text edit boxes must be exact, except for their case. Unfortunately, you have to type them, rather than choose them from a menu. The need for calling shortcuts by name argues for good shortcut naming technique—the more terse and more descriptive the name, the easier it is to use in this context.

You don't have to branch to two shortcuts outside the original Sequence. You may leave either the True or the False Shortcut text edit box blank. If the proper conditionals are met for a blank True or False box, the Sequence will continue to the step after the Decision step. Essentially, you are including one branch in the original Sequence.

Keep in mind that after a True or False shortcut branch is played, the Sequence continues from the step after Decision. If you don't have any steps after it, there's no problem; the Sequence just terminates, after it finishes one of the two outside steps. But if you don't want to return to the original Sequence, you must somehow terminate (cancel) the Sequence after the branch has done its work. An easy way to do this is to create a Message shortcut as the last step in your branch, have the Cancel option chosen, and just click Cancel in the message window.

Decision Tactics *Use Decision to branch a Sequence to one of two other shortcuts depending on the outcome of conditional tests.*

When you start to create a Sequence shortcut with branches (you can nest conditionals several levels), you might want to first sketch a flow diagram of the Sequence. This can help determine whether you want to branch out to two shortcuts or only one—with the default leading into the rest of the Sequence.

Decision can come in handy as a companion to Repeat. You can use Decision to jump out of a Repeat-directed loop in a Sequence (see "Repeat Tactics" later in this chapter).

■ ■ ■ ■ ■

Jump Jump and Decision are two similar shortcuts with different outcomes. Decision moves you to another shortcut, but Jump moves you to another step within your current Sequence. Another difference between Jump and Decision is that Jump branches only if the test condition is true. A false condition just passes execution to the next step in the Sequence. Jump can move backwards or forwards within the Sequence a specified number of steps—handy when you want to replay a step (or steps) without looping. Jump is, in a very limited way, one half of a Repeat.

If you want to use a Jump shortcut to branch to another step in your Sequence, select Jump from the Sequence Tools category of the Extensions submenu of the Define menu within the Sequence edit dialog box. The Jump edit dialog box appears (see Figure 15.17). Choose a logical test from the Jump On pop-up menu.

Jump will branch to another step in your Sequence only if the conditional test you create (for example, the existence of a window, menu

■ ■

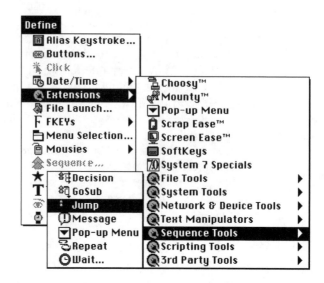

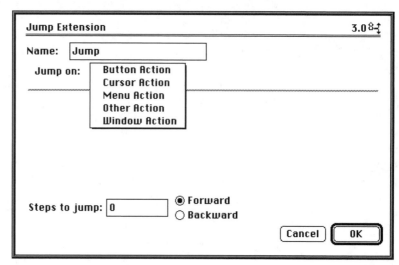

Figure 15.17
Jump edit dialog
box

item, cursor shape, button, and so forth) is true. Enter the number of steps you want to move in the Steps to Jump text box and click on the appropriate radio button to move either forward or backward in your Sequence.

Jump Considerations

You need to know your Sequence to properly count steps. With a long Sequence you might consider printing your Sequence and manually numbering the steps. When counting steps *don't* count the step that

■ ■

you are jumping to as a step, just count the steps you are jumping *over*. Miscounting can produce interesting results.

Remember that Jump only jumps steps when the logical test result is true. Therefore, if you are looking for a negative conditional to be true—for example, a dialog box is not available and the dialog box is available—then the Jump won't occur. Reciprocal conditions are available for almost all the tests, so this shouldn't be a big problem if you design correctly.

Jump Tactics

Use Jump to branch a Sequence to another step within the Sequence, depending on a logical test.

Jump can tricky to manage. When you start to create a Sequence shortcut with its execution jumping or branching due to conditional tests results (you can nest conditionals several levels), we urge you to first sketch a flow diagram of the Sequence. This can help determine whether you want to branch forward or back and how many shortcut steps you want to jump.

Single-Purpose Sequence Controls

QuicKeys 3 retains three very useful single-function Sequence Control shortcuts: Pause, Repeat, and Message. And a new Sequence shortcut has been added: Gosub. These steps perform only one function and do not perform logical tests as conditions of their behavior. As such, they are simpler than the programming Sequence control shortcuts described earlier but provide just as much power. Let's look at these shortcut types in more detail.

Pause

Pause is conceptually a very simple shortcut. Placing a Pause within a Sequence causes the Sequence to halt at that step and wait (while it is waiting the Sequence displays a Playback Palette). You predetermine in which of two ways Pause can wait.

- **Time.** Pause will wait the length of time you choose.

- **Pause and Wait for User.** Pause will flip into the QuicKeys Pause mode. To get it going again, you can press the Pause button on the Playback Palette (or invoke your special Unpause shortcut as explained later in this chapter).

To put a Pause step in a Sequence, choose User/Timed Pause from the bottom of the Define menu of the Sequence editor. The Pause Options dialog box appears (see Figure 15.18). You can then choose how you

Figure 15.18
Pause Options
dialog box

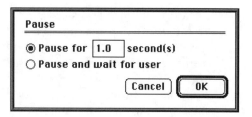

want Pause to pause. If you choose the time option, you can enter the pause time in seconds (and tenths of seconds). You can also press the Pause and Wait for User radio button to pause the Sequence indefinitely until asked to resume.

Timed Pauses

You can use the User Pause Options dialog box to place a timed Pause into a Sequence when the Sequence you've built doesn't work correctly and you suspect that QuicKeys is going too fast for the application it is working in. This is an endemic problem with QuicKeys—it sometimes doesn't realize when an application is creeping along, so it goes right ahead and gives it more steps. Often the application just ignores the QuicKeys messages until it gets its act together, so you find that Sequence steps occur in the wrong places—or do weird things. Placing timed Pauses in a Sequence is like telling QuicKeys, "Hold on, wait for a while, maybe the application will catch up." If the application does catch up in time, then everything is okay; if not, you need a longer pause (or use a Wait step instead).

When you are using the Sequence recorder to create a Sequence, the recorder automatically places a series of timed Pause steps (0.5 seconds long) and Wait steps in your Sequence, for these very reasons. You can consider removing some Pause steps while troubleshooting your Sequence.

Pause and Wait for User

The Pause and Wait for User choice on the Pause Options dialog box makes the Sequence pause and wait for you to tell it to continue. (You can manually pause a Sequence by clicking the mouse while the Sequence is executing.) When your Sequence pauses, a Pause Palette appears that contains only three buttons: Resume, Stop, and Edit (see Figure 15.19). These buttons let you resume the paused Sequence (by pressing the Resume button), stop the Sequence, or open the Sequence editor to edit the Sequence. We can't say enough about the power of a Pause and Wait for User step in a Sequence. It's helped us build some really terrific Sequence shortcuts.

Figure 15.19
Pause Palette

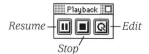

Resume — Stop — Edit

You can use a Wait for User Pause if you have a Sequence that needs user input in the middle. For example, you may have a Sequence that sets up a header for you in a word-processing document. It enters the date and page number but requires you to enter the chapter title before it reformats. You place a Pause and Wait for User step that allows you to type in the chapter name. Then you tell the Sequence to resume. One way to resume the Sequence is to press the Resume button of the Playback Palette that appears when you invoke a Pause. There is another way: make your own UnPause shortcut that you can trigger from your keyboard. Here's how. Select Pause/Unpause Sequence from the Specials submenu of the Define menu in the QuicKeys Editor window. Yup, this is another route to the Pause shortcut that controls the QuicKeys Pause function. But unlike the Pause step available in the Sequence editor, you can give this Pause an invoking keystroke. We like to use our unmodified F15 key for Pause because it's already labeled that way. This shortcut becomes an easy way to unpause a paused Sequence and wait for User mode.

It is worth noting that while you are in a Sequence, your Unpause shortcut is just that: it only functions to resume a Sequence. You can't use it to pause a Sequence (to do that, click the mouse or add a Wait step). However, you can use this shortcut to pause and unpause the Sequence and Real Time recorders.

Pause Considerations and Tactics

Use Pause to suspend a Sequence for a period of time or for user input.

Timed pauses are often used to *debug* (analyze and correct) a Sequence. The sledgehammer approach is to spread many timed Pauses throughout a non-working Sequence (just like the Sequence recorder does). If the Sequence starts working, you know you have a problem with synchronization between QuicKeys and the application. Start taking out (or shortening) the timed pauses until the Sequence stops working. Then you know the last timed pause you removed was necessary (more than one timed Pause may be needed). Yes, it's convoluted and monstrous, but sometimes it's the best possible fix. For more on pauses in debugging, see "Sequence Tips and Tricks" later in this chapter.

In a perfect computing environment, need for a timed Pause would be infrequent. If there is a reason to wait for an application to do something, it is much better to use a conditional step, not a timed step— "Wait until the cursor changes back to a pointer," or "Wait until the document window becomes active."

If you're setting up a Sequence for your own use, user pauses are especially good tools; you know that your F15 key or the yellow bars in the Recorder Palette will unpause the Sequence. Others, however, might not. If you're creating Sequences for others to use, consider preceding these user pauses with a Message shortcut that reads something like "Click OK to close this dialog box, enter the text for the header, then click on the yellow bars in the palette in the corner of your screen." Alternately, you can capture a user's response to the Clipboard with a Message shortcut instead of a pause and incorporate that response into your sequence.

Repeat

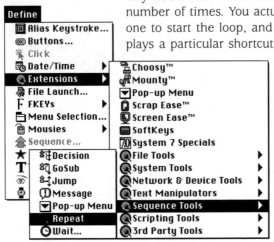

Repeat has two roles; the most important is inside a Sequence, which is why we discuss it here. A Sequence Repeat step loops part of a Sequence a number of times. You actually need two Repeat steps for each loop—one to start the loop, and one to end it. A Non-Sequence Repeat just plays a particular shortcut a specified number of times. Let's get that less important role out of the way first.

Non-Sequence Repeat. You can play any shortcut a number of times, by choosing Repeat from the Sequence Tools category of the Extensions submenu of the Define menu in the QuicKeys Editor window. The Repeat edit dialog box appears with the Non-Sequence button checked in the Function options area, which causes Non-Sequence to be entered into the Name text edit box (see Figure 15.20).

You can play a shortcut by entering its name in the Play the Shortcut Named text edit box. You can then either enter the number of times you want the shortcut played in the Times text edit box or check the Display Dialog Box Asking How Many Times to Repeat checkbox. With this box checked, when you invoke the shortcut you'll get a dialog box asking you to enter the number of times you want the shortcut played.

Sequence Repeat. Here's where Repeat really struts its stuff—as a device that repeatedly executes a segment of a Sequence. You can add a Repeat Shortcut step to a Sequence by choosing Repeat from the Sequence Tools category of the Extensions submenu of the Define menu in the Sequence editor. You guessed it—the Repeat edit dialog box appears. Because this dialog box defaults to the Non-Sequence function, you must choose Begin Repeat from the Function options to create a Begin Repeat shortcut (Figure 15.21).

Figure 15.20
Repeat edit
dialog box for
Non-Sequence

```
┌─────────────────────────────────────────────────────────┐
│ Repeat Extension                                   3.0 ⮌ │
│                                                           │
│ Name:  │Non-Sequence            │                         │
│ Function: ◉ Non-Sequence        ©1991-93 CE Software, Inc.│
│           ○ Begin Repeat            by Gil Beecher &      │
│           ○ End Repeat              Simeon Leifer         │
│ Additional values:                                        │
│    Play the Shortcut named: │              │ │2│  times   │
│       ☐ Display dialog box asking how many times to repeat│
│ Explanation:                                              │
│    Enter the name of the Shortcut and the number of times │
│    to repeat. Select the checkbox to ask how many times.  │
│    Do NOT use within a sequence.                          │
│                                                           │
│                               ┌────────┐ ╔════════╗       │
│                               │ Cancel │ ║   OK   ║       │
│                               └────────┘ ╚════════╝       │
└─────────────────────────────────────────────────────────┘
```

Figure 15.21
Repeat edit
dialog box for
Begin Repeat

```
┌─────────────────────────────────────────────────────────┐
│ Repeat Extension                                   3.0 ⮌ │
│                                                           │
│ Name:  │Begin Repeat         │   Keystroke: │ Unassigned │ │
│ Function: ○ Non-Sequence        ©1991-93 CE Software, Inc.│
│           ◉ Begin Repeat            by Gil Beecher &      │
│           ○ End Repeat              Simeon Leifer         │
│ Additional values:                                        │
│    Repeat items between Begin and End │2      │ times     │
│       ☐ Display dialog box asking how many times to repeat│
│ Explanation:                                              │
│    Place within a sequence where you want the repeat to   │
│    begin. Enter the number of times to repeat. Select the │
│    checkbox to ask how many times.                        │
│                                                           │
│ ┌───────────────┐ ☐ Include in QuicKeys menu ┌────────┐ ╔════════╗ │
│ │ Timer Options │                            │ Cancel │ ║   OK   ║ │
│ └───────────────┘                            └────────┘ ╚════════╝ │
└─────────────────────────────────────────────────────────┘
```

You can either preset the number of times you want Repeat to loop,
by entering a number in the Repeat Items between Begin and End box
field, or you can have Repeat display a window prompting you for the
number of times to repeat.

After beginning a repeat, you must end it, and you do so by placing
an End Repeat shortcut in the Sequence somewhere after Begin Repeat.
Do this by creating a Repeat step as before, but this time click End Repeat
in the Function options.

Repeat Considerations

You can't nest a repeat loop inside another repeat loop, and you can't put an End Repeat before a Begin Repeat (why would you want to?).

The maximum number of times you can have part of a Sequence repeat is 1,215,752. The number displayed in the Repeat Items between Begin and End text edit box defaults to this number, if you enter a greater number.

Repeat Tactics

Use Repeat to loop part of a Sequence. Or use Repeat to play one Non-Sequence shortcut a number of times.

Sometimes you may want to create a Sequence shortcut that performs a task over and over again until it is done—but you don't know how many repetitions it will take to finish the task. Unfortunately, there is no direct way to tell QuicKeys how to do that. But often you can achieve the same result by constructing a repeat pair that will repeat part of the Sequence many more times than necessary to do the job (set Begin Repeat for 1,000,000 repetitions). Then branch out of the repetitions when the task is done, using a Decision shortcut. Here's an example.

Say you have an archive of thousands of messages from an online service. The archive is in your word-processing program (for example, Microsoft Word) and you have massaged the file so that each message constitutes its own paragraph. You want to be able to search through your archive (let's just pretend that the entire archive consists of messages about home brewing), extract all the archives that have the word yeast in them, and paste them to another file.

To do this, you can build a repeat loop in your shortcut that loops 10,000 times, an arbitrarily high number. You'll never get up to 10,000 repetitions, because when the Word Find function gets to the end of the file, the program puts up a dialog box telling you so. You can use this change in windows to trigger a Decision shortcut, which will branch you out of the loop and tell you the Sequence is finished.

Here's the Sequence (see Figure 15.22).

The Decision step that gets you out of the loop watches for the Find window (see Figure 15.23). If the top window is not named Find (in this case, it is a message window telling you that Word has reached the end of the document), then Decision plays the End Sequence shortcut, a Message shortcut that contains a Cancel button to end the Sequence.

The key to making this conditional Repeat escaper is the existence of some change in a window or menu that you can pick up with Decision. If no such change occurs, you stay in the loop. But if one does (as they often do), you've got an out.

Figure 15.22
Sequence for
culling messages

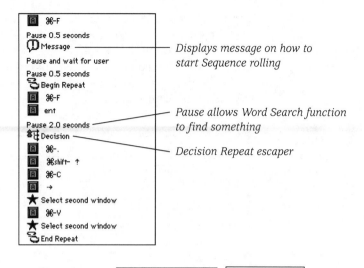

Displays message on how to
start Sequence rolling

Pause allows Word Search function
to find something

Decision Repeat escaper

Figure 15.23
Decision
conditionals

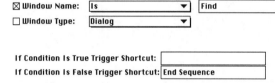

Gosub

Gosub is a special sort of shortcut—a combination branching and single-purpose Sequence control shortcut. Gosub jumps to another shortcut and

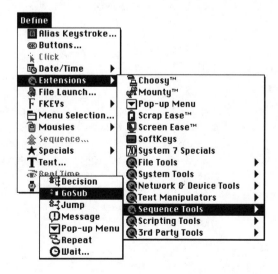

plays it. When that shortcut has completed, execution returns to the step in the original Sequence immediately following the Gosub extension.

If you want to add a Gosub shortcut type to your Sequence, select Gosub from the Sequence Tools category of the Extensions submenu of the Define menu of the Sequence editor. The Gosub edit dialog box is displayed (see Figure 15.24).

Figure 15.24
Gosub edit dialog
box

```
┌─────────────────────────────────────────────────────┐
│ GoSub Extension                            3.0.1 ⌘   │
│                                                       │
│ Name:   │ GoSub                          │            │
│                                                       │
│                                                       │
│ Shortcut to play:  │                        │         │
│                                                       │
│                                                       │
│                                                       │
│                                                       │
│                                                       │
│                                                       │
│                                                       │
│                              │ Cancel │ │   OK   │    │
└─────────────────────────────────────────────────────┘
```

Enter the name of the shortcut you want to branch to in the Short-cut to Play text box.

Gosub Considerations and Tactics

Use Gosub to branch to a specific shortcut or Sequence.

Gosub is very straightforward. All you have to do is name the shortcut you want to branch to. Like Decision, you must enter the exact name of the shortcut or Gosub will not jump. Sadly, this shortcut is also missing a Select Shortcut button that would display a list of available shortcuts, making your work less prone to error.

With complex Sequences, Gosub can be used as a device to separate sections of the Sequence into functional segments. You can have the "mother" Sequence that includes a number of Gosub steps that branch out to other Sequences—so the different parts can be built in manageable chunks.

A Message shortcut displays a message in its own little modal window—
while the window is displayed, you can't do anything else. Although a
Message shortcut can operate outside a Sequence, it is most useful as a
Sequence step, which is why we discuss it here.

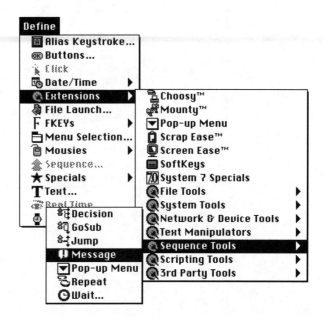

To create a Message shortcut, choose the Message item from the
Extensions submenu of the Sequence Tools category of the Define menu.
The Message edit dialog box appears (Figure 15.25).

The dialog box contains a text edit box where you can enter the
message text that the shortcut will display. Four options appear beneath
the text edit box. When Message is used as a step in a Sequence, these
options control if and how the Sequence will resume.

- **Show OK Button.** Checking this option makes the Message window
  display an OK button. Clicking the OK button closes the Message
  window and resumes the Sequence.

- **Show Cancel Button.** This option remains dimmed until you select
  the Show OK Button option. Checking this option makes the Message window display a Cancel button. Clicking the Cancel button
  closes the Message window and terminates the Sequence.

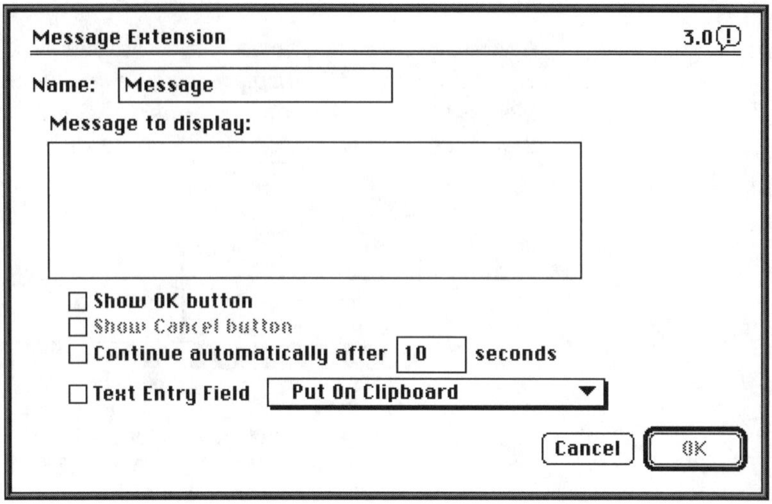

Figure 15.25
Message edit
dialog box

- **Continue Automatically After.** Checking this option makes the Message window disappear and the Sequence resume after the number of seconds that are entered in the accompanying text edit box.

- **Text Entry Field.** Checking this option makes the Message window display a text entry field for user input. Choose from the pop-up menu what the Sequence will do with this input. Choices include placing the input on the Clipboard, typing it out, and playing the shortcut of that name.

Message Considerations and Tactics

Use Message shortcuts to display a message during a Sequence and possibly solicit user input that the Sequence can act upon.

The Message shortcut is straightforward. Note that the Cancel button is only important if the Message shortcut is a step in a Sequence. Clicking Cancel cancels the entire Sequence; clicking OK allows the Sequence to continue.

The ability to enter the name of a shortcut is a way to jump from a Sequence to another shortcut—it's like Decision without logical tests. You have to type the shortcut name perfectly, however, making it less attractive. You can also use Message to terminate a Sequence if you can branch out of the Sequence with a Decision step.

Where Message really shines, though, is in its ability to take user input and put it on the Clipboard. Once it's there, you can use all the conditional shortcuts—Jump, Wait, and Decision—to act on user input.

You can build a shortcut that asks the user what zoom percentage he or she wants in PageMaker and make it happen. Or you can ask for a page number to start a document in Word and have QuicKeys set it correctly and then build a footer that includes it.

With Message and Conditional shortcuts, you can truly make your Mac do double-back flips at a user's behest.

Sequence Tricks and Tips

The best and worst of QuicKeys can be seen in the Sequence. On one hand, you can create Sequences to perform intelligent and complex actions, freeing you from executing long tasks on your Mac by hand. But building a Sequence can be an onerous task because of limitations in the QuicKeys interface—so onerous that many QuicKeys users shun the Sequence altogether. Don't be one of them. Use these tips and tricks to help you become the QuicKeys master.

Quick Extensions

A shortcoming of CE's design of the QuicKeys Editor is how many menus and submenus you must negotiate to choose and use extensions—most Sequence steps are particularly onerous to create because they are buried so deep within the Define menu and their edit dialog boxes are so complex.

For example, suppose you want to include a Sequence step that waits for you to click the mouse before the sequence proceeds. You have to do a lot of digging to get to the right tool: pull down the Define menu of the Sequence editor window, and select the Extensions submenu, the Sequence Tools category, and the Wait extension. When the Wait window opens, use the pop-up menu to select Other Action. From this new dialog box, select the User Event radio button and then select the Click conditional from the pop-up menu.

You can incorporate Sequence shortcuts more quickly into a Sequence by placing the Sequence shortcuts on the top of the Extensions submenu with the Extension Manager (see Chapter 18, *QuicKeys Utilities*). This raises the shortcuts a level in the submenu morass.

Another trick for quickly including Sequence shortcuts is to cut and paste. If you want a step in your Sequence that uses the same type of shortcut that already exists as a step, copy and paste a clone of it and then modify the copy's edit dialog box as necessary.

Advanced Debugging and Editing

If you never make a Sequence that doesn't need editing or debugging, you aren't making many Sequences. Here are a few tricks for subduing the recalcitrant Sequence.

Finding your shortcut. If you have a reasonably large set, one of the maddening properties of QuicKeys is that whenever you open the QuicKeys Editor window, the Shortcuts window displays the beginning portion of the set. So if you are in a heavy editing session on a shortcut, you often have to scroll through your list of shortcuts to open the right one. In some future version of QuicKeys, we hope that CE will include a feature that opens to the editing window of the last shortcut played. But for now, there are two ways to try to massage QuicKeys so that your target shortcut appears in the top screen of the QuicKeys Editor window when it opens.

■ **Use the Filter bar.** If you are editing a Sequence shortcut, choose the Sequence icon on the Filter bar. If your sets are like ours, this will substantially reduce the number of shortcuts displayed. The QuicKeys Editor window retains the Filter bar settings when it closes, so your target shortcut might show up in the top screen.

■ **Rename or rekey your shortcut.** If the first trick doesn't work, change the name or the keystroke of your shortcut so it will fall in the top screen. Remember, you can use the Sort bar to choose how your shortcuts are sorted. Now with your shortcut visible, you can edit it as soon as the QuicKeys Editor window opens.

Debugging 101—two tricks. Here are a couple of little tricks to help debug a Sequence.

■ **Nip it in the bug.** If you are creating a long Sequence, it is sometimes best to build from a central core, testing as you go. This lets you become aware of bugs after only a few additions to the Sequence, so you have a good idea of where the problem is. This is the debug as you build method.

■ **Listen to it.** If a Sequence gets hung up, but you're not sure exactly where, you can sprinkle a few Sound shortcuts at various points in the Sequence. If each Sound shortcut is set to a different sound, you'll quickly hear the silence and know where things ran aground.

Debugging 201—Pauses and Waits. Often a Sequence goes awry because QuicKeys tries to execute the next step in a Sequence before the active application is ready for it. We used to add Pause steps to slow QuicKeys down, but the increased power of the Wait shortcut has made it a valuable tool for this job too. We often use a Pause step when QuicKeys needs to wait a discrete and predictable amount of time before proceeding. Or we use a Pause when we're in a hurry and we just don't want to mess with the more complex task of implementing a Wait step. We prefer a Wait step when the amount of time QuicKeys must wait varies, and, of course, some condition change exists that we can set as a Wait option to trigger the Sequence to resume.

The key here is to remember Don Brown's philosophy of QuicKeys: the better you use QuicKeys, the better you know your computer, the better you use QuicKeys. So first try to figure out what the heck your application and QuicKeys could be fighting about. Then use a Pause or Wait.

- Add Pauses or Waits one at a time, until you get things rolling. Often, Pauses can be one second or less in length, but sometimes applications require much more time to come to their senses.

- When things start working again, you can assume the last Pause or Wait added is *probably* the only delay step you need.

- Go back and get rid of all extraneous Pauses and Waits.

- Reduce the time on any necessary Pause step to a workable minimum. But remember: when an application is crunching on conditions, sometimes those conditions change, so allow for worst-case scenarios.

- See if it makes sense to replace your hard Pause with Wait. Wait steps can be more adaptable than a straight Pause step.

16 Apple Events and Scripting

The introduction of Apple Events and interapplication communication (IAC) in System 7 set the stage for evolution of the Mac. For the first time, the ability existed for applications to interact—to share information and data and thus perform complex operations, such as taking data from a spreadsheet program and using it as input in a project management program. The channel for the communication, IAC, is built into the operating system. The messages that you can send on the channel are the Apple Events.

But when System 7 was first announced, you needed to be quite a programmer to write code that invoked Apple Events. With the first general scripting languages and utilities, such as Frontier, and more recently with Apple's AppleScript, if you have a small facility with programming, you too can write scripts that cause programs to interact and share functions and data.

And while general scripting languages have developed, program-specific scripting has emerged in applications like PageMaker and Excel. You can take advantage of those application-specific scripting languages by invoking them with Apple Event messages.

QuicKeys has evolved to prosper in this new world, providing shortcuts to work with Apple Events, AppleScript, and application-specific scripting languages. Plus, QuicKeys offers QuicKeys Script, its own internal scripting language.

QuicKeys, Scripting, and Apple Events

In this chapter we look at how to use QuicKeys to take advantage of scripting and Apple Events. We start by providing the (considerable) conceptual underpinnings for understanding this complex world. Then we discuss the four scripting and Apple Event shortcuts.

■ Apple Events

■ Finder Events

■ AppleScript

■ DoScript

If you prefer to just build some scripting shortcuts right off, we suggest you jump to "Apple Events Shortcuts" later in the chapter and then come back here to figure out why we did what we did.

At the end of the chapter we investigate QuicKeys' internal scripting language, QuicKeys Script.

Apple Events

Scripting? Apple Events? AppleScript? What do these terms mean? Let's check them out and then see how they relate to QuicKeys.

Apple Events are messages—commands, queries, and responses—sent along Apple's interapplication communication (IAC) channel, the pipeline. A simple example of this would be a message from one application telling another application to print a document. The ultimate promise of this capability is the utilization of different engines within different applications to process data.

An Apple Event can also be a query, requesting a reply from the target application—for instance, asking PageMaker what page it's on or the position of a box. The reply (also an Apple Event) is sent back to the sending application via IAC. It's up to that application to receive the message and—should it so choose—act on it.

With Apple Events you can use Excel to develop numerical scenarios and Chart to graphically depict the results, and then send the chart to Word to include in a letter. To realize the full promise of IAC, applications must be written pretty much from the ground up to utilize Apple Events as a communication protocol. Most applications don't go that far; instead they have been refined to receive and send certain Apple Events. Different applications support different sets of Apple Events.

**QuicKeys
Toolbox**

QuicKeys can send Apple Events to other applications, and other applications can trigger QuicKeys shortcuts with Apple Events, but only if you have the QuicKeys Toolbox loaded (see Chapter 2, *The Old Kit Bag*). To send an Apple Event from QuicKeys, you must also have installed at least one of the four Apple Event QuicKeys extensions discussed in this chapter.

The QuicKeys Toolbox system extension is necessary because QuicKeys, not being an application, can't send Apple Events directly.

QuicKeys sends the Apple Event to QuicKeys Toolbox via CE's own communication system, and QuicKeys Toolbox converts it to Apple Event format and sends it. The opposite is also true: for another application to trigger a QuicKeys shortcut via Apple Events, it sends the message to QuicKeys Toolbox, which passes it to QuicKeys.

QuicKeys Toolbox is an application that's launched by a System extension, so it starts automatically whenever you start your Mac; you can't launch it yourself by double-clicking. This design was due to some vagaries of System 7, but it can be a problem. In its present configuration, if you quit QuicKeys Toolbox, only rebooting can restore it. Why would you want to quit it? One of System 7's new features is its ability to add things like fonts to the System file without rebooting. However, you must close all applications to do so. Or, you might just need the memory for other things. You can avoid this problem by switching QuicKeys Toolbox to the background—a new feature with QuicKeys 3.

AppleScript

AppleScript is a programming language designed for controlling applications via Apple Events. You don't need to use AppleScript to work with Apple Events; it's just one tool for doing so. The purpose of AppleScript is to provide a fairly simple, standard programming language that you can use to control applications on your Mac.

Until System 7.5, AppleScript did not come bundled with your Mac system; you had to acquire it separately. For any application to understand AppleScripts, you must have the AppleScript extension in the Extensions folder of your System folder. This is not the QuicKeys extension called AppleScript; it's a system extension called AppleScript.

When you acquire Apple's AppleScript package, you also receive an application called the Script Editor that you can use to record, write, debug, and execute AppleScripts. The Script Editor can actually work with other scripting languages besides AppleScript, as long as those scripting languages comply with an Apple standard called Open Scripting Architecture (OSA). The most important OSA-compliant scripting language to our discussion is QuicKeys Script, QuicKeys' internal scripting language (see the next section).

With the QuicKeys shortcut, AppleScript (and the AppleScript System extension loaded), you can execute AppleScripts within QuicKeys to control applications. If you're working with a program such as QuarkXPress that can actually execute AppleScripts, you can use either the DoScript or Apple Events shortcut to send those AppleScripts *to the application* for execution.

Program-specific Scripts

As we mentioned above, many programs include internal scripting languages (Excel and PageMaker are two examples). Typically these applications understand one or two Apple Events: doscript and/or evaluate. So you can use one of these Apple Events to send a script written in the application's scripting language. The program recognizes the doscript or evaluate Apple Event and then receives and acts upon the script received. The program-specific script is essentially packaged and sent inside the Apple Event.

Apple Event Suites

Apple Events are organized into functional categories called suites. The most basic suite, Required, includes only four commands:

- Open
- Print
- Quit
- Custom Event

Another basic suite of Apple Events is Core. Many Apple-event-aware applications also recognize nine Core events.

- Get Data
- Set Data
- Delete Element
- New Element
- Number of Elements
- Clone
- Move
- Undo
- Redo

All applications should support these Required and Core events, if possible, but not all programs do.

Sophisticated suites. "Great," you say, "but what about more...well...*useful* Apple Events?" In addition to the two simple suites discussed above, there are two other classes of suites.

■ **Functional.** Functional suites contain Apple Events that are shared by a type of software, such as word processors. In this industry you can't expect different manufacturers to get together and agree on an entire suite, so they often end up supporting parts of different ones. FileMaker Pro, for example, supports subsets of the Database and Table suites.

■ **Custom.** Custom suites include Apple Events designed for a particular application. These suites differ slightly from the application-specific scripting languages discussed above. The commands are actually Apple Events that can be sent individually through the IAC channel. They don't need to be encapsulated, or packaged, inside a doscript or evaluate Apple Event (though they can be).

Because each company is free to define its own set of Apple Events, different applications support different Apple Events, even if the applications do similar things. For example, HyperCard 2.1 defines a group of useful Apple Events for running scripts, evaluating mathematical expressions, and so on (we'll show you how to use one later).

The aete Resource

So how do you know what Apple Events an application understands? Every program that supports Apple Events is *supposed* to have something called an aete (Apple Event Terminology Extension) resource, which describes its supported Apple Events to other applications. When you create an Apple Events shortcut with QuicKeys, for instance, it can look at that resource to see what events are supported; you can choose the one you want from a pop-up menu.

Unfortunately, many applications don't have aete resources, and many of those that do have anemic ones—they don't completely describe the parameters each event needs.

If you're trying to control an application with a missing or incomplete aete resource, we have some bad news for you: you have to read the manuals. Not only that, it's quite likely you'll need to buy or otherwise acquire the manuals from the software publisher (or perhaps print out the documentation from a disk file); many companies don't include scripting documentation with their products.

To be fair, even with a good aete resource, you'll still need to read the docs to work with a program such as QuarkXPress, because its implementation of Apple Events is so robust and flexible. Also, you need to know the appropriate way to format the parameter values for different Apple Events—information that's not provided in any aete resource we've seen.

Wondering what parameter values are? That's next.

Apple Event Anatomy

Whether you get it from aete resource or the manuals, you need to know a few things about an Apple Event to use it. Apple Events messages have a particular structure, consisting of four components.

- **Address.** This is the address of the application you are sending the event to. When you send an Apple Event with QuicKeys you generally don't have to know this address; you can target the application using the Shortcut editor's pop-up menu.

- **Class and ID.** Class and ID together identify the Apple Event; each is a four-letter code. The class is the category the Apple Event belongs to—the suite; the ID is the code name of the actual Apple Event. When you send an Apple Event with QuicKeys, you may or may not have to type in the two four-letter codes for class and ID. Sometimes QuicKeys can look them up from the target application's aete resource.

- **Parameters.** Some Apple Events require additional parameters. The Apple Event to open a document, for instance, requires you to provide the name of the document to open. The Apple Event to quit an application, on the other hand, requires no parameters. You tell an application to quit and call it quits. Robust aete resources give you all the parameters; you just need to fill in the parameters' values.

- **Parameter values.** It's up to you to provide the parameter values—the filename for a file-opening Apple Event, for instance, or the numbers for Excel or HyperCard to calculate. QuicKeys typically offers three ways to incorporate these values: build them into the Apple Event by typing them in the text edit box, select them from a list (a file Open dialog box, for instance), or grab them from the Clipboard when the Apple Event is sent.

Returns

Another aspect of Apple Events that you will run into is the return, or result. The return is simply the response an application makes when it receives an Apple Event. Returns may not be well documented, so you may have to run some tests to discover what the return for an Apple Event is in various situations.

Almost all Apple Events elicit some type of return. Some Apple Events always elicit the same return, whereas others elicit returns that vary depending on the circumstances. For example, when a playbyname Apple Event tells QuicKeys Toolbox to play a particular shortcut, the return is the name of the shortcut played. When an evaluate Apple Event tells Excel to evaluate (calculate) what's on the Clipboard, the return is the result of that evaluation. Often, you will want to ignore the return, but sometimes—when you want to perform an action based on the message that the application returns—it will be critical to your work.

Shortcut Review

Now that you know the basics of scripting and Apple Events, let's take a closer look at the tools QuicKeys provides for working with scripts. QuicKeys works with Apple Events in four different ways, through the four different QuicKey scripting and Apple Event shortcuts.

- **Apple Events.** The Apple Events shortcut sends any kind of Apple Event to any Apple-event-aware application. It's the most general purpose and flexible shortcut, but it's also the most complex.

- **Finder Events.** The Finder Events shortcut sends one of a half dozen Apple Events to the Finder. (This is a special case of the Apple Events extension.) It's very easy to use, because you don't need to target the application (the Finder is where it's going); all you need to do is select one of the available Apple Events from the pop-up menu and specify the files to act on.

- **DoScript.** The DoScript shortcut only sends one Apple Event: doscript. You can use this to send a script to an application in that application's own scripting language. (You can also send AppleScripts using this shortcut, but only to applications that understand them, such as QuarkXPress).

- **AppleScript.** The AppleScript shortcut (in cooperation with the AppleScript System extension) *executes* a script written in AppleScript. Almost every script written in AppleScript sends at least one Apple Event to an application (it's what AppleScript is *for*).

Some functions of these shortcuts overlap. For example, you can send an Apple Event to the Finder using the Apple Events shortcut and choosing Finder from the Send Event To pop-up menu. Or you could use an AppleScript and the AppleScript shortcut to send an Apple Event to the Finder. You can also use the Finder Events shortcut to send an Apple Event to the Finder.

Apple Events Shortcuts

Shortcuts built with the Apple Events extension are the most flexible—and potentially daunting—of the QuicKeys scripting shortcuts. In fact, though, they're not that hard to create, especially when you're working with an application that has a good aete resource.

We'll start with a simple shortcut that tells Excel to open a document. Even if you don't have Excel, we suggest you follow along. We searched far and wide to find an application that 1) has a good aete resource and 2) everybody has. That beast does not exist. Apple Events support is still spotty out there, so we'll show some other examples—both here and in the application-specific chapters—that will help you get a feel for the different ways you might use Apple Events shortcuts.

A Simple Apple Events Shortcut for Excel

The easiest way to learn about Apple Events shortcuts is to build one. We'll start with a shortcut that opens a file using Excel.

1. Launch Excel, then open the QuicKeys Editor.

2. Select Apple Events from the Scripting Tools category of the Extensions submenu of the Define Menu.

3. In the Shortcut edit dialog box, select Excel from the Send Event To pop-up menu.

4. Click the Select Event button. QuicKeys looks at Excel's aete resource and presents you with the dialog box in Figure 16.1.

Figure 16.1
Apple Events
Select Event dialog
box for Excel

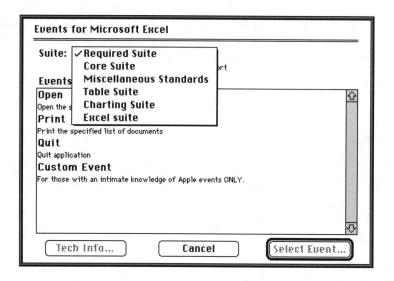

5. Select Required Suite from the pop-up menu, and double-click to select the Open Apple Event. (You can select the event and click the Tech Info button to find out a bit more about the event—its four-letter

class and ID codes, what parameters it requires, etc.) You'll see the Apple Events Shortcut edit dialog box in Figure 16.2.

Figure 16.2
Apple Events edit
dialog box

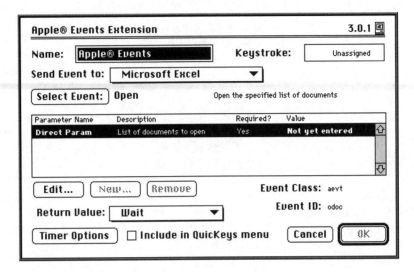

6. Of the four pieces in the Apple Event structure (target, class/ID, parameters, and parameter values), QuicKeys has filled in the first three from Excel's aete resource. To set the parameter value, double-click on the parameter or click the Edit button. You'll see the dialog box in Figure 16.3.

Figure 16.3
Parameter
Specifier dialog
box

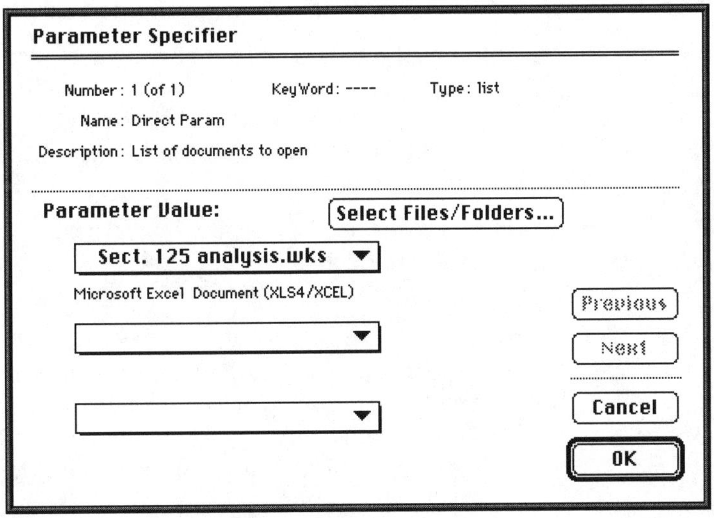

7. Click the Select Files/Folders button, and select the file or files you want to open from the resulting dialog box. Click Done and then click OK to exit the Parameter Specifier dialog box.

8. Give the shortcut a name, and assign a triggering keystroke. Click OK twice to get out of QuicKeys.

Your shortcut's ready to roll. When you trigger it, QuicKeys sends a message to Excel (via QuicKeys Toolbox) telling it to open the specified documents.

Now it's true that you could do all this much more effectively with a File Launch shortcut, but it does clearly show how the Apple Events shortcut works. Let's look at another Apple Events shortcut, this one controlling HyperCard, that goes a little deeper.

A Custom Apple Events Shortcut for HyperCard

HyperCard 2.1 doesn't have an aete resource (it's from Apple; why should it?). Nevertheless, if you have the HyperCard scripting docs, you can control it with a custom Apple Events shortcut—one that you define from scratch based on the HyperCard scripting documentation.

1. Launch HyperCard, and bring up the QuicKeys Editor.

2. Choose Apple Events from the Scripting category of the Extensions submenu of the Define menu.

3. Choose HyperCard from the Send Event To pop-up menu, click the Select Event button (QuicKeys will inform you that there's no aete resource), choose Custom in the resulting dialog box, and click OK. You'll see the dialog box in Figure 16.4.

4. Since HyperCard doesn't have an aete resource, QuicKeys can't fill in the class, ID, or parameters for you. You have to do it yourself. For this example, type misc for class and eval for ID (the entries are case sensitive). This is HyperCard's evaluate mathematical expression Apple Event.

5. Next you need to create a parameter—telling HyperCard what to evaluate. Click the New button to create a new parameter. You'll see the dialog box in Figure 16.5.

6. The field labeled KeyWord is a four-letter code that tells the receiving application what this parameter represents. It's only used for Apple Events that have optional parameters. Most of the time, the keyword for the main (or direct) parameter is ---- (which means, in effect, The receiving application already knows what this parameter is.). Type ---- in this field.

7. To the right of the KeyWord text edit box is the word Type: with a blank area and a pop-up list following it from which you can select a data type. This should be in the documentation (sorry to sound like a broken record!). If the type you want isn't listed, you can choose

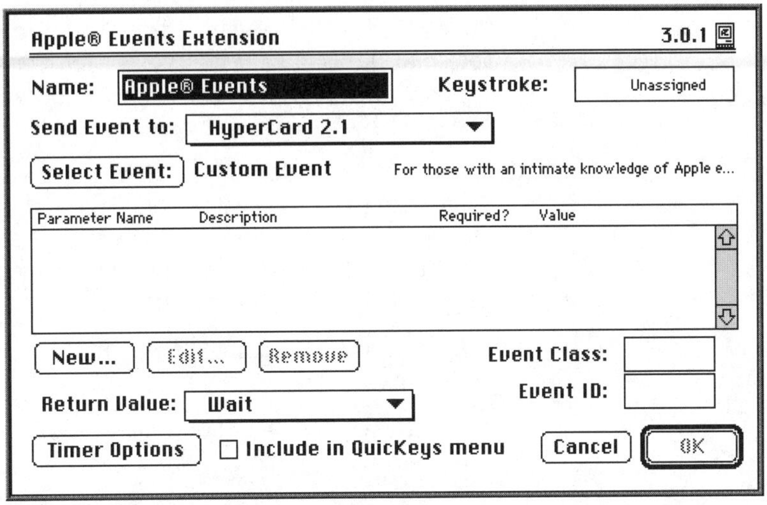

Figure 16.4
Apple Events
Custom Event
editor dialog box

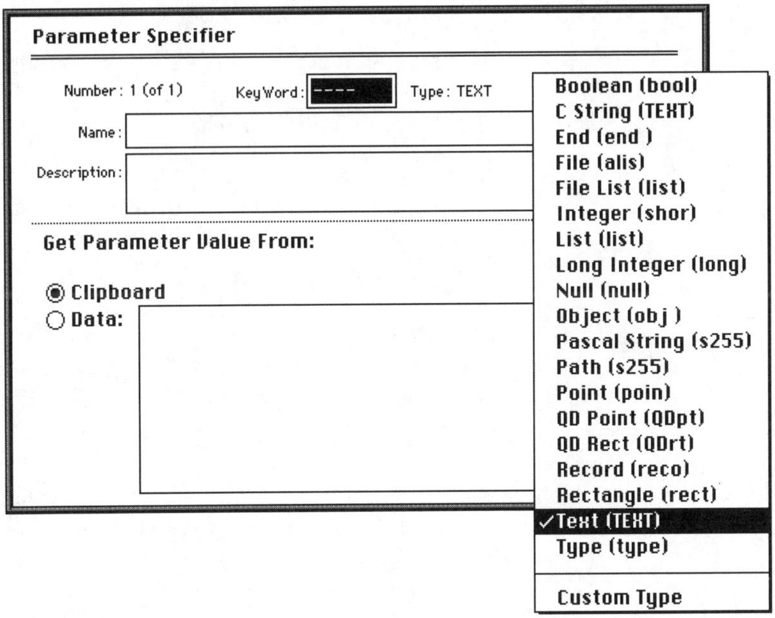

Figure 16.5
Parameter
Specifier edit
dialog box

Custom Type from the list and type it into the resulting dialog box. In this case, select Text from the pop-up menu. The text edit box transforms itself, adding a Get Parameter Value section.

8. In the next two text edit boxes fill in the name and description of your parameter. What you call these are up to you.

9. Now, in the Get Parameter Value From section, you can type some data into the Data text edit box or tell QuicKeys to get it from the Clipboard when you trigger the shortcut. For our example, select Clipboard by clicking on its radio button.

10. Click OK. The dialog box disappears, leaving you with the Apple Events Shortcut edit dialog box. In the bottom left of the text edit box is the Return Value pop-up menu, where you can choose what QuicKeys will do with the response it gets from the HyperCard. Here's what the options mean.

   - **Ignore.** Ignore means, "Send the event and don't wait for a response."

   - **Wait.** Wait means, "Send the event and wait until it's complete, but throw away the response."

   - **Type.** Type means, "Type the text in the current window" (which is a text window, we hope).

   - **Display Full.** Display Full means, "Put up a dialog box describing the event that was sent, plus the response shown, if possible." (This only works for text and numbers.)

   - **Display Minimal.** Display Minimal means, "Put up a dialog box showing the response shown, if possible." (This only works for text and numbers.)

   - **Clipboard.** Clipboard means, "Put the response on the Clipboard."

11. Select Display Minimal from the pop-up menu, and give the shortcut a name and a keystroke; HCard Eval and Control-Option-Command-E would be good (or include the shortcut in the QuicKeys menu). Click OK and you're done (see Figure 16.6).

Leave the QuicKeys Editor window by clicking OK. Leave HyperCard running, and launch a text editor. Type an expression like 94/2. Select it, then copy it to the Clipboard. Trigger your shortcut, and you should almost immediately see the response 47.

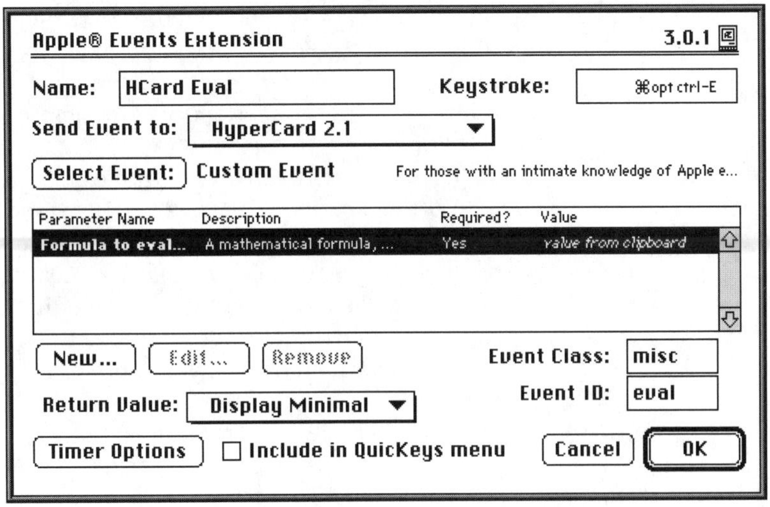

Figure 16.6
Completed Apple
Event edit
dialog box

You can use this method to define Apple Events shortcuts for your favorite applications, assuming that they support interesting Apple Events and that those events are documented somewhere in their manuals. (If they aren't, feel free to call that company's tech support and tactfully suggest they update their manuals. Also see if they can give you the Apple Events parameters.) Happy hunting!

Triggering a QuicKeys Shortcut with an Apple Event

If you have another application that can send Apple Events, like Apple's Script Editor, HyperCard, or FileMaker Pro, or if you would like to be able to trigger a shortcut on another machine over a network, then you can use an Apple Event to trigger a shortcut via QuicKeys Toolbox.

For the moment, we'll use QuicKeys to trigger a QuicKeys shortcut. It's recursive and silly, but it shows you how you can do it.

Display the Apple Events edit dialog box as you did in the last example. Select QuicKeys Toolbox from the Send Event To menu in the Apple Events edit dialog box, then click the Select Event button. You will see a pop-up list of event suites and a list of their events.

Select the QuicKeys suite, as the Required suite doesn't mean much to QuicKeys Toolbox. You'll see a number of QuicKeys-specific Apple Events listed. Select PlayByName. Click Select Event, and you'll see that all the class, ID, and parameter information has been filled in for you. All you need to do is fill in the parameter value. Double-click on the parameter, type the name of the shortcut you want to run, and click OK.

Select the Ignore or Wait return type, since shortcuts don't return anything anyway. Presto! You can now run a shortcut by typing...a shortcut. This may seem a wee bit strange, but keep in mind that you can use this to run a shortcut on a remote computer via the Remote Application option on the Send Event To pop-up menu. Make sure program linking is active on that machine, then on your computer, select QuicKeys Toolbox on the remote machine, and the rest is easy.

One extremely useful application of this technique: create a sound on your colleague's computer that's a recording of his or her phone ringing. Make a shortcut on that machine that plays the sound. Use an Apple Event shortcut to trigger the Sound shortcut on the remote machine. This is most amusing if you can see and hear your colleague from your desk.

For an example of how truly useful it is to trigger QuicKeys via Apple Events, see "Triggering Shortcuts with Apple Events" in Chapter 22, *QuicKeys and FileMaker Pro*.

Apple Events Tactics and Considerations

Use Apple Events shortcuts to send Apple Events to applications.

With all the different tools built into QuicKeys for controlling applications, why do you need to control them via Apple Events? There are (at least) four reasons.

- **Speed.** With more complex operations involving multiple steps, an Apple Events shortcut can often operate much faster than a Sequence shortcut, which must navigate its way through the interface, waiting for screen updates and the like.

- **Reliability.** Apple Events shortcuts don't pose the problems of waiting for an application, finding windows, menus, and buttons that might have moved; and the like, so they can be more reliable and easier to debug than Sequence shortcuts.

- **Interactivity.** Since you can get responses from an application with Apple Events, your shortcuts can react to those responses. With standard QuicKeys shortcuts, for instance, there's no way you can ask PageMaker what color is applied to a box. With an Apple Events shortcut you can.

- **Flexibility.** You can do things with Apple Events shortcuts that simply can't be done with other QuicKeys shortcuts. In QuarkXPress, for instance, you can control an individual page element by name (HeadlineBox, for instance), which you can't do with other shortcut types.

So when should you use Apple Events shortcuts? We're going to surprise you for once by *not* giving a categorical response. It all depends—on what you're trying to do, what application(s) you're working with, how well they implement Apple Events, and how robust their internal scripting language is.

Apple Events are so powerful and flexible that asking what you can do with them is like asking what you can do with your Mac. Enjoy!

Finder Events Shortcut

QuicKeys is nothing if not thorough. Included among its scripting and Apple Events extensions is an extension that sends Apple Events to the Finder—naturally called the Finder Events shortcut. This shortcut can be seen as a subset of the Apple Events shortcut, since it performs the same function as the Apple Events shortcut, but with a (much) more narrow focus.

Given its more focused purpose, the Finder Events shortcut is easier to use than Apple Events. The shortcut can send one of six Apple Events to the Finder.

- Show Clipboard

- Sleep

- Get Info

- Show

- Open

- Print

To create a Finder Events shortcut, from the QuicKeys Editor window, select Finder Events from the Scripting Tools subcategory of the Extensions category of the Define menu. Figure 16.7 displays the Finder Events edit dialog box.

Give the Finder Events shortcut a name and select an event to send from the Finder Events pop-up menu. Note that the Sleep event works only with PowerBooks. Assign a keystroke, and you're done.

Finder Events Tactics and Considerations

Use the Finder Events shortcut to send one of a few Apple Events to the Finder.

Why would you want to send an Apple Event to the Finder? It lets you use the Finder's file management tools while you are in other applications—to open, select, print, or get information on folders, documents, and applications. The Finder traditionally has been a unique part of the

Figure 16.7
Finder Events edit
dialog box

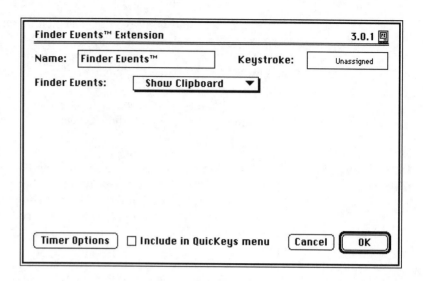

Macintosh operating system that could not be changed, just used. Hence, the paltry nature of the Apple Events it supports under System 7.1 and earlier system versions.

Luckily, the new version of the Mac operating system, System 7.5, includes what is called a scriptable Finder. This means that you can control the Finder in more ways with Apple Events. (Many of the events were already available, but undocumented.)

The new scriptable Finder essentially makes the Finder Events shortcut obsolete. You can still use it to send its six poky little Apple Events, but none of the new Apple Events or objects that the Finder now recognizes can be sent with this shortcut—for that you have to use the Apple Events shortcut.

AppleScript Shortcut

QuicKeys' AppleScript shortcut executes scripts written in AppleScript. For it to work, you must have the AppleScript system extension in the Extensions folder of your System folder. That extension doesn't come with System 7 or 7.1. It is bundled with System 7.5.

We cannot teach you all there is to know about AppleScript in this chapter. We know that's a bit of a cop out, but it's just too complex. If you are interested in finding out more about AppleScript, we suggest you take a look at *The Tao of AppleScript* by Derrick Schneider or *The Complete AppleScript Handbook* by Danny Goodman. Not only are these useful references, they contain disks with AppleScript examples.

If you're writing AppleScripts, we strongly recommend you use the Script Editor that comes with the AppleScript package. Once you've got the scripts all debugged, you can use an AppleScript shortcut to execute them.

Running a Script Using the AppleScript Shortcut

To create an AppleScript shortcut, choose AppleScript from the Scripting category of the Extensions submenu of QuicKeys' Define menu. You'll see the dialog box in Figure 16.8.

The two radio buttons, Text and File, provide options for where the shortcuts finds its script.

- **Text.** If you choose Text and then click the Modify Text button, a text edit box opens in which you can write your script. The script's size can be no more than 2K.

- **File.** If you choose File you can have the shortcut execute a script that's been saved as a text file (an AppleScript saved as a compiled script in the Script Editor works too). The file size for this shortcut can be up to 32K.

Figure 16.8
AppleScript edit
dialog box

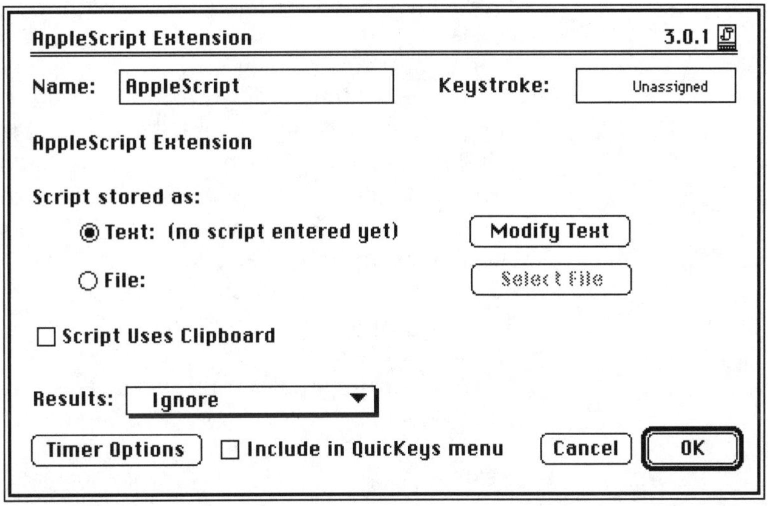

You can incorporate the contents of the Clipboard into your AppleScript when it's executed using the Script Uses Clipboard checkbox. To access the Clipboard contents, your AppleScript must begin with an On Open QKClipboard command, followed by its requisite End Open command at the end of your AppleScript. Then you use QKClipboard in the script where you want the Clipboard inserted.

For example, the following script (an adaptation from *The QuarkXPress Book* by David Blatner) tells QuarkXPress to rotate every picture box in a document to the value found on the Clipboard.

```
On Open QKClipboard
   tell Application QuarkXPress®
     set rotation of every picture box¬
     of every page of document1 to QKClipboard
   End Tell
End Open
```

The Results pop-up menu gives four options of what you should do with any results the application sends back. These work just like the options described for the Apple Events shortcut earlier in the chapter.

As usual, enter a name and a keystroke sequence for your shortcut, and your AppleScript shortcut is done.

AppleScript Tactics and Considerations

Use AppleScript shortcuts to run AppleScripts from anywhere.

AppleScript is a remarkably powerful language for controlling the applications on your Mac. With it, you can bring the capabilities of many different programs to bear on your particular problems.

In general, though, to run AppleScripts you have to use Apple's Script Editor—jump to that application, load the script from disk, and click the Run button. It's not the most elegant approach to automation.

That's where QuicKeys' AppleScript shortcut comes in. You can use it to run any AppleScript, at any time, without launching another application. If you need the flexibility of AppleScript—its programming constructs, such as variables, conditional execution, loops, repeats, and the like—and you also want one-key execution, the AppleScript shortcut provides both.

When writing AppleScripts, we suggest that you stick to the Script Editor with its debugging tools, scrolling text box, and non-modal windows to write and debug your AppleScript scripts and save them as text files if you want to trigger them with QuicKeys. Writing scripts directly into the shortcut is tricky, because you manually enter text that you must debug by hand (no debugging tools) and write blindly, because the AppleScript edit dialog box is modal (it cannot be moved around the screen and often hides the window that you want to use for writing your script). But, of course, if you are a good programmer, you'll find our advice annoying and write your scripts directly, anyway.

DoScript Shortcut

The DoScript shortcut sends a text script written with any application-specific scripting language to that application using the doscript Apple Event. The receiving application only needs to understand one Apple Event: doscript.

Sending a Script Using DoScript

Like the AppleScript extension, DoScript supports sending either small scripts entered in the shortcut itself or script text files that can be sent by the shortcut. To create a DoScript shortcut, select DoScript from the Scripting Tools category of the Extensions submenu of the Define menu in the QuicKeys Editor window, and then select the target application from the Send Script To dialog box that appears. Click OK. The DoScript edit dialog box then appears (see Figure 16.9).

Figure 16.9
DoScript edit
dialog box

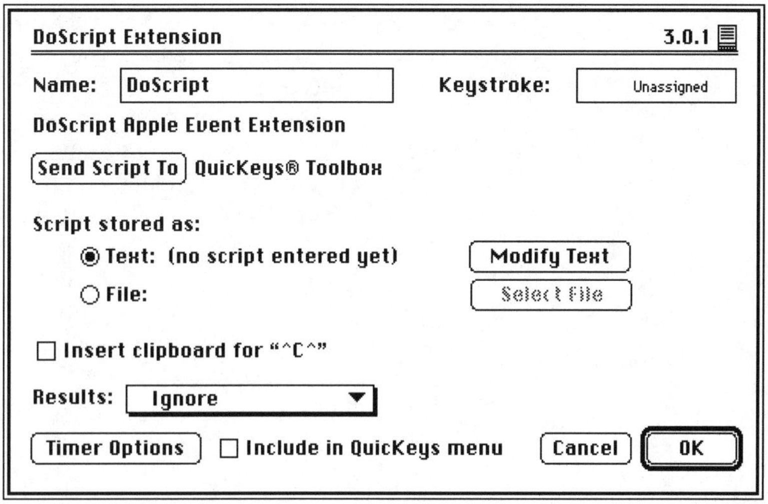

The DoScript edit dialog box bears a striking resemblance to the AppleScript edit dialog box, which is not surprising—both send scripts. But the nature of the scripts (AppleScript versus application-specific scripts) differs slightly, a fact that is reflected in the dialog boxes.

Unlike AppleScripts, which are executed by the AppleScript System extension (the target is specified within the AppleScript code), application-specific scripts must be sent to their target applications. Clicking the Send Script To button makes a dialog box appear from which you can select this target—on your computer or on remote machines.

The Script Stored As options are identical to those in the AppleScript shortcut.

If you check the Insert Clipboard for "^C^" checkbox, QuicKeys inserts the contents of the Clipboard into the script wherever you enter ^C^.

The Results pop-up menu is identical to the one in the AppleScript shortcut.

DoScript Tactics and Considerations

Use DoScript to send an application-specific script to an application.

Doscript seems to be the black sheep of Apple Events. Many books on AppleScript don't document the doscript Apple Event at all. Perhaps this is because doscript exists only for applications that don't follow Apple's dream of all applications supporting a thousand Apple Events. Applications like PageMaker that have internal scripting languages may recognize very few Apple Events and rely on doscript as their Apple Event doorway into and out of IAC. The doscript Apple Event lets a PageMaker user package an alien (PageMaker) script inside an Apple Event. Like a virus, the doscript command encapsulates the alien code of the application's script so it can be sent along the IAC channel. This sounds rather threatening, but in fact it's great—it gives you the power to run application-specific scripts from anywhere.

To use a DoScript shortcut, you need to know the application's scripting language. You thought Apple Events were badly documented by applications? Wait until you try their internal scripting languages! All we can suggest is when the documentation fails, give the vendor a call. Documentation for QuicKeys Script, the internal scripting language of QuicKeys, is better than most (see the next section).

QuicKeys Script

QuicKeys Script, CE's OSA-compliant internal scripting language, comes with QuicKeys 3. Essentially, QuicKeys Script provides a text-based method of describing shortcuts. QuicKeys Script does not contain any functionality beyond that in QuicKeys itself.

Why would you want to describe QuicKeys shortcuts using a text-based command language? It's great if you want to run QuicKeys shortcuts from other applications via Apple Events.

You could always create the shortcut normally, of course, and trigger it with a playbyname Apple Event sent from the other application to QuicKeys Toolbox. But you're relying on that shortcut being there to trigger. If you instead define the shortcut using QuicKeys Script, all the instructions in the shortcut are included in the script itself, so all you need is QuicKeys Toolbox and QuicKeys. It doesn't matter what short-cuts have been defined on that particular system.

We discuss this question in more detail in "QuicKeys Script Tactics and Considerations" later in this chapter.

Creating QuicKeys Scripts

Because QuicKeys Script is OSA-compliant, it can be written using an OSA-compliant script editor, like AppleScript's. Creating a QuicKeys Script with Script Editor offers a number of advantages, including working in a non-modal window, script recording, debugging tools, and the capability to run the script right from the editor. These advantages have prompted us to look at QuicKeys Script's use with the Script Editor in this section. Keep in mind that you don't need AppleScript or the Script Editor to use QuicKeys Script. You can write a QuicKeys Script in any text editor. And you can send it to QuicKeys Toolbox from any application that can send Apple Events via the doscript Apple Event.

The documentation for QuicKeys Script does not exist in the printed materials that come with QuicKeys. In the QuicKeys Script Info folder in the QuicKeys Tools folder you will find extensive documentation on QuicKeys Script—you just have to print it or view it in the reader if you want to save a tree. Some example scripts have been included in the QuicKeys Script Info folder, but, unfortunately, they can only be opened with the Speech Macro Editor, the OSA-compliant script editor that comes with Plain Talk, Apple's speech recognition software.

Recording an Example Script

In this section we use the Script Editor to record a two-step sequence—choosing the Word Count command from the Tools menu of Microsoft Word and clicking the Count button. As you may recall, this is the example Sequence we recorded in Chapter 14, *The Sequence*. No, it's not that we lack creativity (though that's arguably true); we chose the same Sequence so we can compare the Sequence as it appears in QuicKeys shortcut steps to how it appears in QuicKeys Script. So even if you don't have Script Editor, you can check out the resulting QuicKeys Script we create to see how it corresponds to the identical Sequence in QuicKeys.

When you open the Script Editor (see Figure 16.10), you can see a small menu on the bottom-left of the window that lets you choose whatever OSA-compliant script languages you have installed. Choose QuicKeys from this pop-up list to write QuicKeys Scripts.

Now you can get down to recording a script in QuicKeys Script. First, make sure that Microsoft Word is running. Then, switch back to the Script Editor and click the Record button. The now-familiar QuicKeys Recording Palette appears.

Figure 16.10
The Script Editor
window

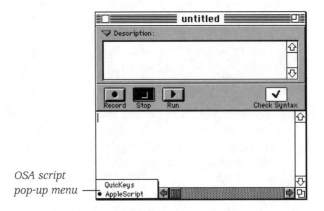

*OSA script
pop-up menu*

Switch back to Word by choosing it from the Application menu. Choose Word Count from the Tools menu and click on the Count button when the dialog box appears. Then click the Stop button (the one with the square on it) on the Recording Palette. You are transferred back to the Script Editor, which now displays your Sequence in QuicKeys Script.

```
Menu "Microsoft Word 5.1" Exactly From "#-16489"
Wait Application "Microsoft Word 5.1"
Menu "Word Count…" Exactly From "Tools"
Pause 0.5
Wait Window Name_Is "Word Count" Dialog
Click (48, 117 Top_Left) - (0, 0 Mouse)¬
   Window #1 ("Word Count") Button #1 ("Count")
Pause 0.5
```

Compare this script to the QuicKeys Sequence shown in Figure 16.11.
The first two lines of the QuicKeys Script switch to Microsoft Word. Those steps aren't necessary in the QuicKeys Sequence since at the start of the recording there, Word was already the top active application.
The rest of the steps in QuicKeys Script correspond directly to each of the steps in the QuicKeys Sequence (except the last step in the QuicKeys

Figure 16.11
Sequence in
QuicKeys

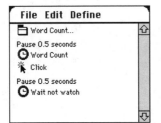

Sequence, a Wait step, is not recorded in the QuicKeys Script; we don't know why). The syntax for the different text representations of shortcuts can be found in the QuicKeys Script documentation that comes with QuicKeys.
If you play the QuicKeys Script, it acts just like the Sequence.

QuicKeys Script Tactics and Considerations

Use QuicKeys Script to write text-based shortcuts.

Why would you want to use QuicKeys Script instead of the more usual method of making shortcuts? We asked Don Brown, the creator of QuicKeys, that very question. He told us that CE's initial reason for creating QuicKeys Script was an Apple requirement that QuicKeys have an OSA-compliant scripting language before Apple would license a limited version of QuicKeys for speech recognition.

But he went on to tell us, "If people have another program with the ability to send scripts to other programs (like FileMaker does, for example), you can put QuicKeys Scripts in there. Without such a textual language, other applications would be limited to telling QuicKeys to play pre-existing sequences, which means that the FileMaker file isn't completely self-contained (QuicKeys must have that sequence loaded). Yes, if all you want to do is record things and play them back, the normal QuicKeys Editor is going to be easier to use. But, it's easier to interface with other applications through a text-based language."

You don't need the Script Editor to use QuicKeys Script. For example, we took the QuicKeys Script we created using the Script Editor and pasted it into a DoScript shortcut targeted to QuicKeys Toolbox. When we triggered the shortcut, we got exactly the same results as when we ran the script in the Script Editor. Or, as Don Brown suggests, you can send QuicKeys Script from another application, like FileMaker Pro. For an example of how that's done, see "Triggering Shortcuts with Apple Events" in Chapter 22, *QuicKeys and FileMaker Pro*.

What an Event

Although this is the biggest chapter in the book, we've barely skimmed the surface of what you can do with Apple Events and scripting. Even with the current (mediocre) state of Apple Events support on the Mac, you can do wondrous things. As more applications support Apple Events and as their support improves, we're hoping to see a world where the only application you ever use is QuicKeys, with all the other applications struggling away as subordinate slaves, subject to the whims and fancies of your QuicKeys shortcuts.

17 Keystroke Strategies

Remember when you first used a Mac? You were probably a total vermin abuser like the rest of us. If you wanted to open a new file, you drove your little mouse up to the File menu and chose Open. If you wanted to copy something, you made that poor rodent grab Copy from the Edit menu. Most of the time your keyboard was for entering data, and your mouse was for issuing commands.

Then you realized that you could use the keystroke shortcuts for these commands. Command-O and Command-C went through the keyboard, and the mouse got a vacation.

The keystrokes you used were mostly preset—hard-coded into your System and applications. If you're like us, you figured these keystrokes were determined in long sessions between programming wizards and young execs with MBAs and doctorates in Computing Science. In raucous meetings, they must have thrown at each other reams of studies on primate behavior, human-machine interaction, and the medical aspects of keyboard and mouse design, in their Herculean labors to develop the perfect keystroke system. And it was all lorded over by the gods on Olympus (read: Apple), who brought the Law of the Human Interface Guidelines down from the mountain top.

Now you can throw all that out the window. Welcome to the acme of the shortcut mountain. The keystrokes are yours.

In this chapter we discuss different schemes for your keystrokes that trigger shortcuts. We suggest a number of groups of shortcuts that you may want to consider having in your sets. Finally, we introduce some third-party and user-created keyboard enhancements to help you remember where all those keystrokes are hiding.

Choosing Keystrokes

What a shortcut does and what keystrokes trigger the shortcut should be complementary. It eases memorization if you standardize each shortcut type's keystrokes (group them on the keyboard). For example, you don't want to have Control-W open Microsoft Word, and Control-Option-F8 open PageMaker. First you need to categorize your shortcuts, then figure out the best ways to trigger them, to help you remember where they are.

Okay, okay. If you're the kind of person who has only a few shortcuts and you take an oath that you'll never use any more, you can trigger them nearly arbitrarily; there'll be few enough that you'll probably remember them all. But if you're like the rest of us, it's impossible to use just one, so the best policy is to start with a plan. That plan involves the marriage of your shortcuts and your keyboard.

Your Keyboard

Just to review, there are two types of keys on your keyboard: character keys and modifier keys. The character keys (letters, numbers, Tab, Delete, Page up, and so on) usually do something when you press them; the modifier keys (Control, Command, Shift, and Option) must be pressed in conjunction with a character key for something to happen. Caps lock is a modifier key which most applications don't use. QuicKeys doesn't use it, so it is essentially a dead key in this discussion.

There are many different Mac keyboards. Don's first Mac keyboard (on his 128K Mac) had no keypad, no Control key, and no function keys. Don's current extended keyboard has 44 additional character keys (function keys, arrow keys, keypad keys, and so on), plus a Control key. It's a totally different environment. Then there are PowerBooks...PowerBook keyboards are a lot like the standard Apple keyboard in that they lack a keypad or function keys (unless you have a new one) but that do have that important Control key and arrow keys.

The Control key is so important that Steve believes it is a shoe-in for the Mac features Hall of Fame (Windows/DOS boxes only have three modifier keys—Control, Alt, and Shift—making it difficult to create sensible keystroke strategies on that lesser platform). Luckily, Apple has recognized its value, so only a few of you out there have Macs that lack this key. Next we'll discuss you have-nots.

An aside to the basic keyboard folk. We wish that everyone who crosses a Mac with QuicKeys also has the benefit of an extended keyboard. Basic keyboards (those that lack the Control key, function keys, and so forth) severely limit the number of available keystroke combinations for shortcuts, in two ways (see Figure 17.1).

Figure 17.1
Basic keyboard

- **Keystroke combinations.** It's difficult (and a waste of time) to quantify this handicap exactly, but here's a rough sketch: Microsoft Word, the Mac application that probably hogs the most keyboard shortcuts (it uses 227 by default), leaves around 1,055 combinations for you to play with when you have an extended keyboard. That number shrinks to about 129 for a basic keyboard—only 12 percent of 1,055. 129 keystrokes seems like a lot of shortcuts, except for appropriateness.

- **Appropriateness.** You do not want to be a slave to your keystroke possibilities. You need a large, varied potential-keystroke pool to choose from, so you can define easy-to-remember keystrokes. Your keystroke paradigm might be based on geography (where the key is located), modifier combination, or something else. Limiting the number of keystroke combinations *severely* limits your ability to exploit different keystroke grouping schemes.

If you have a basic keyboard, you cannot fully utilize much of the information in the rest of this chapter. If you also have a large number of shortcuts, you can use some of the keystroke-layout strategies we suggest, but you won't be able to exploit them fully. You may have to rely on visual devices (templates, keypad stick-ons, and so forth) to remember your invoking keystrokes (see "Keyboard Enhancements" later in this chapter).

Extended keyboards. Many folks who have extended keyboards don't press some of their keys very often. How many programs use the Esc (Escape) key? How many support Page up, Scroll lock, and Delete? How many applications treat the keypad numbers differently from the standard keyboard numbers? More applications do all the time, but do all of them? QuicKeys gives you the ability to unlock the potential keystroke combinations that lie dormant in your extended keyboard. And you can exploit this large number of combinations so that it is particularly advantageous to your setup.

Keystroke Considerations

Good keystrokes meet some basic standards.

They must be easy to remember. Once you get started you won't stop. You are going to have an abundance of shortcuts and even with the best visual-aids in the world, you want to be able to recall your shortcuts instantly.

They must acknowledge any keystroke shortcuts in your System and applications. You don't want to name a shortcut Command-S unless it has something very fundamental to do with saving a file. Every application has keystroke equivalents, and many of these equivalents follow a protocol that has been developed for the Mac. You don't want to arbitrarily map over any of these with QuicKeys shortcut keystrokes. And you can take advantage of the already-laid foundation to suggest keystrokes for your shortcuts.

They (usually) must be easy to use. Pressing Control-Option-M is relatively easy. Pressing Command-Control-Shift-Page up is relatively difficult. The ease of pressing a keystroke should be a consideration in making that keystroke part of your Shortcuts set.

Remember Mnemonics

We're experts at this. Don has been accused of not being able to remember his own name, and if his mother hadn't sewn it onto his clothes when he went to camp, he probably would have forgotten it. So he's pursued memory aids with some vigor.

Mnemonics are strategies that help you remember things (from Mnemosene, the Greek goddess of memory). In theory, many different mnemonic devices can trigger memory, and we're sure that we haven't tried some at one time or another for our shortcuts—but we've tried a lot. We've evolved a synthesis of different keystroke strategies that use the following mnemonic devices.

The alphabet. The alphabet is an obvious choice. That's why Command-S saves and Command-O opens. We think about our applications and utilities by name, so using the alphabet keys to represent them makes sense. So it's P for PageMaker, X for Excel, Q for QuicKeys, F for Freehand, D for DiskTop, and so on. (Steve's shortcut to call up DateBook Pro is Control-C—because the name of the calendar program he used four years ago started with C!)

Of course, the problem with the alphabet is that some letters are more popular than others. P, Q, and S seem to be the fashion among whoever thinks up application names. This inherent problem with alphabet-based systems can be mitigated carefully applying modifier keys.

Key names (and connotations). Heck, they're written right on them! No one in her right mind is going to assign the Page down key to the Line Up Mousie shortcut. Let these keys express themselves, follow their bliss, be what they want to be! These keys, at least in a minimally modified manner, will help you remember what they are—if you play to their strengths. Help, Page up, Page down, Delete, and so on, can also be employed to trigger tasks that can be easily associated with them in memory. For example, we use Delete plus some modifiers to shut down our Macs.

For some reason our Apple extended keyboards have Undo, Cut, Copy, and Paste printed under the function keys F1 through F4. We don't know what overworked design team came up with this, and we don't know of many applications (except for QuicKeys' default Universal Set) that support it. And why should they? It's arbitrary. We say ignore it.

Geography. Location, location, location! Grouping like-minded shortcuts together can be a great memory aid and make access very rapid. It can also be a memory-boggler to have your shortcuts all jammed together like 1950s tract houses. In this case, it is usually advisable to have some additional stimulus to trigger your memory (see "Keyboard Enhancements" later in this chapter).

If you place complementary shortcuts together (for example, Shut Down and Restart, or your different Choosy printer selections), you are better able to remember where they are because they comprise an area of the keyboard.

One good key in an area can influence others around it. Don uses Control-Option-Delete to shut down his Mac. He uses it at least once a day; it's his "let's get the hell out of here" keystroke. Because that connection is so strong in his mind, he's tied Control-Option-= to his Restart shortcut. The Equals (=) key doesn't seem to correspond to the restart function at all, but because it's adjacent to Delete, it's very easy to remember.

That's probably also the source of the QuicKeys standard Command-Option-. (period) shortcut for toggling QuicKeys on and off. Command-. (period) is the key to make things stop happening on the Mac (like Control-C on IBM machines), so Command-Option-. (period) is a natural keystroke (for some people) to stop QuicKeys.

Modifiers. Using the same modifiers for the same class of shortcuts helps keep things nicely pigeonholed and can therefore jog the memory.

Don uses specific modifier combinations to correspond to certain emotional and functional qualities of his shortcuts. For example, his Control-Option-Command combinations connote power; he uses them for shortcuts that he wants to think about before using. Control-character key signifies application. His Control-Option-character key means utility, and so on. We discuss this strategy in more detail in "Putting It All Together," later in this chapter.

Accepted (albeit sometimes bizarre) practice. One aspect of memory is that once you've got it and you use it, it doesn't easily disappear. We could make up a very illogical anti-mnemonic system, and you would probably memorize it if you used it repeatedly. But luckily, we don't have to invent an illogical system because someone (CE Software) already has. If you based your Universal set on the default sets that CE Software supplies as part of their package, you started on the wrong foot.

When you first install QuicKeys, you're supplied with a little Universal set (15 shortcuts). You can open a More Universal Set (38 shortcuts) to transfer additional shortcuts. Many shortcuts in these sets are appropriate to have, but their keystrokes often leave something to be desired (see Figure 17.2).

There are a few basic problems with the keystrokes in the automatically loaded Universal Set. Some keystrokes are identical to shortcuts in some applications, rendering the applications' keystrokes useless. Some are not based on any mnemonic system. For example, what is the connection between the Spacebar and the QuickReference Card, or Return and the QuicKeys Editor window? However, Steve still uses the latter because he's always used it, he's comfortable with it, and (in a final defense of this peculiar behavior) he says, "That's the way it came."

Figure 17.2
Automatically
Loaded Universal
shortcuts

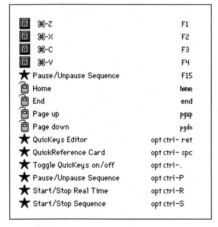

So we can try to be a Henry Higgins to your Eliza and clean up your act, but if you are comfortable with what you already use, you might be better off starting there and merely adapting some aspects of our *incredibly more logical* approach.

Complements Applications and Accepted Protocols

Your shortcut keystrokes can conflict with or complement those shortcut keystrokes already in most applications.

Keystroke conflicts. What if your application has a built-in keystroke, Command-Option-Return, that makes a new paragraph, but leaves the cursor at the end of the old one (as Microsoft Word does)? What if your Universal Set (like Steve's...) has a shortcut that uses Command-Option-Return to trigger the QuicKeys Editor window? The Universal Set takes precedence over the application's shortcut, so you will get the QuicKeys Editor, not a new paragraph.

What if you now make an application-specific shortcut that uses that same Command-Option-Return to do something else (for example, to enter three Returns)? The shortcut from the application set takes precedence. Here's the precedence of keystrokes.

- The application set takes precedence over the Universal Set.

- The Universal Set takes precedence over the application's built-in shortcuts.

If there are duplicate (or triplicate) invoking keystrokes, only one is played, and it will be a shortcut. Of course you can toggle QuicKeys off, and the current application's keystroke will then take precedence.

In some circumstances, you may *want* to map over an application's keystroke. Sometimes applications have duplicate keystrokes for the same command, so you can use one of them for a shortcut. Or sometimes the application's shortcut is active at times different from when you want your shortcut to be active, so you can often access both functions with one keystroke.

Keystroke complements. An application's shortcut keystrokes can often suggest keystrokes for your shortcuts. Microsoft Word, like most applications, will click a default button (double-outlined) in a dialog box if you press the Return key. Steve often uses the Replace dialog box (see Figure 17.3), but unfortunately its default button is Find Next and not what he usually presses, Replace All. So Steve set up Command-Return to trigger a Button shortcut that presses Replace All, *his* default button. He is able to remember it because of its relation to the usual keystroke in this situation (Return).

For an even more innovative solution to this Change All problem, see "A Smart Change All Button" in Chapter 19, *QuicKeys and Word*.

Figure 17.3
Microsoft Word's
Replace dialog box

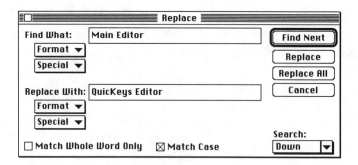

Ease of Use

Spreading your fingers over an extended keyboard involves physical limitations. Some keystroke combinations are just easier to hit, because they naturally fit where our fingers go. Some keystroke combinations are appropriate because they are adjacent to complementary keystrokes: once our fingers have already moved to a new spot, these likely keys are close by.

Finger stretch. Have you ever had your hands so entangled while hitting three keys that you contemplate hitting the fourth key with your nose? Some modifier combinations are naturally easy to press; others are relatively difficult. You probably know what works best for you, but we came up with our own unscientific survey (see Table 17.1).

Table 17.1	Keystroke difficulty—modifiers with various keys			
	None	**z**	**F1**	**Clear**
⇧	1	2	2	2
⌥	1	2	2	2
⌃	1	2	2	2
⌘	1	2	2	2
⇧ ⌥	1.5	2	3	3
⇧ ⌃	1.5	2	3	3
⇧ ⌘	2	3	3	3
⌥ ⌃	1	2	2	2
⌥ ⌘	1	2	2.5	2.5
⌃ ⌘	2	2.5	2.5	2.5
⇧ ⌥ ⌃	2	2.5	3	3
⇧ ⌥ ⌘	2	2.5	3	3
⌥ ⌘ ⌃	1	2	2	2
⇧ ⌥ ⌘ ⌃	2.5	2.5	3	3

Higher numbers indicate more difficulty

⌃ –Control
⌥ –Option
⌘ –Command
⇧ –Shift

You generally choose your often-utilized keystrokes from the easy modifier combinations. However, you can make difficult keystrokes work to your advantage by making them trigger potentially dangerous shortcuts. For example, Don uses Shift-Option-Command-Control for experimental temporary shortcuts. Besides being difficult to press (and remember), thereby ensuring some safety, the difficult keystroke combination is easy to pick out in the QuicKeys Editor window—which aids housekeeping tasks.

Putting It All Together

Obviously, with all these factors influencing shortcut inclusion and keystroke designation, developing an overall shortcuts environment calls for more art than science. Building a shortcuts system often involves a fair amount of trial and error, experimentation and evolution. In this section, we'll show you the logic of our approach and how it evolved to meet the vagaries of our work. Table 17.2 gives you a succinct picture how we categorize shortcuts within our system. You can borrow from our approach, and customize it to your situation.

Table 17.2	Functional categories in our shortcut system
Set	**Shortcut function**
Universal	Open applications
	Open documents
	Open utility programs
	Move to folders
	Open anything
	Adjust and control the Mac
	Adjust and control windows
	Press buttons
	Change printers
	Control QuicKeys
	Standardize shortcuts between programs
Application	Operate controls and commands
	Perform tasks in applications
	Perform tasks between applications
	Perform miscellaneous tasks

We should mention that when we first wrote about keystroke strategies many years ago, there was no Instant QuicKeys (see Chapter 18, *QuicKeys Utilities*). Instant QuicKeys was developed to address the need for quickly developing useful shortcuts and giving them a coherent and ordered set of triggering keystrokes. While it isn't perfect, it can be very helpful to some.

We work in an office environment in which 10 Macs are connected in a network that also contains five printers, three scanners, and two IBM clones. Each Mac has been customized by its operator to perform best for that individual's requirements. However, since we often work on each other's machines, we've found that standardizing certain aspects of the computing environment—especially applications and utilities—has substantially increased productivity and made the atmosphere somewhat less...tense.

Here's how our system works. Remember—the application shortcuts, the application sets, and the Universal Set all have to complement each other.

Make Up Your Universal Set

Our Universal Set contains the bulk of our shortcuts, even though we have healthy application sets for many different applications. The Universal Set is a good place to start refining your shortcuts environment.

Open applications. We like to use the alphabet to remember our application keystrokes: our application keystroke assignments tend to be permanent, and an alphabet-based mnemonic is easy to remember. We use the Control key as the modifier of choice to open applications; it doesn't conflict and is easily accessible (see Figure 17.4).

To switch between open applications, we use the ProcessSwap Next Application and Switch Back shortcuts (Steve actually prefers MasterJuggler's app-switching menu, which has nothing to do with QuicKeys, so it doesn't conflict with these shortcuts). These seem natural to trigger with our Right and Left arrow keys with Control-Option as the modifier. The scheme fits neatly into switching between windows in a single application, which uses the same keys but the modifiers Option-Command (see "Adjust and Control Windows" later in this chapter).

Figure 17.4
Opening applications

Switch Back	opt ctrl- ←
Next Applicatio	opt ctrl- →
Aldus FreeHand 4.0	ctrl-F
Kid Pix	ctrl-K
Aldus PageMaker 5.0	ctrl-M
Navigator 3.2	ctrl-N
Adobe Photoshop™ 2.5	ctrl-P
QuarkXPress®	ctrl-Q
Smartcom II	ctrl-S
Quicken 4	ctrl-U
Microsoft Word 5.1	ctrl-W
Microsoft Excel	ctrl-X

Open documents. Because we work on books divided into chapter files, we often have a number of documents that we want to be easily accessible on our Macs over several weeks or months. However, these docs are rarely permanent and often have similar names; therefore, an alphabet system isn't appropriate. Instead we use function keys and a template device to aid in their recall. Don uses Control-Shift with function keys for opening documents. When he runs out of function-key combinations with Control-Shift (which often happens), he adds Control-Command. When you have so many often-accessed files that this system breaks down, it is time to forget about targeting the files and instead start targeting their folders. To do that, see "Move to folders" later in this chapter. SoftKeys Palettes may also help, if you like them.

Open utility programs. We categorize our helper programs as utilities. This group includes many of the applications that live under the Apple menu (the former Desk Accessories), as well as what most users commonly think of as utilities (ResEdit and StuffIt Deluxe, for example). We even stick in access to the Control Panels folder here, maybe because it lives on the Apple menu.

We think of our utility programs by their names (as with applications), so we use Control-Option with the alphabet keys to trigger them (see Figure 17.5). If you don't have too many applications or too many of these utilities, you won't run out of appropriate invoking letters, and so you can class these with the applications, using Control as the only modifier. However, if you have as many of both categories as we do, you'll find it helps to use Control-Option. It's easy to hit.

Figure 17.5
Opening utilities
and desk
accessories

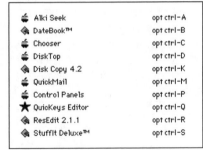

Alki Seek	opt ctrl-A
DateBook™	opt ctrl-B
Chooser	opt ctrl-C
DiskTop	opt ctrl-D
Disk Copy 4.2	opt ctrl-K
QuickMail	opt ctrl-M
Control Panels	opt ctrl-P
QuicKeys Editor	opt ctrl-Q
ResEdit 2.1.1	opt ctrl-R
StuffIt Deluxe™	opt ctrl-S

Some of our utility launchers are actually Sequences, because they open the utility and then click an appropriate button to get into it.

Move to folders. Here's a shortcut type that some people haven't discovered: the Folder (formerly called Location) shortcut. When you're in an Open dialog box or a Save dialog box, Folder moves you to a specific folder. We'd never want to assign a File Launch shortcut to open each individual illustration in a book, for instance, but we often need to access the folder; hence, the value of the Folder shortcut. It's a great shortcut.

And don't forget one of its best features: the option that opens the folder itself when the shortcut is triggered in the Finder.

There is some difference of opinion in our office as to the best keystroke scheme for different Folder shortcuts. Don, because he relies on a template, uses Control with a function key (see Figure 17.6). Steve relies on SuperBoomerang, a utility that includes a function very similar to the Folder shortcut. He triggers his folders with an alphabetic keystroke scheme (Command-M for his Macworld folder, Command-T for his Temp folder, and so on). SuperBoomerang works within Open dialog boxes and Save dialog boxes, so the keystrokes are only active while the dialog box is open. If you tend to think of your folders by name and you don't have too many of them, you could use a similar alphabetic keystroke scheme in QuicKeys, perhaps employing Control-Option-Shift as modifiers.

Figure 17.6
Accessing folders

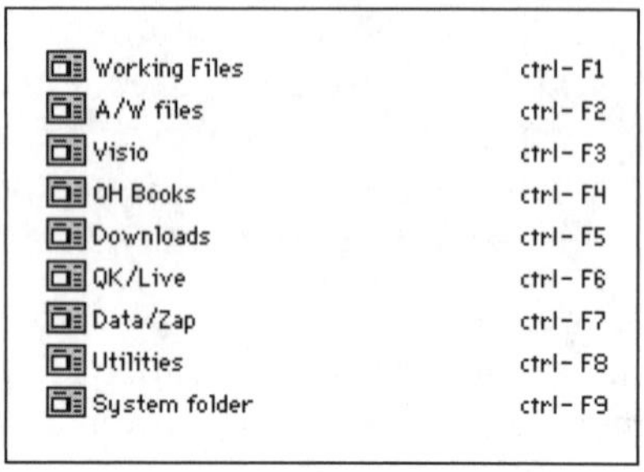

Working Files	ctrl- F1
A/W files	ctrl- F2
Visio	ctrl- F3
OH Books	ctrl- F4
Downloads	ctrl- F5
QK/Live	ctrl- F6
Data/Zap	ctrl- F7
Utilities	ctrl- F8
System folder	ctrl- F9

Open anything. We can't leave this group of opening shortcuts without mentioning one of Don's favorites: the Transfer shortcut (for more on Transfer, see Chapter 5, *Shortcuts That Launch and Open*). Transfer launches files by displaying an Open file dialog box. Because Transfer is not target-specific, you only need one in your Universal Set. Don uses F14 (Scroll lock) to trigger Transfer, because it is easy to hit and we don't need to lock scrolling in any of our work (see Figure 17.7). Steve doesn't think this is very mnemonic (and he's right). But Don has F13, F14, and F15 reserved for System-wide tasks, and F13 and F15 perform the jobs that are printed on them, leaving F14 open.

Figure 17.7
Open anything
shortcut

★ Transfer   F14

Adjust and control the Mac. We group these geographically, using the number keys at the top of our keyboards. Such a distribution lets us easily mark their location on our templates. We use Control-Option as the modifier combination because we associate that combination of modifiers with utilities, which is how we think of adjustments (see Figure 17.8).

The first three shortcuts are SpeakerChanger extensions: the first sets the level to zero, the next two toggle the speaker up and down. Then we have a third-party freeware extension, BitDepth, which shows

Figure 17.8
Adjusting the Mac

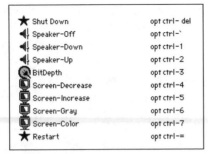

the bits per pixel that our monitors are currently displaying. The next two shortcuts increase or decrease the monitor's bit level, using the Screen Ease extension. Two Screen Ease shortcuts that switch to grays or color follow. The final two are shortcuts Specials to turn the Mac on and off. At first their keystrokes may seem a bit weird, but they are based on Shut Down being tied to the Delete key (a fairly straightforward association). The Equals (=) key, adjacent to Delete, then works well for Restart.

Adjust and control windows. A large variety of window shortcuts reside in our Universal Set (see Figure 17.9). Their keystrokes seem to be scattered all over the keyboard, but they actually inhabit only three areas.

Figure 17.9
Adjusting and
controlling
windows

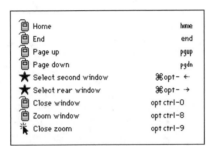

The Page up and Page down Mousies are remapped to the correspondingly-named keys on the keyboard, as are Home and End. This serves their functional purposes and also standardizes these functions between applications.

Zoom window and Close window use Option-Control plus numbers at the top right of the keyboard, for the same reason we gave for the Mac adjustment shortcuts: we think of them as utilities. Close window comes in handy sometimes, because some applications use Command-W to close a window and some use Command-. (period). Steve uses Command-` for Close Window, because it's like clicking in the upper-left corner and most applications don't use that combination for anything else (PageMaker is the primary exception).

CloseZoom is our own Mousie that clicks on the bottom-right corner of the active window (in the size box) and pulls it all the way to the upper-left corner, essentially shrinking the window size as small as it can be. The Select Rear Window and Select Second Window Specials let you either step through your open documents or toggle back and forth between the top two docs in an application. These we use constantly.

These last two keystrokes fit snugly into the ergonomics of the Mac keyboard. It's comfortable to rest your left hand on the three lower-left corner keys (Control-Option-Command), which makes it extremely simple to press Command-Option-Right arrow to page through open docs in an application. Control-Option-Right arrow is set up to page through open applications (see "Open applications" earlier in this chapter).

Press standard buttons. We don't use these much because DialogKeys is often better and you can often activate buttons with application-specific keystrokes, but occasionally they come in handy. Don has a bank of them—that use his utility modifiers—in his function keys (see Figure 17.10). If you want standard Button shortcuts in your arsenal, you might want to use alphabetic keystrokes (C for Cancel, Y for Yes, and so on) with your own modifiers. And some folks (Steve is among them) swear that the Esc (Escape) key is the only key to use for a Cancel Button shortcut.

Figure 17.10
Pressing buttons

Change printers. We often printers switch, and the Choosy extension makes it so effortless that these shortcuts get quite a workout. First on our list is a Choosy shortcut that doesn't change printers, but reports on which one is already chosen. Don keeps Choosies in the function keys, where his template crib sheet jogs his memory for the less utilized ones (see Figure 17.11). Steve puts his Choosy shortcuts on the QuicKeys menu, which he accesses as a pop-up via Control-Option-clicking (see "Configure CEToolbox" in Chapter 4, *The QuicKeys Cockpit*).

Figure 17.11
Changing printers

Control the QuicKeys program. We probably have more QuicKeys control shortcuts than most people, but they get used a lot (see Figure 17.12). Their keystrokes break down into three areas.

Figure 17.12
Controlling
QuicKeys

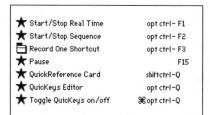

- Function keys with the Control-Option modifier.

- The Pause shortcut, which unpauses Sequences. We like to be able to trigger it quickly, so we use the F15 key, which has Pause written on it.

■ The other three Specials are variations on the Q key. Toggle Short-cuts On/Off uses the power modifier combination, because you don't want to trigger it thoughtlessly.

A note about the QuickReference Card: we don't trigger it except when we want to puzzle over it. But some folks actually use it for its intended purpose—triggering shortcuts—especially if they have a bushel of shortcuts that they don't use often enough to remember their key-strokes. If you often access your shortcuts using the QuickReference Card, you will probably want to assign an easily accessible keystroke (like F14) to display it; or, if you use Control-Option-Q for the QuicKeys Editor window, Control-Option-R might be right for the QuickReference Card.

Standardize shortcuts between programs. This is a potpourri, because it depends completely on the vagaries of various programs. The category is also redundant with other categories mentioned in this section; there-fore, many shortcuts we list here have been seen before. Nevertheless, these shortcuts are useful—they sweetly mollify your computing envi-ronment, taking off some of the rough edges left by the programmers (see Figure 17.13).

Page up and Page down are not supported in all applications. By assigning these Mousies to the extended keyboard keys of the same names, you guarantee the func-tion in any application (like the QuicKeys Editor window). Steve often applies Page up and Page down shortcuts to the 3 and 9 keys on his numeric keypad, mimicking their operation in Microsoft Word. The other stan-dardizations consist of menu items that we employ in many programs. By using Shift-Control with an appropriate alphabetic key, we are able to recall them instantly.

Figure 17.13
Standardizers

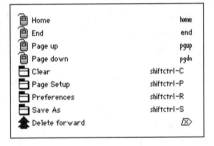

The Delete Forward Sequence makes your Delete forward key do what it is supposed to do—in most applications. It consists of two steps: move the cursor one character to the right, then hit Delete. If you have any appli-cations that support this feature internally (like Microsoft Word) and you want to let it operate, you can put an Alias shortcut in the application-specific set that maps the Delete forward key to the Delete forward key.

This preempts the Universal Set Sequence from occurring in that particular application.

Make Up Your Application Sets

Our application sets are not overflowing, but the shortcuts inside them are customized to make their applications zing. You'll find good workhorse shortcuts in the chapters dealing with specific applications, so we'll just provide a strategic overview here.

Operate controls and commands in specific applications. How do you use the application? Where do you find yourself using the mouse repeatedly? Where do you perform the same actions over and over again? These are the places for shortcuts. See the chapters on specific applications for some good examples of this category. Using those examples as a guide, customize your applications to your work.

Set up your keystrokes to minimize hand movement. For example, working with Navigator (a communication program for CompuServe) involves a lot of screen scrolling and moving from message to message or field to field. Most of our navigating through Navigator is done with our keypad; the right hand sits on it, and the right arm hardly moves through an entire session.

Perform tasks in specific applications. Most applications have tasks that beg to be performed by shortcuts. If you work on multiple projects in one application, you might want to keep their respective shortcuts in different sets. Give the specialized sets obvious names like Word-shortcuts, Word-ComputerHealth, and Word-DTPSurvivalGuide. When you start working with a particular project, you can open the appropriate specialized set and copy its shortcuts into your basic Word set. If your basic Word set contains any specialized shortcuts from the most recent project, these can be deleted.

Some specialized long Sequences (that we perform occasionally) reside in application sets. These can be big processing engines that search through a document, copy text, paste it in another doc, and then repeat.

Since we use these infrequently, we keep track of them with the Comments box via the QuicKeys Editor window. Often these long Sequences are dangerous, so we trigger them with the Control-Command-Option modifier combination that signals, "Pay attention." If the Sequences are temporary, we add the Shift modifier to the combination which gives us the four-modifier "Hey, this is only temporary" classification.

Perform tasks between applications. These shortcuts are often long Sequences that move text or graphics from one application to another, manipulate them, and then move them back again. They should usually reside in the set of the originating application. Treat them like the long Sequences described in the last section, and don't forget to use the Comments box to keep track of what they do.

Miscellaneous tasks. Here are a few screwball shortcuts we couldn't live without (see Figure 17.14). Often, when you type on an extended keyboard, your right-hand pinkie overshoots Delete and lands on Help, making some programs spin into Help mode. So we've mapped Delete to the Help key, giving us two keys that perform the Delete function (Delete and Help). We get the Help function through Command-Help. We admit that this is not the most user-friendly setup for a novice who sits down at one of our machines, but it works for us.

Figure 17.14
Miscellaneous task
shortcuts

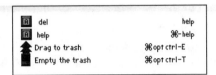

del		help
help		⌘-help
Drag to trash		⌘ opt ctrl-E
Empty the trash		⌘ opt ctrl-T

Trash It is a Click shortcut that lives in the Finder set and drags whatever is under the cursor to the Trash. Don uses the last shortcut, Empty Trash, to empty the Trash, using an Apple Event. Steve doesn't like emptying the Trash without a more rigorous fail-safe mechanism, so his Empty Trash shortcut is in the Finder set: you must be in the Finder for it to work, but he uses a simple Control-T, so it's pretty dangerous in its own right.

Different Strokes

One of our technical editors (okay, okay, it's Dave Loverink) believes we are snobs because we can't see out of the keystroke-trigger, hyper speed lane we madly drive in (even though he admits he prefers driving there himself). Dave suggested that one of QuicKeys' strengths is its ability to trigger shortcuts in a variety of ways, ways that some folks may legitimately prefer over keystrokes. Because we wanted our manuscript back (and because he's right), we make this admission: we use other triggers, too.

We introduced the rich variety of shortcut triggers in Chapter 3, *The Gateway to QuicKeys Knowledge*, and commented on a few of our non-keystroke triggers in Chapter 4, *The QuicKeys Cockpit*. You may want to use non-keystroke triggers to help you fire off shortcuts without having to resort to memory, or you may want to give some of your shortcuts a number of different triggers, so you can fire them in different ways. We urge you to explore all types of triggers to see which best fit your working style. Here's a quick rundown on ways you might liberate yourself from keystrokes.

QuicKeys menu. When he wants to change printers, Steve triggers a Choosy shortcut from the QuicKeys menu, which he usually accesses from the CEToolbox pop-up menu. We love the CEToolbox pop-up menu and have standardized on Control-Option as our modifiers to invoke it (see "Pop-up Menu Configuration," in Chapter 4, *The QuicKeys Cockpit*). Don sometimes likes to put application-specific shortcuts that he creates specifically for one project on the QuicKeys menu, so he won't have to remember a keystroke trigger for them. When the project ends, he deletes the shortcuts.

Timer. Some shortcuts need timer triggers to fulfill their intended function. Our office-mate Glenn creates Message shortcuts on timers to remind him of appointments because he doesn't use a calendar program. He uses a timer to trigger a File Launch shortcut to launch America Online so it can proceed with a scheduled FlashSession. Don plays sounds at intervals to remind him to stretch and rest.

SoftKeys Palettes. CE Software claims that a great body of QuicKeys users begged for SoftKeys Palettes and now uses them preferentially to trigger their shortcuts. Although slow, SoftKeys Palettes can be just the thing for those new to QuicKeys or those who just don't easily remember keystrokes. If you want to give SoftKeys Palettes a try, we suggest you jump in with both feet by using Instant QuicKeys to develop a complete palette system.

QuickReference Card. When all else fails you can do what we do— invoke the QuickReference Card to peruse your active shortcuts. We trigger the display of the QuickReference Card with a keystroke and then click on the name of the appropriate shortcut to trigger it. Naming your shortcuts descriptively helps you use this method successfully. If you have a bunch of shortcuts, liberal use of comments can also assist in locating the correct shortcut.

More different strokes. You can use a Message shortcut to display a text box where you can type in a shortcut's name and trigger it. You can create a QuicKey icon that can be placed in the Apple menu or double-clicked in the Finder. You can send an playbyname Apple Event to QuicKeys Toolbox to trigger a shortcut. If you have an AV Mac, you can trigger shortcuts by voice. All these methods may have their uses in your Mac world. Don't forget 'em.

Keyboard Enhancements

Third-party vendors market various products that add to the efficiency of your Mac working environment. The next sections describe a few commercial and shareware products that help you remember where you put each of your shortcut keystrokes.

Multicomp Keystroke Catalog

For a long time, Don kept track of his shortcuts mapped to his function keys with the F-key Flipbook, a set of long, thin, plastic pages, hinged at the top, that sits at the top of the keyboard. The Flipbook came with two fine-line permanent markers and an eraser to prove they're not so permanent after all.

What Don liked about the Flipbook was its choice of materials perfectly suited for the job. The permanent inks didn't smear, the plastic pages were easy to read, and the eraser expunged unwanted entries without marring the plastic surface. Plus, he was able to pick up more pens from a stationery store to further differentiate between keystrokes. What Don didn't like about the Flipbook was that its design didn't really suit his computing environment—he didn't want to flip pages. So he adapted: the top page of the Flipbook was reconfigured to allow notation of both his Universal Set's and Microsoft Word set's activating function keys.

Perhaps the folks at Muticomp heard him whine because they have introduced some new products that fit his style perfectly: a single plastic panel that fits above his function keys and is ruled to accept function-key-triggered-shortcut notations for up to six different modifier-key combinations, and a small strip that accepts up to three different combinations that fits below the function keys. And because these products use the same easy-to-mark plastic and are less expensive than the five-panel version, Don (Mr. Cheap) is happy. However, if you have an overload of application-specific shortcuts triggered by function keys, the larger Flipbook might be for you.

Hooleon

Hooleon Corporation in Cornville, Arizona, manufactures a passel of different keyboard-enhancement devices. Unfortunately, they are much more IBM- than Mac-oriented. Their off-the-shelf Mac arsenal includes do-it-yourself keyboard labels and Dvorak keyboard labels. They also stress their custom work: imprinted snap-caps, printed keyboard labels, and the like, which might come in handy in a mega-Mac office that uses many standardized shortcuts.

The Frugal Shortcut

If you've got the tools, some motivation, and a few hours, you can create a couple of spiffy enhancement devices yourself.

Wrap-around plastic template for the extended keyboard. Print out the function key wrap-around template, using the Template Printer (see Chapter 18, *QuicKeys Utilities*). Get an Exacto knife, a metal ruler, a piece of acetate, a couple of fine-line permanent markers (in various colors), and an eraser. Oh yeah, and maybe some very thin chart tape. Anything you don't have is available at a good stationery store.

Put the acetate over the template, and cut the acetate to conform (don't forget to cut out the long holes for the function key groups). Then use the chart tape to divide the top of your keyboard into five (or so) horizontal sections. Chuck the paper template into the alternate universe, place the acetate on the keyboard, write your most popular modifier combinations on the left and right, and then fill in your shortcuts (see Figure 17.15).

Figure 17.15
Frugal function
key template

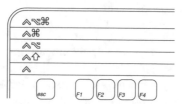

Your own keyboard labels. If you've got a steady hand, you can make your own keyboard labels with a drawing application, a laser printer, and some laser-compatible label (sticky-back) paper. We'd use sheets that are already die-cut to the correct dimension ($7/16 \times 1/2$ inch), but we can't find them. As it is, we use uncut label paper and cut the little labels out. But first we cover the printed area with wide pieces of transparent tape to protect the labels from our greasy fingers.

Set up your artwork as shown in Figure 17.16. We've found that Helvetica Narrow is the most pleasing font (it matches the type that's already on the Mac keyboard). The 5-point shortcut names are tiny, but we can read them. Each of the three vertical positions corresponds to a different modifier combination. We use Control at the top, Control-Option in the middle, and Shift-Control at the bottom.

Figure 17.16
Frugal key labels

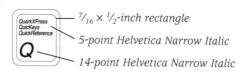

18 QuicKeys Utilities

QuicKeys has taken a few knocks in its time. "It's great, but I can't figure it out quickly enough to make my own shortcuts." "The QuicKeys extensions are too hard to install and select." "I can't share my Shortcut sets easily with another user." "I've got a bunch of shortcuts...but I can't remember their keystrokes!" At one time, all these complaints were legitimate. So Don Brown and his engineers at CE responded. Where they couldn't change the program, they provided some additional utilities to make life with QuicKeys easier. No, these aren't perfect solutions, but they go a long way to meeting most users' needs.

This chapter describes the contents of the Utilities menu, including these applications.

- **Instant QuicKeys.** A shortcut-creation engine, Instant QuicKeys provides a way for you to build a series of shortcuts and learn about QuicKeys' features at the same time.

- **QK Extension Manager.** The Extension Manager helps install QuicKeys extensions and controls their subsequent placement on the Extensions submenu of the QuicKeys Editor's Define menu.

- **QK Shortcut Installer.** The Shortcut Installer helps you install new shortcuts as well as package shortcuts so you can give them to other users.

- **QK Template Printer.** The venerable Template Printer lets you display your keystroke assignments in a printable template.

You can access all these utilities from the Utilities menu in the QuicKeys Editor window.

■ ■

**Instant
QuicKeys**

If you have never used QuicKeys, you may want to start with Instant QuicKeys, and even if you're a more advanced user, you might want to give it a go. Instant QuicKeys includes a tutorial section that explains how to use the utility effectively.

Instant QuicKeys is constructed around a HyperCard-like system of windows. You navigate around the program using buttons that take you to any of 10 sections. Note that the shortcut sections differ somewhat from their categories in the Define menu, since the goal is to get up to speed rapidly. After you have built all your shortcuts, you move to another section where you can assign keystrokes to them. A section is also provided where you can place your newly minted shortcuts on SoftKeys Palettes.

To start building shortcuts, you choose Instant QuicKeys from the Utilities menu; the Instant QuicKeys Welcome window appears (see Figure 18.1).

Figure 18.1
Instant QuicKeys
Welcome window

You can click the IQ Tutorial icon to display a straightforward 10-page tutorial on the utility, or you can click the Continue icon to enter Instant QuicKeys itself. We'll leave the tutorial for you to discover on your own.

When you click on the Continue Arrow icon, the Instant QuicKeys Quick Reference Guide appears (see Figure 18.2). The Quick Reference Guide displays the navigation icons that appear on bottom of the introductory windows of subsequent Instant QuicKeys sections. This card

■ ■

Figure 18.2
Instant QuicKeys
Quick Reference
Guide

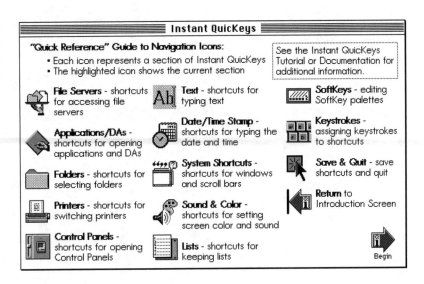

provides the only concise key to the meaning of these icons, so it is too bad you cannot return to it directly from the subsequent sections.

Clicking on the Begin Arrow icon moves you to the introductory card for the first functional section, Network Drives.

Functional Sections

Each functional section has its own shortcut-building edit dialog box that creates appropriate shortcuts based on the configuration of your Mac. You can skip any category by selecting the Skip button at the bottom of the section's introductory screen. You can also go to another category by clicking its icon on the bottom of the dialog box (keep Figure 18.2 handy).

The different functional sections are implemented intelligently, with many built-in aids to ease the process of developing shortcuts customized to your environment. For example, the Applications section searches through your designated drive and displays your applications; the Printers section scans the network and lists all available printers and drivers.

After you have built the shortcuts you want, you can move on to the subsequent sections to give them triggering keystrokes or place them on SoftKeys Palettes.

Assigning Keystrokes

The Keystroke Assigners contains such an array of tools that it could be a utility itself. When you choose the Keystroke Assigner icon from the bottom of one of the section introduction windows and then click the Continue button on the resulting window, the Keystroke Assigner window appears (see Figure 18.3).

Figure 18.3
Keystroke Assigner

Keystroke display area ——

Unassigned shortcuts area ——

Trash Can ——

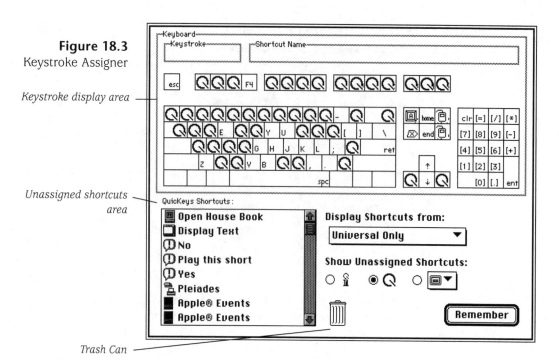

This window is itself fairly daunting, but even more complexity is hidden from view. The best way to understand it is to break it down into two areas: keystroke display and unassigned shortcut display. You can use both these areas to drag and drop shortcuts, thereby assigning them triggering keystrokes.

Keystroke display area. The Keystroke display area consists of the Display Shortcuts pop-up menu, the keyboard layout, and the keystroke and shortcut name display boxes. The keyboard layout graphically displays what keys trigger what shortcuts. If a key (with or without modifiers) triggers a shortcut, an icon is displayed on that key. Often the icon is a large Q, but sometimes the icon for the shortcut type is displayed instead (we'll illustrate how that works later).

■ **Display Shortcuts pop-up menu.** From the pop-up menu you can choose which sets of shortcuts are displayed on the keyboard layout. The pop-up menu gives the option of displaying just the Universal Set or any other sets you have installed in your Keysets folder (you can't display sets stored elsewhere). When you choose one of the application-specific sets, both that set's shortcuts and the Universal Set's shortcuts are displayed together. This pop-up menu can also affect the display of untriggered shortcuts in the Shortcuts window (see the next section, "Unassigned Shortcut display area").

- **The keyboard layout.** The keyboard layout displays icons on keys that trigger shortcuts. The icon is either a large Q or one of the icons that represents a type of shortcut (like the icons you see in the QuicKeys Editor window). You can change the display by pressing modifier keys. Which icons are displayed follows a rather bizarre set of rules. If a key only triggers one shortcut, then when you press the modifiers for that key's shortcut, it displays the shortcut type icon; otherwise it displays the big Q. If a key triggers more than one shortcut, it always displays a big Q, no matter what modifiers you press. See the next item for a continuation of this process.

- **The keystroke and shortcut name display boxes.** When you point the mouse to a key on the keyboard layout, the key is displayed in the Keystroke box. When you also press a modifier, the modifier is also displayed. When this combination (the key and modifier) represent a shortcut trigger, the icon for the shortcut type and the shortcut's name are displayed in the Shortcut Name box.

There is one more twist in the Keystroke display area. If you click one of the keys that has an icon on it, all of the shortcuts that use that key to trigger it are displayed (see Figure 18.4). You can change the keystroke modifiers by double-clicking on a shortcut, or you can drag and drop a shortcut to another key to assign a different keystroke (or you can drag it to the Trash). See "Dragging and dropping shortcuts" later in this chapter.

Figure 18.4
Shortcuts triggered
by the Q key

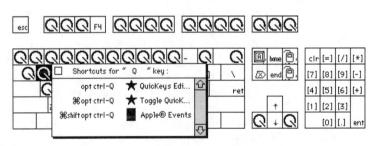

Unassigned Shortcut display area. The Unassigned Shortcut display area consists of a scrolling display window and three radio button options to choose which shortcuts are displayed there. Only shortcuts that have no keystrokes are displayed. The radio button choice and layout is a little odd.

 Clicking the first radio button causes the untriggered short-cuts you've created in Instant QuicKeys to be displayed in the Shortcut Display window.

Clicking on the second radio button causes the untriggered shortcuts from the sets chosen in the Display Shortcuts pop-up menu to be displayed.

 Choosing an item from the pop-up menu next to the third radio button causes the untriggered shortcuts you've cre-ated in that section of Instant QuicKeys to be displayed.

Once you have untriggered shortcuts displayed, you can drag and drop them to the keyboard display to assign them keystrokes.

Dragging and dropping shortcuts. Assigning keystrokes is easy. Just drag the shortcut from the Shortcut Display window onto a key on the keyboard display. Instant QuicKeys displays a dialog box in which you then can apply modifier keys (see Figure 18.5). You can even bypass this dialog box by pressing the modi-fier keys while dragging the name on top of the key.

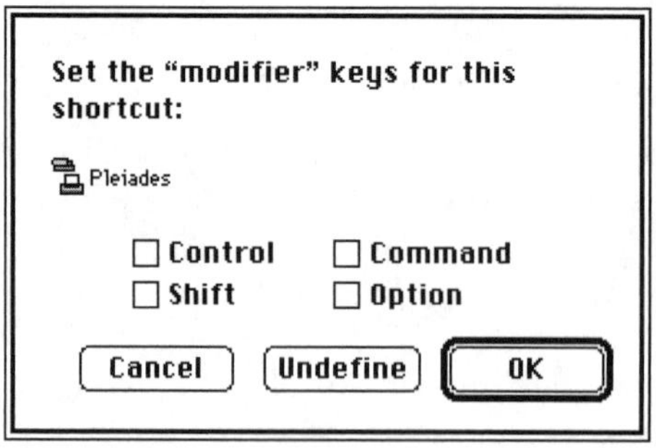

If you want to get rid of a shortcut, just drag it to the Trash Can.

This drag-and-drop tech-nique also works with short-cuts that already have triggering keystrokes. You can drag and drop the shortcuts that appear when you click a key on the keyboard display (see Figure 18.4). These shortcuts can be dragged to other keys to reas-sign their triggers or to the Trash Can to get rid of them.

When you are finished assigning keystrokes, press the Remember button to close the Keystroke Assigner window.

Figure 18.5
Keystroke Assigner edit dialog box

> Set the "modifier" keys for this shortcut:
>
> Pleiades
>
> ☐ Control ☐ Command
> ☐ Shift   ☐ Option
>
> [Cancel] [Undefine] [OK]

Creating SoftKeys Palettes

The Edit SoftKeys Palettes section of Instant QuicKeys contains a set of ten SoftKeys Palette shortcuts that correspond to the 10 functional sections of the utility. The shortcuts that you have made in Instant QuicKeys are automatically included on these palettes. There is also a "mother" palette that can be used to trigger any of the 10 functional palettes. For more about SoftKeys Palettes, see Chapter 13, *Shortcuts That Control QuicKeys*.

When you choose the Edit SoftKeys Palettes icon from the bottom of one of the section introduction windows and then click the Continue button on the resulting window, the Edit SoftKeys Palettes Tree window appears (see Figure 18.6).

Figure 18.6
Edit SoftKeys
Palettes Tree
window

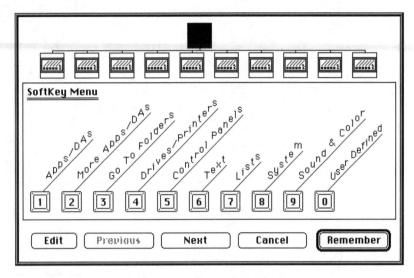

The top icon represents the mother palette with the 10 functional section palettes underneath. To edit one of the palettes, click on its icon and then click on the Display window (the one with the numbers across the bottom) below it. A SoftKeys Palette edit dialog box like that in Figure 18.7 appears.

The scrolling window on the left contains shortcuts you can drag and drop to the palette list on the right. By clicking one of the three radio buttons you can alter which shortcuts are displayed.

 Choosing the first radio button causes just the shortcuts you have in your sets that are appropriate to this particular functional section to be displayed. For example, if you are in the Sound & Color Palette, only your Screen Ease and SpeakerChanger shortcuts are displayed.

Choosing the second radio button causes just the shortcuts you have created in Instant QuicKeys to be displayed.

Choosing the third radio button causes all of your shortcuts that have no triggers to be displayed.

Figure 18.7
SoftKeys Palette
edit dialog box

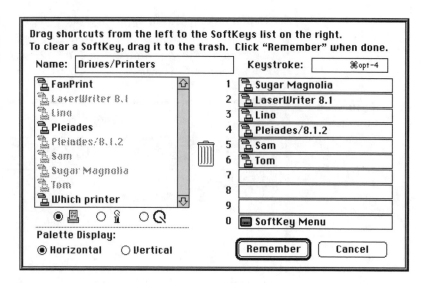

> Drag shortcuts from the left to the SoftKeys list on the right.
> To clear a SoftKey, drag it to the trash. Click "Remember" when done.
>
> Name: Drives/Printers   Keystroke: ⌘opt–4
>
> FaxPrint   1 Sugar Magnolia
> LaserWriter 8.1   2 LaserWriter 8.1
> Lino   3 Lino
> Pleiades   4 Pleiades/8.1.2
> Pleiades/8.1.2   5 Sam
> Sam   6 Tom
> Sugar Magnolia   7
> Tom   8
> Which printer   9
>   0 SoftKey Menu
>
> Palette Display:
> ● Horizontal ○ Vertical   [Remember]   [Cancel]

Shortcuts on the right-hand palette list can be also dragged to different positions on the list. When you have finished dragging and dropping shortcuts, you can choose whether you want the palette to be horizontally or vertically oriented, and you can change its keystroke (it will still be triggered by the mother palette) and name.

We don't use SoftKeys Palettes often. But this hierarchical arrangement with a mother palette triggering function-specific palettes is pretty clever and may work well for you. It gives you a concise method of triggering a large number of shortcuts using very few keystrokes.

Extension Manager

The Extension Manager provides an easy way to add new QuicKeys extensions to QuicKeys. You can also turn off extensions, make them appear on the top of the Extensions submenu, and find out information about them. One more time with feeling: QuicKeys extensions are not system extensions, they are a group of shortcuts that are characterized by the ability to add them into or take them out of the program, unlike the other shortcuts that are "hard-wired" into QuicKeys.

Using the Extension Manager

You can open the Extension Manager by selecting it from the QuicKeys Utilities menu. The Extension Manager edit window appears (see Figure 18.8).

The Extension Manager displays your installed QuicKeys extensions—each followed by a Preferred checkbox—and provides a row of buttons

Figure 18.8
Extension
Manager

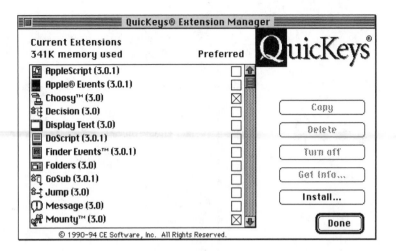

that offer you choices of how to manage your extensions. The Install button is always active. The other buttons are activated when one or more extensions is highlighted (you highlight more than one by Shift-clicking on the additional extension). Here's what the options do.

Copy button. Using the Copy button, you can export extensions to a floppy disk or hard drive. When you highlight one or more extensions and click on the Copy button, a standard Save dialog box appears. Choose where you want to save the extension, how you want to name it, and click Save.

Delete button. When you highlight one or more extensions and click on the Delete button, a warning dialog box appears asking you if you know what you are doing. You do, so click Delete and your extension will be no more. Click Cancel if you want to give your extension a last-minute reprieve.

Turn Off (Turn On) button. By highlighting one or more extensions and then clicking the Turn Off button, you can turn off little-used extensions and save system memory, since these extensions remain on your Mac but are not loaded at system startup. The same button (with a new moniker, Turn On) lets you then turn the extensions back on when needed.

Get Info button. A final use of the Extension Manger is to get information about an extension. Using the Get Info button lets you learn how much memory the extension uses, where it is typically stored (for example which category), what it requires, such as QuicKeys Toolbox, and what it does.

■ ■

Install button. If you press the Install button, a dialog box appears (see Figure 18.9). By selecting an extension in the top list and clicking Add (or just double-clicking the extension), the extension will be added to the Extensions to Install list. When you have added all the extensions you want to install, click the Done button.

Figure 18.9
Dialog box for choosing files

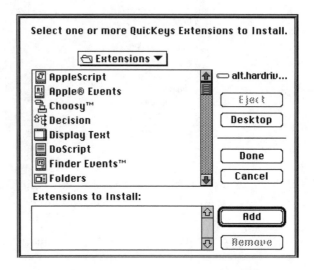

Preferred checkbox. By checking the Preferred checkbox, you can assign extensions to the top of the Define menu's Extension submenu. When the box is unchecked, the extension is displayed in its appropriate category within the Extensions submenu.

Real World Extension Managing

When you install or delete an extension, or turn one on or off, the changes are not made until you reboot. However, copying extensions and making changes in the Extensions menu with the Preferred checkbox make changes without a restart.

Back in the good ol' days, independent programmers like Simeon Liefer used to create nifty QuicKeys extensions that were available from online sources like CompuServe, but we haven't seen a new third-party extension in years. We can only hope that they will soon appear. When they do, use the Extension Manager to install them.

One of the main benefits of using Extension Manger to manage your extensions is that you can save memory, since every extension takes up valuable system heap space, even though you may never use

■ ■

it. When you only have 4Mb of RAM on your PowerBook, such conservation of resources becomes crucial.

Make an inventory of those extensions you use, and turn off all others, such as those advanced shortcut types QT Movie, Apple Events, Finder Events, AppleScript, or DoScript. You can also turn off those shortcut types that have limited or specialized uses, such as NetModemChoosy if you are not working on a network or Mounty, for the same reason. Remember that when you have turned off an extension, it is not available, so check your Sequences carefully to make sure that none of your temporarily unavailable extensions are in use.

You an also install extensions by dragging their icons on top of the Extension Manager's icon in the Finder.

Shortcut Installer

Shortcut Installer should be called something like the Installer Utility because it not only installs shortcuts, but QuicKeys utilities, sets, and extensions, plus system control panels and system extensions as well. Some Shortcut Installer functions overlap with the Extension Manager (like QuicKeys extension installation and information display). But it is a different beast, supporting both drag-and-drop and scripted installation.

The Shortcut Installer offers three ways to install shortcuts.

■ **Drag and drop.** You can simply drag a folder containing new sets or shortcuts (or the individual sets or extensions) and drop it or them on top of the Shortcut Installer icon (or its Alias). The Shortcut Installer window appears, containing the installable items (see Figure 18.10).

Figure 18.10
Shortcut Installer window

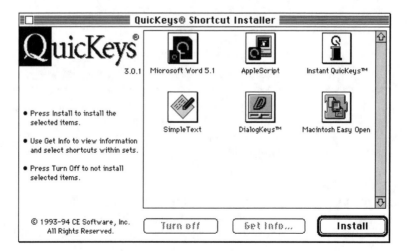

- **Script files.** Double-clicking on a Shortcut Installer Script file launches the Shortcut Installer containing the installable items named in the script.

- **Manual installation.** If you simply choose Shortcut Installer from the QuicKeys Utilities menu, an edit dialog box similar to that you used within the Extension Manager appears (see Figure 18.9). After you choose the items you want to install and click Done, the Shortcut Installer window appears, containing the items you chose.

The Shortcut Installer window has three buttons at the bottom.

- **Turn Off.** Selecting an item (or more than one item with a Shift-click) in the Item window activates the Turn Off button. If you click it, the item goes gray and when you click the Install button it will not be installed.

- **Get Info.** Selecting an item (or more than one item with a Shift-click) in the Item window activates the Get Info button. If you click the button, a dialog box appears for each selected item, providing information including the item's size and description. If the item is a set, a scrolling list of all the shortcuts in the set is displayed.

- **Install.** Clicking the Install button installs all the items that have not been turned off.

The Shortcut Installer is a good-looking installation cannon, but a bit of a loose one. On one hand, the ability to drag and drop items onto it, or run it through a script, is pretty elegant and easy. On the other hand, the ability to choose any application as one of its installation items is rather bizarre. Of course this comes in handy if you want to have an application like FileMaker Pro show up on your QuicKeys Utilities menu, because the Shortcut Installer installs all chosen applications in the Utilities folder of the QuicKeys folder, and anything in there shows up on that menu. You might find this to be a feature....

If you want to delve into the mysteries of writing scripts for the Shortcut Installer, see the documentation included in the Shortcut Installer Scripts file in QuicKeys Programmer Files folder in the QuicKeys Tools folder.

Template Printer

The Template Printer was designed to help you keep track of your shortcuts' triggering keystrokes. The idea is simple: print out a illustration of the keyboard layout with the names of the shortcuts printed on the keys that trigger them. The shortcut name takes on text styles to represent the different modifier keys used to trigger it.

When you launch the Template Printer by choosing it from the QuicKeys Utilities menu, nothing appears. Well, that's not quite true, your Menu bar changes, displaying a File and Edit menu on the left and the application icon for the Template Printer on the right. To make the Template Printer work, you must make sure the Preferences are set correctly and then choose the sets you want to print the triggers for.

Setting Preferences

When you select Preferences from the File menu, the Preferences edit dialog box appears. This dialog box contains four areas of options (see Figure 18.11).

Figure 18.11
Template Printer
Preferences edit
dialog box

```
┌─────────────────────────────────────────────────────────────┐
│  ┌─Preferences: ──────────────────────────────────────────┐  │
│  │ ☐ Always include Universal Set when opening application sets│
│  │ ☐ Show CEToolbox Keys with Universal Set                │  │
│                                                               │
│  ┌─Print Template: ──────────────┐  ┌─Print Style: ─────┐    │
│  │                               │  │ Font: [ Helvetica ]│    │
│  │ Extended Keyboard             │  │                    │    │
│  │   [ Choose Template ]         │  │ Size: [ Other ] 6  │    │
│  └───────────────────────────────┘  └────────────────────┘    │
│                                                               │
│    ┌─Template Styling: ──────────────────────┐   ┌────────┐  │
│    │ Command: [ Bold ]   Control: [ Shadow ] │   │   OK   │  │
│    │  Option: [ Italic ]   Shift: [ Outline ]│   └────────┘  │
│    └──────────────────────────────────────────┘  ┌────────┐  │
│                                                   │ Cancel │  │
│                                                   └────────┘  │
└─────────────────────────────────────────────────────────────┘
```

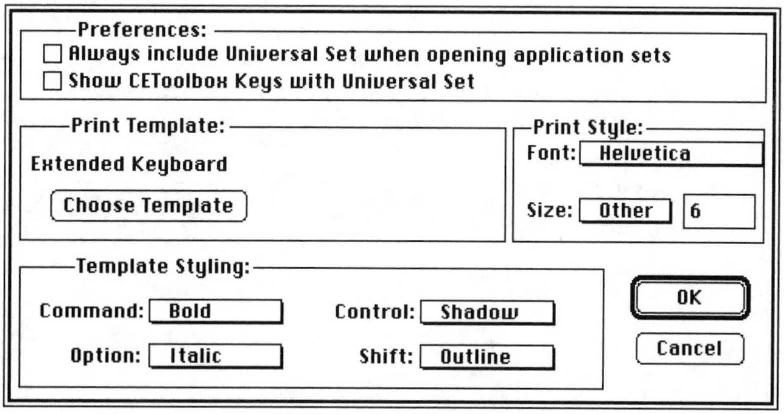

Preferences. The Preferences section at the top contains two checkboxes. The top box includes the Universal Set when you open any application sets (see "Opening Sets" later in this chapter). If you check this box and then open an application set, the Universal Set shortcuts are displayed in the Shortcuts window along with the application's shortcuts. The bottom checkbox doesn't do anything—maybe CE will fix it someday.

Print Template. The Print Template area controls the template you use to print from. Different keyboard layouts are included. Templates for the standard Apple keyboards come with the program, stored in the Templates folder in the QuicKeys folder. You choose a template by clicking the Choose Template button and then selecting the proper template from the open dialog box. The path is System Folder:Preferences:QuicKeys folder:Templates.

Print Style. The Print Style area controls the font you use and its size. You may need to make the font size very small if you want to see enough of your shortcuts' names to recognize them.

Template Styling. Using the four pop-up menus, you can choose which type style (for example, bold or italic) will represent a modifier key. The preset choices work as well as any (which is to say not very well at all). Unfortunately there's no option to use colors (for those of you lucky enough to have color printers), which would make the templates much more useful.

Opening Sets   Once you have set your preferences, you need to open one or more sets to print. There are two opening options: Open Set and Open Installed Set. Choosing the Open Set option invokes an Open File dialog box where you can choose the set you want to open. The Open Installed Set menu item has a submenu from which you can choose an installed set to open. When you open an application-specific set, a Shortcut window much like that shown in Figure 18.12 appears.

Figure 18.12
Shortcut window

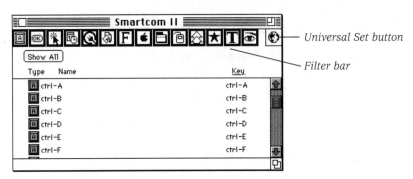

The Filter bar works just like its counterpart in the QuicKeys Editor window. Clicking different buttons representing different types of short-cuts enables you to create subsets of your shortcuts. Only the shortcuts displayed in the window will print.

If you had chosen the Include Universal Set in application set in the Preferences dialog box, your Universal Set shortcuts would also be displayed in this Application Set Shortcut window. However, you can achieve the same end by clicking on the Universal Set button in the Filter bar (the button on the right with the world on it). This button does not appear in the Universal Set Shortcut window.

Template Printer Theory and Practice

The theory of the Template Printer rests on your being able to distinguish between modifier-key combinations through the use of type styles. In practice, this doesn't work too well, especially when there are multiple modifiers. Bold outline italic type is difficult to distinguish from outline italic type. Also, your shortcuts typically will not fit inside the key areas and are therefore truncated with ellipses at the end. The template is more effective if you keep your shortcut names short and descriptive, and your type small. And be sure to set the orientation of your printer to horizontal.

We think there are two good ways to use Template Printer.

■ Print your keyboard template enlarged 400 percent on a laser printer. Then cut the margins off the pages and glue them all to a piece of board (like foamcore), creating a giant wall chart of your shortcuts.

■ Use the Wrap-around Extended Keyboard feature and cut out the template that circumscribes your function keys. This template also includes notations for the top row of the lower keyboard keys—making these keys more attractive for shortcut keystrokes.

By the way, the Template Printer contains a surprise. Open it, choose About Template Printer from the Apple menu, then don't use your mouse or keyboard for 30 seconds, and you'll see what we mean. During the surprise, press Command-Option-Shift-Spacebar to drop in a ready-made visual critique.

19 QuicKeys and Word

Microsoft Word has so many shortcuts, it might seem that to add more would be gilding the lily. And besides that, Word has its own built-in capability to assign keystrokes to commands and to add items to its menus, so what does it need QuicKeys for? The answer is that there are plenty of situations in Word where QuicKeys shortcuts are indispensable. You can also use shortcuts to duplicate some of Word's more popular shortcuts in other programs—standardizing these shortcuts throughout your computing environment.

You might want to change some of the Word shortcuts discussed below from job to job. A good strategy to handle this is to reserve certain keystroke combinations for designation on a job-by-job basis. Store each job's shortcuts in their own set (Word-QuicKeys Book or Word-Zap!, for example), and just copy them to the mother set when you begin that job.

Checking Out Your Open Docs

If you're like us, you open a lot of documents simultaneously in Word. If you're *really* like us, you lose track of which docs are open. You can just press on Word's Window menu, and you'll see a list of your open docs. Or you can step through the open windows if you have the Select Rear Window Special shortcut in your Universal Set. But that might be too slow for some of you. Instead, especially if you are a complete anti-mouser, you can build this shortcut. We admit it's pretty funky, but if you record it well, it works all right.

Open Docs is a Real Time shortcut (we've included this for Don Brown) that clicks on the top of your Window menu for three seconds. We'd use a Click shortcut to do this, but there is no way to make a Click hold down the mouse button for a predetermined length of time. The whole art of making this shortcut (or any Real Time shortcut) is to set up your recording mechanism and your environment for complete efficiency during the recording process. We suggest you use a Start/Stop Real Time shortcut and the Recording Palette to initiate and terminate the recording. Have your pointer already on top of the Window menu, and let 'er rip. There's no way to edit a Real Time shortcut, so you may have to try it a few times to get it right.

Fixing Transposed Characters

We've known a lot of different folks who have come up with this shortcut independently of each other. That shows you how ubiquitous the need for it is.

This Sequence (see Figure 19.1) fixes common typographical errors where two characters are transposed. All you have to do is click between the two offending letters to place an insertion point, press the invoking keystroke for the shortcut, and watch as your typo is corrected to what you intended it to be.

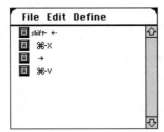

Figure 19.1
Sequence for fixing typos

File   Edit   Define

shift← ←·
⌘-X
→
⌘-V

The steps in the Sequence just use Word's keyboard shortcuts to cut one letter and paste it into its correct position. We find that we use this shortcut often enough that Don has assigned an unmodified function key to it, in the Word set. Steve uses Command-1 (the number at the top of the keyboard), because it's so easy to press with his left hand—no real mnemonic there.

Choosing Styles

We work with different styles when we are putting a book together; styles are integral to our whole production process, so using them accurately is a must. Versions of Word 5 and beyond offer an internal method of changing styles with a user-defined keystroke, so if you use just one set of styles for most of your work, you may want to consider Word's method. First choose Commands from the Tools menu. In the Commands edit dialog box select Apply Style Name from the scrolling Command window, then select your style from the pop-up menu that appears and assign the style a keystroke.

However, Word's method does not provide enough flexibility for the high-pitched, wildly competitive, mega-post-deadline environment we work in. With different books we may have totally different sets of style names. Being able to invoke each style with a keystroke and easily switch to a new set of styles is a must.

You can easily assign your most used styles to keystrokes with a simple QuicKeys Sequence (see Figure 19.2). The first and the last steps

Figure 19.2

Sequence for changing to style Normal

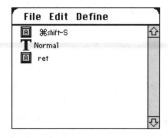

of the Sequence are the same for all of these shortcuts; the middle step changes to reflect the name of the style you want to choose. So you can create one of these Sequences, copy it, paste a number of them into the same set in the QuicKeys Editor window, and then just redefine the middle step. Give each one a different name and invoking keystroke, and you have a complete set.

For our projects, we usually assign about eight most most used styles (out of around 30) to shortcuts. Don likes to use non-modified function keys to invoke them. Just make sure your cursor is in the paragraph you want to style, press the shortcut keystroke, and the style changes almost instantaneously. We enter the other 22 styles manually because they don't come up too often. If one did, we'd build a Sequence shortcut for it, too.

The advantage to using shortcuts to apply styles rather than Word's internal method becomes obvious when we switch to another project that contains a set of styles with completely different names. We build a set of style invokers for that project and save it as its own set. Then we open the Microsoft Word set in the QuicKeys Editor window, select all the Style shortcuts (Shift-dragging does this almost instantly), and delete them. We then open our set with the other project's style Sequences, copy them all, and paste them into the Word set. This takes about 30 seconds, far less time than it would take to change all the style-applying commands in Word.

Don't overlook the advantages of this quick restyling capability for production situations. If your writers don't style their copy (or if they style it incorrectly), you can take their files and process them on a Mac that has these Style shortcuts loaded. You can zip through the documents, restyling paragraphs with a keystroke as you go.

Sometimes our styles contain text entries. For example, we have a style named Bullet, which begins with a bullet (•) followed by a tab. Including this bullet character with its style can be automated with a special Sequence shortcut (see Figure 19.3).

■ ■

Figure 19.3
Changing to
style Bullet and
typing text

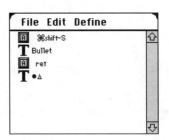

■ ■ ■ ■ ■
Word Count

We never write to length; *we* always let our work expand or contract to meet the needs of the material. But some of you might write to length much of the time, and so you find yourself using Word Count.

Word's Word Count feature works just great, but you have to go through two steps to make it work: choose Word Count from the Tools menu (or use the keystroke shortcut), and then click the Count button. You can automate this operation with a two-step Sequence of a Menu Selection shortcut and a Button shortcut.

■ ■ ■ ■ ■
**A Smart
Change All
Button**

In Chapter 17, *Keystroke Strategies,* we discussed a Button shortcut that Steve created to click the Replace All button in Word's Replace edit dialog box—he clicks Replace All much more often than the default button, Find Next (see Figure 19.4). He's forever pressing Return and getting the next occurrence, rather than the global change he's after. So he triggers a Button shortcut with Command-Return that clicks Replace All.

Figure 19.4
Replace edit
dialog box

	Replace	
Find What:	invoke	**Find Next**
Format ▼		Replace
Special ▼		Replace All
Replace With:	trigger	Cancel
Format ▼		
Special ▼		
☐ Match Whole Word Only ☐ Match Case		Search: Down ▼

But there's a problem with this: Word has a command triggered with Command-Return that gives you a new paragraph with the same style as the previous one. Steve's shortcut overrides it, so when he

■ ■

presses Command-Return and the Replace dialog box isn't displayed, he just gets a beep.

The solution takes advantage of the Decision extension. First, make a Sequence like that depicted in Figure 19.5.

Figure 19.5
Replace Sequence

Use Command-Return as the keystroke

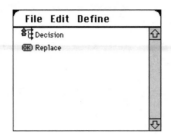

The Decision extension's Window Action logical test is the heart of this Sequence (see Figure 19.6); it makes a decision based on the name of the active window. If the window is named Replace, the Sequence is satisfied, and so control passes to the next step (because the If Condition Is True Trigger Shortcut text box is blank), in this case clicking the Replace All button.

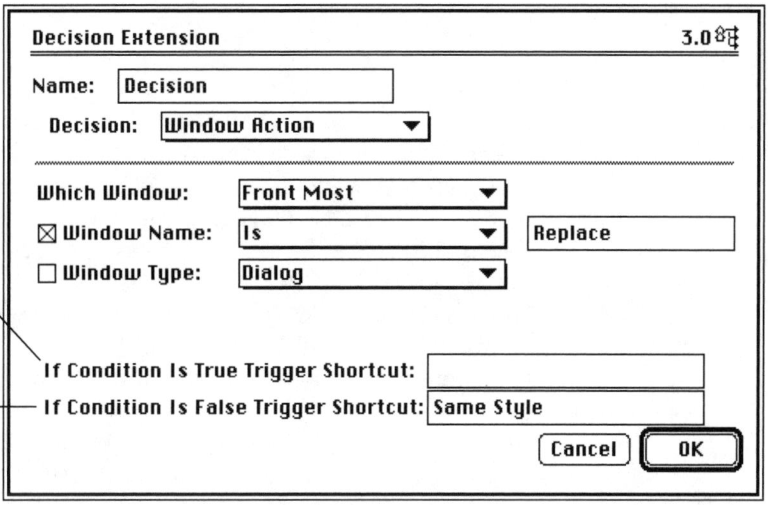

Figure 19.6
Decision
Extension's
Window Action
edit dialog box

If criterion is met this left blank, control passes to the next step in the Sequence.

If the criterion is not met, this shortcut is played.

Decision Extension   3.0

Name: Decision

Decision: Window Action   ▼

Which Window: Front Most   ▼

☒ Window Name: Is   ▼   Replace

☐ Window Type: Dialog   ▼

If Condition Is True Trigger Shortcut:

If Condition Is False Trigger Shortcut: Same Style

Cancel   OK

The If Condition Is False Trigger Shortcut (if the active window is *not* named Replace) passes control to a shortcut named Same Style (see Figure 19.7). The Same Style shortcut types Command-Return, which Microsoft Word recognizes as its command to create a new paragraph with the same style as the previous one.

Of course, once this is all set up, it's invisible to the user. So Steve can eat his cake and have it, too.

Figure 19.7
Same Style Alias
Keystroke edit
dialog box

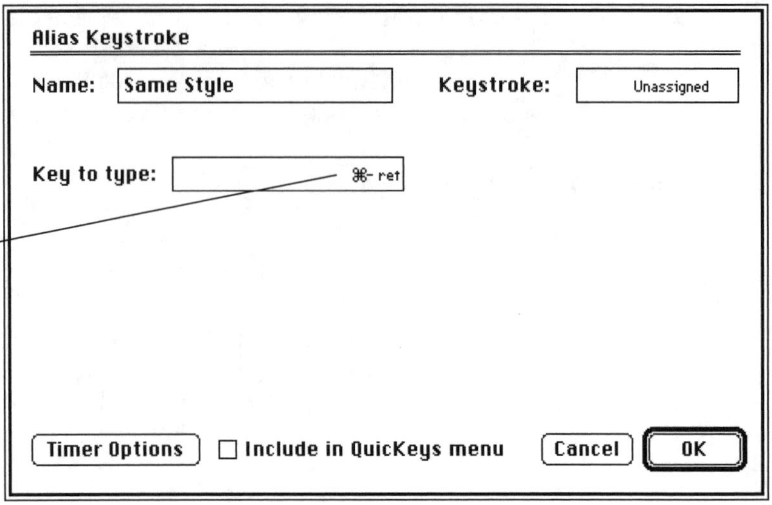

Alias Keystroke

Name: [Same Style]   Keystroke: [Unassigned]

Key to type: [⌘-ret   ]

*Presses Command-
Return if the active
window is not named
Replace*

[Timer Options]   ☐ Include in QuicKeys menu   [Cancel] [OK]

Expanding New Documents

No matter what application you are in, you may often want to enlarge a document window to the full size of your display. In the old days, you needed QuicKeys to zoom a Word window with a keystroke, but now Word has a command, Zoom to Fill Screen, that you can choose from the Commands edit dialog box and put on one of Word's menus (Window makes sense to us). You can also assign it a keystroke (see "Making Sequences with Word's Shortcuts", next, for more on working with Word's commands).

When you open documents in Word, they open to whatever size they were when you saved them, but a new document opens smaller than we would like. So we have a two-step Alias Keystroke Sequence triggered by Command-N. The first step presses Command-N, opening a new document, and the second step presses the keystrokes we assigned to the Zoom to Fill Screen command in Word. Now our new documents fill our screens.

Making Sequences with Word's Shortcuts

The more shortcuts you build into an application, the easier it is to create sophisticated Sequences: you have a wealth of tools available. But you have to know the keystroke shortcuts to use them. That's not easy in Word because you can assign Word shortcuts over 200 standard shortcuts, plus there are many additional commands available.

Word's built-in shortcuts. An easy way to access Word's shortcuts is to first make a list of them. Word has automated that process for you: choose Commands from Word's Tools menu (or press the key combination Command-Shift-Option-C). The Commands dialog box appears (see Figure 19.8). Click the List button on the bottom of this dialog box, select All Word Commands in the subsequent dialog box and Word opens a new document that lists your commands.

Figure 19.8
Commands dialog
box

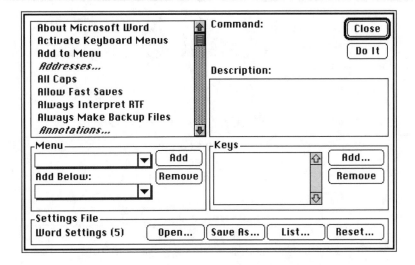

Some commands have keystroke shortcuts, and some do not. You can give a command a keystroke shortcut in Word by highlighting the command in the Commands dialog box. Then click the Add button in the Keys section. Word prompts you for the keystroke and alerts you if that keystroke is already taken by another Word command.

If you're not quite sure what a Word keystroke does, there's a tool to find out. It's hidden in the Command list: Command from Key Assignment (you can press the Do It button to execute it from there, put it on a Word menu, or assign it a keystroke). Trigger this command, and Word prompts you to press a keystroke. Press one, and Word tells you what command it's invoking.

Of course, you could use QuicKeys to assign a keystroke to a Word command; however, we feel it is good practice to use the mother application for functions that can also be performed in QuicKeys—unless there is good reason to assign the capability only through QuicKeys.

Sequences with Word's shortcuts. Many of Word's functions have redundant access: you can get them either from a menu, by pressing the keystroke shortcut, or by using the Toolbar's buttons. We generally use the keystroke to include these functions in Sequences. It's easier because of the Insert Keystroke button in the QuicKeys Sequence editor.

Let's build a sample Sequence, to explore how Word's shortcuts come in handy. When we make a table of contents for a book, we style lines differently, depending on their head levels (see Figure 19.9).

Figure 19.9
Partially formatted table of contents

Instant QuicKeys 268
Functional sections 269
Assigning keystrokes 269
Keystroke display area. 270
Unassigned shortcut display area. 271
Dragging and dropping shortcuts. 272

But eventually we give all the page numbers a standard character style and point size. This Sequence uses a number of Word's shortcuts to help us do that (see Figure 19.10).

Figure 19.10
Table of contents reformatter

File Edit Define
Begin Repeat
[1]
⌘shift- ←
⌘opt-V
[7]
↓
[1]
⌘shift- ←
ret
End Repeat
Moves cursor to the end of the line
Selects the number
Copies the formatting
Moves to the front of the line
Drops down to the next line
Moves cursor to the end of the line
Selects the number
Applies the preselected formatting to the selection

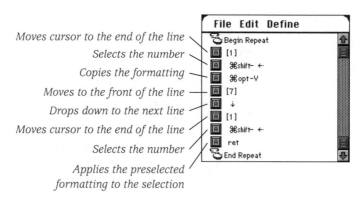

To make the Sequence function, you must style the page number in the first line the same way you want all the other numbers styled and then leave the cursor somewhere in the first line.

The Table-of-contents Sequence uses a Repeat shortcut set to 100 times, to move it along. If we have more than 100 lines in the table of contents, we trigger the shortcut again; if not, when it reaches the end of the table of contents, the Sequence beeps at us until we click the mouse button and cancel it.

Standardizing Word's Shortcuts Throughout Your Applications

Because Word holds the batting title for shortcuts, if you use Word frequently you may just want to take some of its keystrokes and apply them to identical functions in your other applications (see Table 19.1). Or you can redefine your favorite Word shortcuts to other keystrokes and standardize those throughout applications.

How you standardize depends on what functions you want to standardize and how they are handled in various applications. If the function is handled identically in all your applications, like a menu item in the same menu (for example, Save As), you can just make a Menu Selection shortcut in the Universal Set. If the function is located in different menus or dialog boxes in different applications, you may have to combine a Universal shortcut with overriding application shortcuts in some situations.

Table 19.1	Popular Word shortcuts
Function	**Keystrokes**
Save As	Shift-F7
Page Setup	Shift-F8
Plain Text	Shift-F9
Bold	Command-Shift-B
Italic	Command-Shift-I
Underline	Command-Shift-U
Left Justify	Command-Shift-L
Right Justify	Command-Shift-R
Center	Command-Shift-C
Go Back	Command-Option-Z
Select Paragraph	Shift-Command-Down arrow
Select to the End of Sentence	Shift-Command-[1] (on keyboard)
Select to the Beginning of Sentence	Shift-Command-[7] (on keyboard)

20 QuicKeys and PageMaker

While PageMaker is fairly well endowed with keyboard shortcuts, there's no shortage of areas where QuicKeys can speed your page-layout work. A number of menus items, in our opinion, absolutely *need* new or different keyboard shortcuts; there are some handy Sequences for setting up your work area; and using PageMaker's internal scripting language, you can control almost every aspect of PageMaker's operation—including doing things that you can't do via the normal controls.

Choosing Tools

If you have a smaller screen (or even if you don't), you just gotta get the toolbox out of the way and select tools with keystrokes. PageMaker includes keyboard shortcuts for this—Shift-F1 through F8 (see Table 20.1). That's all well and good, but try reaching Shift-F1 with one hand, much less Shift-F8.

Table 20.1	PageMaker's built-in tool-selection keystrokes
To select this tool	**You press Shift plus**
Pointer	F1
Diagonal line	F2
Horizontal/vertical line	F3
Text	F4
Rotate	F5
Rectangle	F6
Oval	F7
Cropping	F8

Steve's solution to this finger-stretching dilemma is to choose tools using the first eight function keys, without the Shift key. Set up eight Alias Keystroke shortcuts in the PageMaker set that look like those in Figure 20.1.

Figure 20.1
Alias Keystroke shortcuts for selecting tools in PageMaker

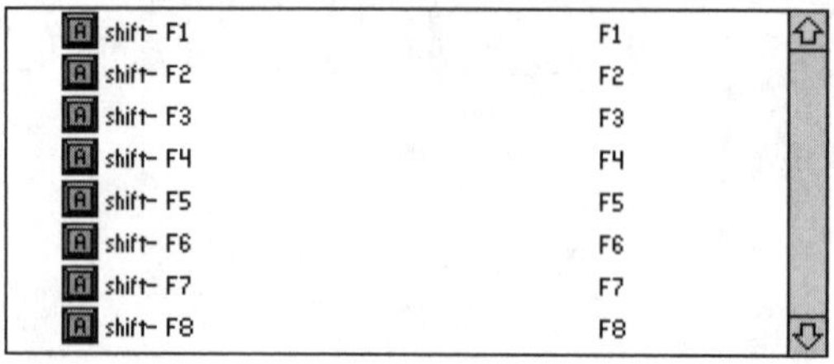

shift~ F1	F1
shift~ F2	F2
shift~ F3	F3
shift~ F4	F4
shift~ F5	F5
shift~ F6	F6
shift~ F7	F7
shift~ F8	F8

With these Alias Keystroke shortcuts, you can select tools without the Toolbox visible and without permanently stretching your left hand.

Toggling the Scroll Bars

Another way to make more space to see your publication is to turn off the scroll bars. This would be fine, since you can still get around with key-click combinations and the Option grabber hand—except that turning off the scroll bars also turns off the Page Number icons, which is annoying in longer documents where PageMaker's Command-Tab page-turning doesn't suffice.

So, set up a Menu Selection shortcut to turn the scroll bars and Page icons on and off (see Figure 20.2).

Figure 20.2
Menu Selection edit dialog box for scroll-bar toggler

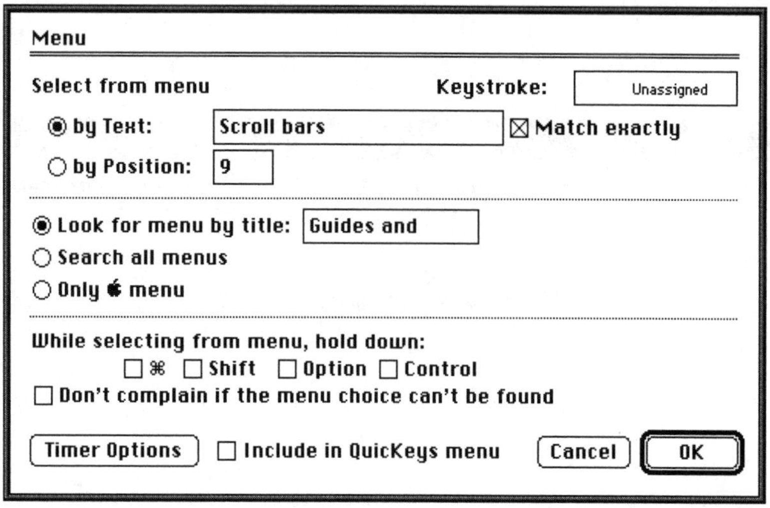

Menu

Select from menu Keystroke: Unassigned

◉ by Text: Scroll bars ☒ Match exactly
○ by Position: 9

◉ Look for menu by title: Guides and
○ Search all menus
○ Only menu

While selecting from menu, hold down:
☐ ⌘ ☐ Shift ☐ Option ☐ Control
☐ Don't complain if the menu choice can't be found

[Timer Options] ☐ Include in QuicKeys menu [Cancel] [OK]

Using Power Paste

When you copy an item and paste it in PageMaker, it pastes the copy a bit offset from the original (if that position is visible in the window). If you hold down Option while choosing Paste, however (or if you press Command-Option-V), the copy pastes directly on top of the original. It's called power paste.

Move that copy, then power paste again. The second copy lands as far from the first as the first lands from the original. Keep power pasting, and you've got step-and-repeat duplication.

Once you've used power paste, you'll never use regular Paste again. So use an Alias Keystroke shortcut to reassign Command-V to invoke Command-Option-V—the power-paste keystroke.

Kerning with Arrows

In PageMaker, Command plus the Right and Left arrow keys (the ones in the inverted T shape) are positive- and negative-kerning keys. For Word users, this is infuriating. Command-Left arrow and Command-Right arrow should move you left and right, one word at a time (PageMaker accomplishes this with the Command key, plus either 4 or 6 from the keypad). So you go to move the cursor a word left or right, and you get kerning instead.

The solution is to set up Alias Keystroke shortcuts, as described in Table 20.2, and to use the normal Delete key-based kerning keystrokes described in Table 20.3. To mimic the normal selection operation, adding the Shift key selects a word at a time.

Table 20.2 — Keys to move and select by word

Bracketed numbers indicate keys on the numeric keypad.

Key combination	Invokes
Command-Left arrow	Command-[4]
Command-Right arrow	Command-[6]
Command-Shift-Left arrow	Command-Shift-[4]
Command-Shift-Right arrow	Command-Shift-[6]

Table 20.3 — PageMaker's kerning keys

Keystroke plus Delete	Result
Command	decrease spacing 1/25 em
Option	decrease spacing 1/100 em
Command-Shift	increase spacing 1/25 em
Option-Shift	increase spacing 1/100 em
Command-Option-K (no Delete key)	remove all kerning

Closing Windows

If you use a Mousie shortcut to close the currently active window, be aware that your shortcut will close any open palettes (Styles or Colors) before it closes the main document window. And since PageMaker remembers whether or not the palettes are open for each document, if you close a palette and then close the document window with a blazing fast double-press of your Close Window shortcut, PageMaker will ask if you want to save changes. The change it's referring to is closing the palette.

You can get around this instead by using a Menu Selection shortcut to choose Close from the File menu. You can hide and close the palettes with PageMaker's built-in keystrokes—Command-Y for Styles, Command-K for Colors, and Command-' for Measurements.

Expanding Palette

PageMaker's Styles palette comes up in a tiny size that's fine if you only have a few styles. If you have a lot of styles, however, you may want the Styles Palette to extend all the way down the right side of the screen, as narrow as it can be (see Figure 20.3).

Positioning the Styles Palette here covers up the right scroll bar, but cool PageMaker users never use scroll bars anyway; they use

Figure 20.3
PageMaker's Styles
Palette

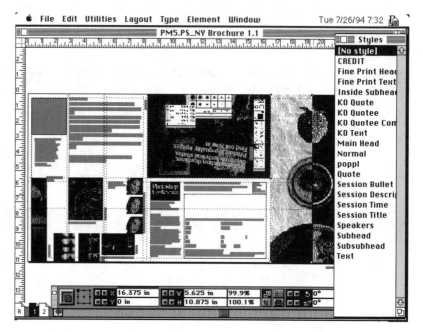

Command-click zooming and the Option-drag grabber hand to get around the page. The palette also covers the Window-sizing icon, but you can use the Tile and Cascade commands on the Window menu to rearrange windows when necessary.

If you want your Styles Palette to look like the one in Figure 20.3, create a Sequence shortcut made up of the two Click shortcuts shown in Figure 20.4. The setup shown there works on an Apple 13-inch RGB display.

Figure 20.4
Styles Palette
shortcut steps

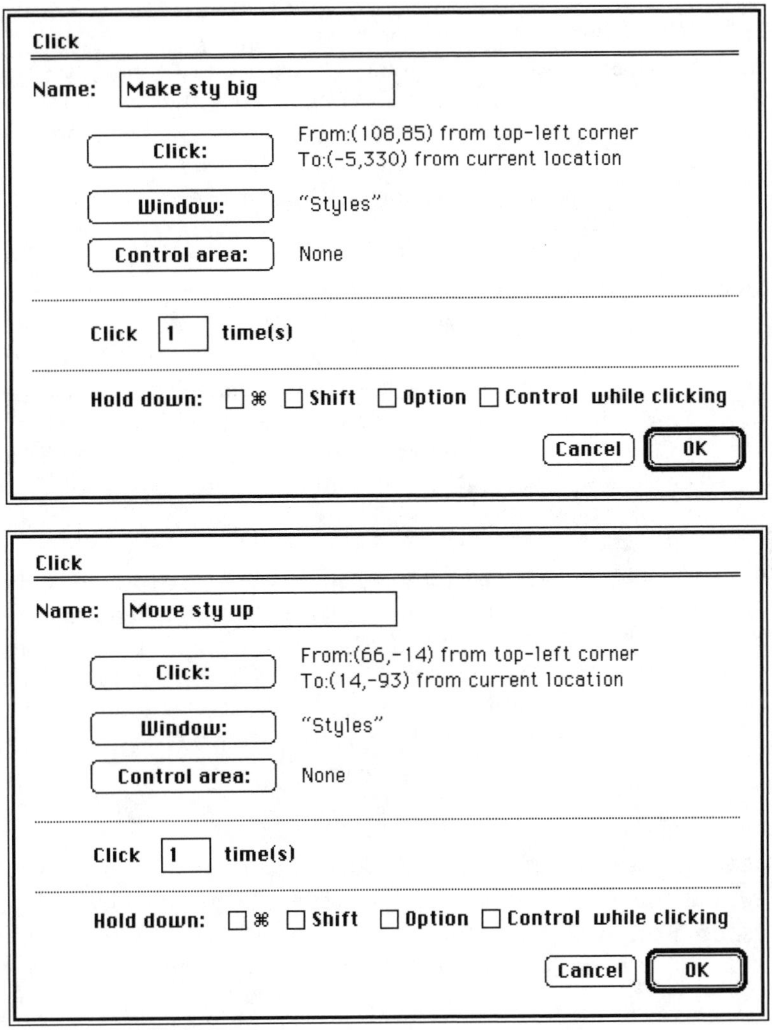

Click

Name: | Make sty big |

Click: — From:(108,85) from top-left corner
To:(-5,330) from current location

Window: — "Styles"

Control area: — None

Click | 1 | time(s)

Hold down: ☐ ⌘ ☐ Shift ☐ Option ☐ Control while clicking

[Cancel] [OK]

Click

Name: | Move sty up |

Click: — From:(66,-14) from top-left corner
To:(14,-93) from current location

Window: — "Styles"

Control area: — None

Click | 1 | time(s)

Hold down: ☐ ⌘ ☐ Shift ☐ Option ☐ Control while clicking

[Cancel] [OK]

If these coordinates don't work on your monitor, create your own two-Click Sequence using the Sequence recorder. The first click of the Sequence drags the palette to the upper-right corner of the window; the second grabs the bottom-right sizing box and stretches the palette.

PageMaker remembers the location of the Styles Palette when you open and close the palette, but it doesn't remember the location between sessions. When you quit PageMaker, then relaunch, the Styles Palette goes back to its original diminutive size; hence the need for this shortcut.

Fit In Window for All Pages

It's a common situation: you've been working on different pages at different magnifications, so every time you change pages you need to switch to Fit in Window view, then zoom in where you want to go. You can change all the pages in a publication to Fit in Window view by pressing Option while choosing Fit in Window (from the Page menu). In our opinion, that's worth a keystroke. Steve uses Command-Control-W.

Reversed Type

Every type style in PageMaker has a keyboard shortcut—Command-Shift-U for underline, Command-Shift-I for italic, and so on. The one type style that doesn't have a shortcut is Reverse, which (besides bold and italic) is the one most people use most.

It's easy enough to assign a Menu Selection shortcut to Reverse, but which keystroke should you use? Command-Shift-R is already taken for Align Right, so Command-Shift-V is a good choice.

Making Fractions

There's no automatic way to make fractions in PageMaker, but by putting the numerator in superscript, the denominator in subscript, replacing the slash (virgule) in between with a fraction slash (solidus), and adjusting your superscript and subscript controls, you can create a good-looking fraction. Table 20.4 shows a Sequence shortcut to do it for you, assuming that you have selected the whole fraction and there's a space to the left of the fraction.

Measurements Palette as Dialog Box

PageMaker's Measurements Palette is a great tool, but there's no doubt that keeping it on screen all the time slows things down. For that reason, Steve prefers to treat it like a dialog box rather than a palette—bringing it up to do his work and then close it again. Table 20.5 shows the keys

Table 20.4	Sequence for making fractions	
Shortcut type	**Entry**	**Action**
Alias Keystroke	Command-T	Open Type Specs dialog box
Button	Options...	Open Type Options dialog box
Text	<tab>60<tab>30<tab>0	Enter superscript and subscript values
Alias Keystroke	Option-Return	Close dialog boxes
Alias Keystroke	[4]	Move cursor off fraction
Alias Keystroke	[6]	Move cursor next to fraction
Alias Keystroke	Shift-[6]	Select numerator
Alias Keystroke	Command-Shift-=	Put numerator in superscript
Alias Keystroke	[6]	Move past slash
Alias Keystroke	Shift-[4]	Select slash
Alias Keystroke	Shift-Option-1	Replace virgule with solidus
Alias Keystroke	Command-Shift-[6]	Select denominator
Alias Keystroke	Command-Shift-(hyphen)	Put denominator in subscript
Alias Keystroke	[6]	Move cursor to right of fraction

Table 20.5	Alias Keystroke shortcuts for the Measurements Palette	
Triggering keystroke	**Action**	**Explanation**
Command-'	Command-' then Command-`	Open the palette and make it active
Command-Enter	Return then Command-'	Apply changes and close the palette

that our cohort Ole Kvern (PageMaker Thunder Lizard extraordinaire) built to make the Measurements Palette act like a dialog box.

So to use the Measurements Palette, Steve presses Command-' (bringing up the palette and making it active), does his work, then presses Command-Enter (applying the changes and closing the palette).

Custom-to-Pica Vertical Rulers

If you work with leading grids like we do, you know what a pain it is to constantly toggle back and forth between Custom and Pica settings for your vertical ruler (in Preferences). Here's a little conditional setup that toggles for you—very quickly.

First create a sequence like the one in Figure 20.5.

Figure 20.5
Custom/Pica Sequence

File Edit Define
Preferences...
Decision
ret

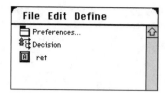

This Sequence opens the Preferences dialog box, makes a decision about what to do, and then once it's made, presses Return to close the dialog box.

Now, how about that decision? Take a look at the dialog box in Figure 20.6.

Figure 20.6
Custom or Pica Decision shortcut

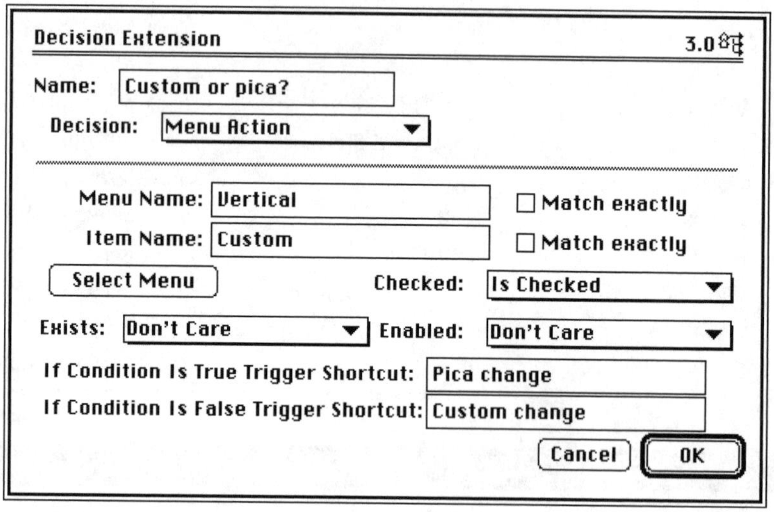

Decision Extension
3.0
Name: Custom or pica?
Decision: Menu Action
Menu Name: Vertical
Match exactly
Item Name: Custom
Match exactly
Select Menu
Checked: Is Checked
Exists: Don't Care
Enabled: Don't Care
If Condition Is True Trigger Shortcut: Pica change
If Condition Is False Trigger Shortcut: Custom change
Cancel
OK

This Decision shortcut looks to see if the Custom option in the Vertical Ruler pop-up menu is checked. If it is, it triggers Pica Change (a pop-up menu shortcut that selects Picas). If it isn't—if some other measurement system is chosen—it triggers Custom Change (another Pop-up Menu shortcut that selects Custom). Figure 20.7 shows the Custom Change shortcut.

Steve uses Command-Option-R to trigger this shortcut, because he thinks it's similar to PageMaker's built-in Command-R shortcut for turning Rulers on and off.

Scripting in PageMaker

PageMaker only understands two Apple Events (aside from the boring core suite)—doscript and evaluate. Both do the same thing; they allow you to send a script to PageMaker in its native scripting language. When you buy PageMaker, you'll find a card in the box for a free copy of the scripting manual. If you haven't sent it, do so, and you'll know most of what you need to know to control PageMaker via scripting. In the meantime,

Figure 20.7
Pop-up Menu
shortcut to select
Custom from the
Vertical Ruler pop-
up menu

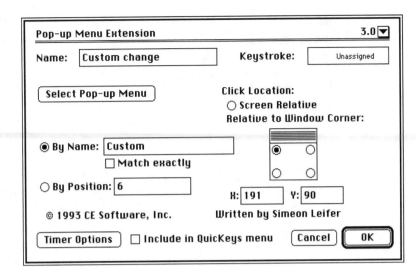

here are a couple of scripting tips you can use with PageMaker and QuicKeys.

Percentage Magnification

You may already know that you can zoom in to arbitrary percentages (and go beyond the normal 400 percent limit to 800 percent) using PageMaker's magnifying glass tool (hold down Command and Spacebar to get this tool; add Option to zoom out). But what if you want to zoom to some arbitrary percentage, like 473 percent, numerically? Here's a two-step sequence to do it.

The first step is a Message shortcut, as in the dialog box in Figure 20.8.

This shortcut brings up a dialog box asking "Zoom to what percentage?" with a text entry field where the user can type a number. QuicKeys puts the number on the Clipboard, ready for use by a DoScript shortcut (Figure 20.9).

The script in this shortcut is incredibly simple: view ^C^. View is a PageMaker scripting command, and, since the Insert Clipboard for ^C^ box is checked, ^C^ inserts the contents of the Clipboard (which we just put there with the Message shortcut).

Trigger this sequence (Control-Z is a good keystroke), and you get a dialog box asking for the zoom percentage. Type it, press Return, and PageMaker dutifully zooms in. As is normal with PageMaker, if you have anything selected on the page, that selection is centered in the zoomed window.

■ ■

Figure 20.8
Message shortcut
to ask for
percentage

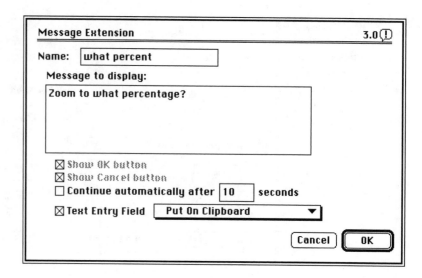

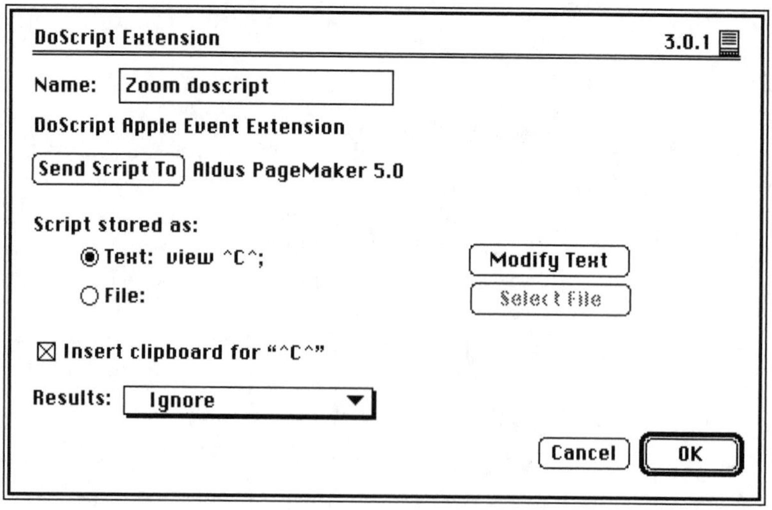

Message Extension   3.0 ⓘ

Name: │what percent│

Message to display:

┌──┐
│ Zoom to what percentage?   │
│   │
│   │
│   │
│   │
└──┘

☒ Show OK button
☒ Show Cancel button
☐ Continue automatically after │10│   seconds
☒ Text Entry Field   │Put On Clipboard   ▼│

[Cancel]   [OK]

Figure 20.9
DoScript shortcut
to zoom to
selected
percentage

DoScript Extension   3.0.1 ▤

Name: │Zoom doscript│
DoScript Apple Event Extension

[Send Script To] Aldus PageMaker 5.0

Script stored as:
   ◉ Text: view ^C^;   [Modify Text]
   ○ File: [Select File]

☒ Insert clipboard for "^C^"

Results: │Ignore   ▼│

[Cancel]   [OK]

■ ■ ■ ■ ■

**Suppress
Printing for
Page Elements**

One useful feature found in QuarkXPress but not (or at least not easily)
in PageMaker is the ability to suppress the printing of page elements.
So a box, text block, or whatever on the page, visible on screen, doesn't
print. This is handy for putting notes and such into templates that other
people will use.

■ ■

It turns out that in fact PageMaker does support this feature, but only through a script command: Suppressprint. You can set up DoScript shortcuts to turn print suppression on and off for selected elements. Figure 20.10 shows the DoScript shortcut edit dialog box.

Figure 20.10
DoScript shortcut
for suppressing
printing

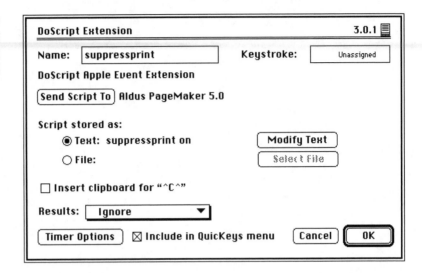

The script in this shortcut is two words: suppressprint on. Create another shortcut with the script: suppressprint off. Then, in PageMaker, select the elements whose printing you want to suppress, and trigger the Suppressprint shortcut. The object(s) look the same (in fact there's no way to tell that the print bit has been set, aside from querying PageMaker with a script), but they don't print. Use the Suppressprint Off shortcut to make them print again.

Steve prefers to access these shortcuts from the QuicKeys menu, because he doesn't use them very often.

21 QuicKeys and Excel

Like many other Mac programs, Excel has a myriad of keyboard shortcuts of its own for its most used features. Plus, to make it work like the Windows version of Excel and Lotus 1-2-3, Microsoft added the ability to access all menu commands with the keyboard by pressing the Slash key (/) followed by a sequence of letters corresponding to with menus, items, buttons, and so forth. This means that your hands may not need to leave the keyboard at any time.

Nevertheless, as we have seen elsewhere in this book, there are many reasons to use shortcuts. This chapter will explore those which hold true in Excel.

- To remap Excel's keyboard shortcuts with more mnemonic substitutes

- To create shortcuts left out by Microsoft

- To create editing Sequences

Excel's Menu Keys

Since you can do almost everything in Excel from the keyboard, the best way to get started is to practice. Turn the Command Underline feature on (see Figure 21.1) and begin to use it. Excel menus change when you have Command Underline turned on. Instead of mousing to Save As on the File menu, you can type /FA; or you can type /RE instead of choosing Replace from the Formula menu.

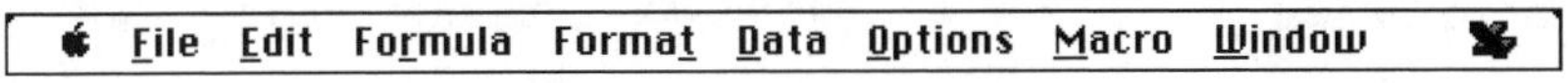

Figure 21.1
Accessing Excel menus from the keyboard

＊ **File Edit Fo_rmula Forma_t Data Options Macro Window** 🐛

291

To turn on Command Underline, select the Workspace command from the Options menu (see Figure 21.2) and click the On radio button in the Command Underline section at the bottom of the dialog box. This lets you see what keys to press to activate menus. Even if you don't use the Slash key technique much initially, you're likely to learn the keys by osmosis.

Figure 21.2
Excel's Workspace edit dialog box

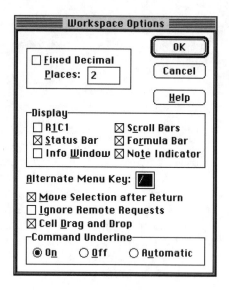

So once again, why use shortcuts? Consistency is one reason. You can build shortcuts to align cell entries, for example (see below), using easy-to-remember keystrokes. Before we get to that, though, a little philosophy.

Print Preview

Print Preview is so often used that it really deserves a more straightforward keyboard shortcut than /FV. Command-Option-P is a great keystroke for a Print Preview Menu Selection shortcut.

Paging and Scrolling Up and Down

In Excel, you move the position of the current selection when you use the Page up, Page down, Up arrow, and Down arrow keys. If you want to move your view without moving the selection point (to Shift-select a range of cells, for instance) and without using the scroll bars, you can use Page Up, Page Down, Line Up, and Line Down Mousies shortcuts (see Figure 21.3).

Figure 21.3
Some movement shortcuts

Page up
⌘-pgup
Page down
⌘-pgdn
Line up
⌘- ↑
Line down
⌘- ↓

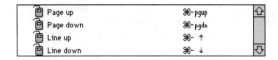

We had to dig to find modifier key combinations for these Mousies that didn't map over existing shortcuts in Excel. We use Control-Command, but Control-Option-Command will also do. Now we can move around the worksheet without resorting to the scroll bars.

Aligning Text

To center text in a cell, you normally type /TAC and then press Return—not exactly what you'd expect. How about remapping the command so Word's standard Command-Shift-C centers cells (a Click shortcut used to select the Center Alignment button on the tool bar)? See Figure 21.4.

Figure 21.4
Click to center a cell in Excel

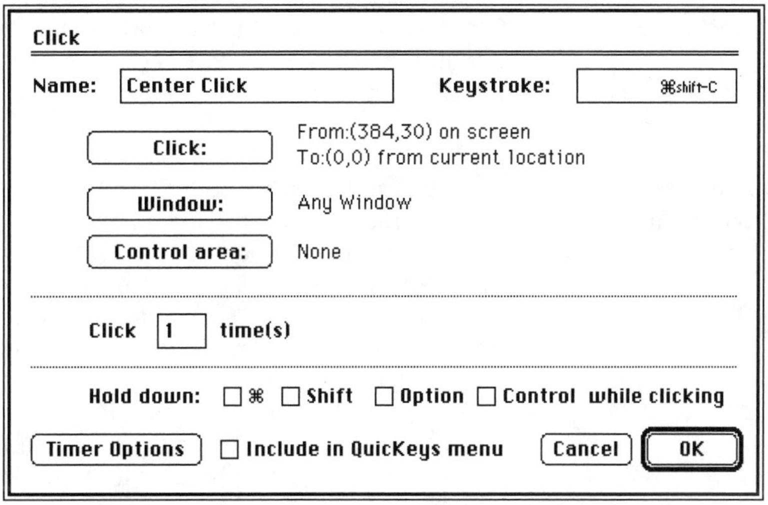
Click
Name:
Center Click
Keystroke:
⌘shift-C
Click:
From:(384,30) on screen
To:(0,0) from current location
Window:
Any Window
Control area:
None
Click
1
time(s)
Hold down:
⌘
Shift
Option
Control
while clicking
Timer Options
Include in QuicKeys menu
Cancel
OK

To create shortcuts for right- and left-aligning cells, copy this Click shortcut and paste it back into your set twice. Double-click on each new shortcut, and change the names, keystrokes, and the x-coordinate of the click definition to conform to your monitor (the Excel toolbar buttons' coordinates shift depending on the monitor's size). An easy way to determine the values to offset the x-coordinate for the two outside buttons is to use Corner, the shareware INIT discussed in Chapter 7, *Shortcuts that Mimic the Keyboard and Mouse.* The values that work on my 13-inch, 640 × 480-pixel display are shown in Table 21.1.

Table 21.1	Text alignment shortcuts			
Alignment	Keystroke	x=	y=	
Left	Command-Shift-L	360	30	
Center	Command-Shift-C	384	30	
Right	Command-Shift-R	408	30	

Paste Function

It's impossible to remember all of Excel's myriad functions. With the Paste Function command on the Formula menu, you don't need to—Excel presents you with a cataloged list of all available functions, along with their arguments. Unfortunately, there is no keyboard shortcut for Paste Function. This is an excellent place to use a Menu Selection shortcut—assign Paste Function a keyboard command.

Make a Menu Selection shortcut for Paste Function with a keystroke of Option-Command-F. This can now be used at any time, even when editing in the formula bar, to bring up the Paste Function dialog box and insert a function with all its arguments.

Comment/ Uncomment

Excel won't let you enter an incorrect formula. This is good policy to minimize errors, but it means you need to type each formula exactly right before leaving the editing line. This is not realistic, since people don't always have the information needed to do it correctly. To store a temporary formula, we fool Excel into thinking of the formula as text by typing a character in front of the equal sign which starts every formula. Adding and deleting this extra comment character requires some attentive mousing, but creating two small shortcut Sequences to comment and uncomment is quite simple. For our comment character, we prefer the bullet (Option-8), because it shouts, "Comment," to us whenever we see it.

To add the bullet as your comment character, your Sequence should include these steps.

1. A Click step that clicks at the far left side of the Formula bar (the flashing insertion point appears in front of the equal sign). Figure 21.5 shows you the Click Location dialog box for this Formula Start Click step for one of our monitors.

2. A Text step that types the bullet character in front of the formula.

Figure 21.5
Clicking at the
beginning of the
formula

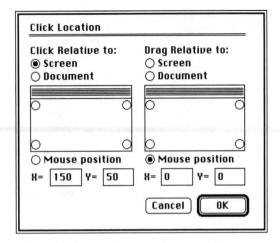

3. An Alias Keystroke step that presses Enter to accept the change. Remember to hold down the mouse button while pressing Enter to place that keystroke in the Key To Type text field.

To create a Sequence (see Figure 21.6) that uncomments the formula, copy the Comment Sequence and make a few changes.

1. Again, begin with the Formula Start Click.

2. Include an Option-Right Arrow Alias Keystroke step to move the insertion point in the Formula bar between the first and second characters.

Figure 21.6
Uncommenting a
formula

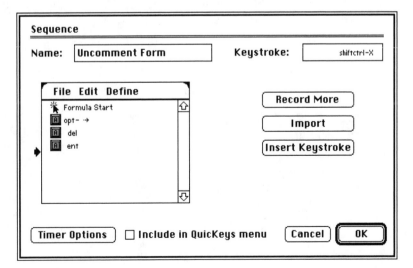

3. Make another Alias Keystroke step that deletes the extra character.

4. Use the same Alias Keystroke step as before to type Enter to accept the change.

These two Sequences, or modifications of them, are excellent for use in macros to skip certain cells containing commands you may not always want executed; for instance, the = STEP() command for debugging.

Repetitive Editing

Shortcuts for sophisticated editing within cells? You bet. Say you've got a list of names in a column and you want to split the first and last names into separate cells. Hours of repetitive editing? *Au contraire*: one shortcut.

If we remember that the Formula bar in Excel is a little word-processing area that acts a lot like Word, things will be easier. Here's what the Alias Keystroke-based Sequence should do (see Figure 21.7).

1. Press Command-U. This activates the Formula bar and places the insertion pointer at the end of the formula (a name, in this case).

2. Press Command-Shift-Left arrow. As in Word, this selects the word to the left of the insertion pointer (the last name).

3. Press Command-X to cut the last name.

4. Press Delete to remove the space between the first and last names.

5. Press Tab to move one cell to the right. The first name is now in the original cell.

6. Press Command-V to paste the last name into the current cell.

7. Press Return to accept the entry and move down one row.

8. Press Left arrow to move to the next cell to be processed.

Figure 21.7
Name splitting

If you really want to automate this process, place a Repeat shortcut at the beginning and end of the Sequence. QuicKeys will keep fixing up those names until you tell it to stop. For more on using Repeat, see Chapter 15, *Sequence Shortcuts*.

Now it's true that you can do this same maneuver a lot faster using Excel's text functions, but you may be able to create the shortcut and run it faster than you can figure out how to use those Excel functions. The fastest way to create this Sequence is to go through the eight steps while running the Sequence recorder. However, this results in some unnecessary Wait and Pause steps, which considerably slow down the execution of the finished Sequence. Just edit these out at the same time you add your Repeat steps, and the Sequence will move along smartly.

Day and Time Stamp

Use this Alias Keystroke Sequence to put the current day and time into a given cell (see Figure 21.8). This Sequence can be created quickly with the Sequence recorder.

1. Type Command--(hyphen) to enter the current date.

2. Type a space to separate day from time.

3. Type Command-; to enter the current time.

4. Press Enter to accept the entry.

Figure 21.8
Entering date and
time

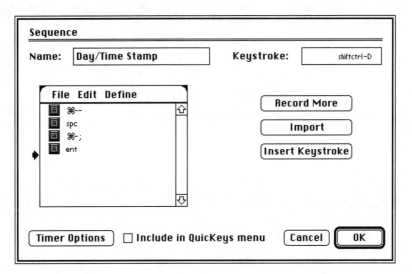

Pasting Values and Formats

The Paste Special command is one we use constantly. First you copy some cells containing formulas, and then you paste only the formulas, values, or formats (see Figure 21.9).

Figure 21.9

Paste Special
dialog box

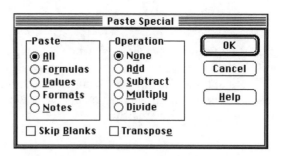

We use these functions so often that we've created shortcut Sequences for the four most common Paste Special setups, as show in Table 21.2.

These Paste Special Sequences consist of three steps each—select Paste Special, press a keyboard shortcut that selects the appropriate radio button option (through Excel's Command Underline feature) and then press Enter. You can't use Button shortcuts for the second step because they don't seem to work in this dialog box.

Table 21.2	Paste Special shortcuts	
Keystroke	**Pastes**	
Option-Command-R	Formulas	
Option-Command-V	Values	
Option-Command-T	Formats	
Option-Command-N	Notes	

Format Broadcaster

Sometimes we have spiffy formatting for a cell, that we want to apply to other areas within the spreadsheet. The usual method for doing this is to copy the cell, select the target cells to be formatted, and then apply a format-only Paste Special. We've already shown you how to speed up this process by creating a format-only Paste Special shortcut. Now here's a way to use another Sequence shortcut to make things even faster.

This Sequence copies the formatting of a cell (or cells) you've highlighted and pauses for you to select a target cell (or cells). Then that target is given the same format as the original cell. We made this Sequence by importing the three steps of our format-only Paste Special shortcut into the new Sequence (see Figure 21.10).

Figure 21.10

Importing shortcuts into our Format Broadcaster Sequence

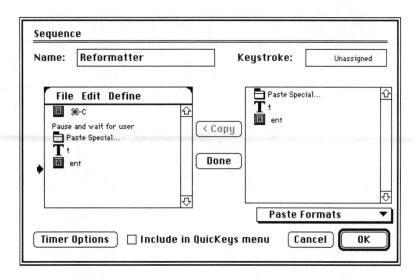

The Pause step that is built into this Sequence is a little tricky. It would be nice just to pause for a short period of time (five seconds, for example) while you select the target cells. But you can't do a timed Pause step, because you usually drag the mouse to select the target cells, and clicking the mouse during a Sequence interrupts the Sequence.

Instead, you must include a Pause and Wait for User step, which means that the Sequence must be manually unpaused to get it to perform the rest of the Sequence. The easy way to do that is to click the Pause/Resume button on the Sequence Playback Palette that appears when you trigger the shortcut. Or you can have a Pause/Unpause shortcut (the Pause Special) in your Universal Set that you can trigger after you select the target cells. F15 is a good choice for this shortcut, because the key has pause written on it.

Excel and Apple Events

Excel has a pretty good arsenal of Apple Events (and—what a surprise—a robust if flawed aete resource to accompany them). Among other things, you can execute any Excel macro with an Apple Event.

To see the Apple Events that Excel supports, launch Excel, then create an Apple Events shortcut (from the Scripting Tools category of the Extensions submenu of the Define menu). Select Excel as the target application, then click Select Event.

The Apple Events that Excel supports are divided into several suites, the most complete being the Core suite. The Apple Event that's of most importance, however, is in the Excel suite: Evaluate. That's next.

Excel's Evaluate Apple Event

Excel's Evaluate Apple Event will crunch any formula you send it (any valid formula, that is) and send back the result. You can also use it to trigger macros you've defined within an Excel worksheet.

There's only one problem (it took us several days to figure this out): Excel's aete resource has an error, so if you create an Evaluate Apple Event, it just plain doesn't work. To be precise, the aete defines the data type of the event's one parameter to be ****. In fact, it should be of type TEXT. There's no way to fix this if you define the Evaluate Apple Event by selecting it in the Select Event dialog box; QuicKeys doesn't let you change the parameter's type.

The solution is to create a custom Apple Event shortcut instead, much like the one we created for HyperCard in Chapter 16, *Apple Events and Scripting*. Figure 21.11 shows the dialog boxes for creating this shortcut.

Notice that the Event ID for this Apple Event is mcro. This may explain why Microsoft tech notes we've downloaded call it GetMacro instead of Evaluate. In any case, this shortcut takes anything from the Clipboard and sends it to Excel to evaluate (or if it's a macro, to execute). Excel sends back the result.

To use it, copy some expression in a format Excel understands—like sqrt(44) or 2437/57—then trigger the shortcut. You'll see a dialog box like the one in Figure 21.12.

To make this shortcut really useful, include it in a Sequence. Steve has one where the first step is a Command-C Alias Keystroke step, which copies whatever's selected to the Clipboard. Then comes the Evaluate shortcut (with Return Value set to Clipboard) and a Decision shortcut to branch the sequence based on what's in the Clipboard. The possibilities are endless.

Running Macros with Apple Events

You can use the very same Apple Event shortcut we just created to trigger macros that you've defined in Excel. Just use this parameter value:

```
run(macrosheetname!macroname)
```

For instance, run **(MyMacros!CleanUp)**. If there are special characters in the macro name (spaces or whatever), enclose the name in quotation marks.

There are a few things to be aware of when running Excel macros via Apple Events, however (we learned these from several postings on CompuServe by Don Birmingham—71360,653). First, Excel seems in some situations calculate differently, or at least in a different order,

Figure 21.11
Setup for a custom
Excel Evaluate
Apple Event

Apple® Events Extension   3.0.1

Name: `ExcCust Eval AE`   Keystroke: [Unassigned]

Send Event to: [**Microsoft Excel** ▼]

[**Select Event:**] **Custom Event**   For those with an intimate knowledge of Apple e...

Parameter Name	Description	Required?	Value
expression	expression to evaluate	Yes	*value from clipboard*

[New...] [Edit...] [Remove]   Event Class: `XCEL`

Return Value: [**Display Full** ▼]   Event ID: `mcro`

[Timer Options] ☒ Include in QuicKeys menu   [Cancel] [OK]

Parameter Specifier

Number : 1 (of 1)   KeyWord: `----`   Type : TEXT ▼ ☒ Required

Name: `expression`

Description: `expression to evaluate, or macro to run`

Get Parameter Value From:

◉ **Clipboard**
○ **Data:** [   ]   [Previous]
                                          [Next]
                                          [Cancel]
                                          [OK]

Figure 21.12
Results dialog box
from the Evaluate
Apple Event
shortcut

QuicKeys/Apple Event Information:

**ExcCust Eval AE sent a Custom Event Apple Event to
Microsoft Excel
The return value was:
6.6332495807108**

[OK]

when you run macros via Apple Events. Watch out! Also, if the macro takes a long time and you've set the Return Value to Wait, QuicKeys might tire of waiting and proceed on its merry way. A workaround for this: have your macro finish by creating a new document, and use a Window Action Wait shortcut instead.

Howard Hansen contributed a significant portion of this chapter. Howard is a Seattle-based Macintosh consultant specializing in Microsoft Excel programming, training, and consulting.

22 QuicKeys and FileMaker Pro

Even though FileMaker Pro features a healthy number of keyboard shortcuts and a robust internal scripting language, QuicKeys can be a useful adjunct to FileMaker in a variety of ways. Simple Alias Keystroke shortcuts for keyboard navigation within the program are handy, especially to select items from the Script menu. More complex macros can save a lot of time when you're processing database information, especially record-to-record data. In the range between the simple and the complex, various utility operations can make data entry and manipulation more efficient. And for the more adventurous, FileMaker Pro provides extensive support for Apple Events, including the ability to send an Apple Event from within a FileMaker Pro script.

Menu Shortcuts

Although most FileMaker Pro commands have their own triggering keystrokes, three of the commands we use most often don't. And FileMaker Pro scripts either don't have activating keystrokes or have keystrokes we don't like. We choose these menu items with Menu Selection shortcuts.

Commands. Importing and exporting records is one of the most common activities for many FileMaker Pro users, but you must select these commands from a submenu of the File menu. We set Control-Command-I as Import Records and Control-Command-E as Export Records. The entries that QuicKeys automatically makes in the Menu Selection text edit box work fine to select these submenu items. Likewise, we often find ourselves choosing Find Omitted from the Select menu after we've just made a Find. Our Menu Selection shortcut, triggered with Control-Command-F, works just fine.

Scripts. FileMaker Pro's internal scripting capability works great, but its hard-wired feature of assigning Command-1 through Command-0 as triggering keystrokes for the first 10 scripts on the Scripts menu certainly lacks elasticity. So we trigger our favorite scripts with Menu Selection shortcuts. Don uses Control-Option-Command as his modifier keys with the first letter of each script's name as a trigger.

Switching Layouts

Okay, okay. We usually say you should preferentially use a program's internal method of performing an action, rather than using QuicKeys, and now we are going to contradict that—with good reason. We often work with FileMaker Pro files that contain many layouts, and we switch between these layouts frequently. You can script FileMaker to switch to a layout, but as we said in "Menu Shortcuts" earlier, we end up building a shortcut to trigger the script. Since we would use a shortcut anyway, we just build Pop-up Menu shortcuts to switch to our most popular layouts, but we have to tweak them *just right* to make them work. When you click the Select Pop-up Menu button in the Pop-up Menu edit dialog box and then choose a layout, QuicKeys makes some entries in the edit dialog box that look something like those in Figure 22.1.

If you trigger this shortcut it doesn't work—instead you can see the cursor trying to find the pop-up menu about an inch to the right of the pop-up menu. Editing the x-coordinate of the click location sets things right. To account for the distance of approximately 72 pixels (one inch),

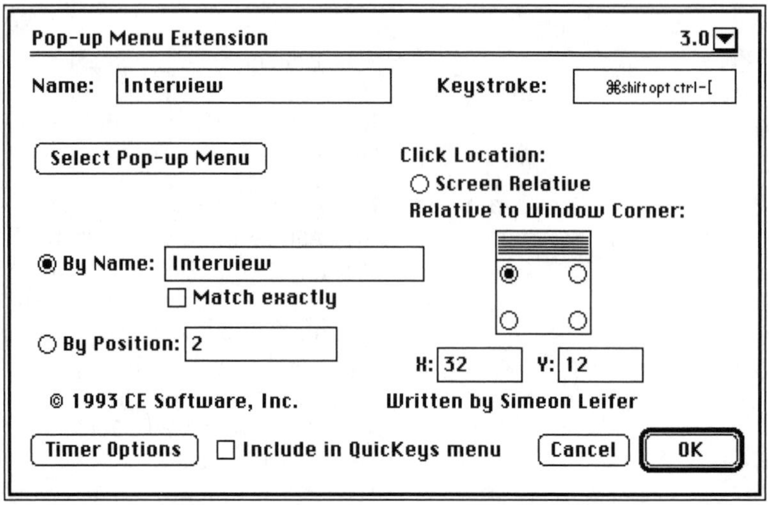

Figure 22.1
Pop-up Menu edit dialog box with automatic entries

Figure 22.2
New and improved
x-coordinate

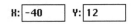

just subtract 72 from 32. If you enter –40 as the x-coordinate (see Figure 22.2), the shortcut works perfectly.

Paging Through the FileMaker Book Icon

The book metaphor (see Figure 22.3) is used by FileMaker to move from record to record (in Browse mode) or from layout to layout (in Layout mode). FileMaker has built-in key commands for moving through the book as an alternative to mousing through it. Command-Tab moves to the next record (or page) and Command-Shift-Tab moves to the previous.

But many users want to avoid mental confusion and save all tabbing for moving between fields, rather than records. Plus, with the Page

Figure 22.3
Moving through
records and
layouts

up, Page down, Home, and End keys available and so logically associated with the Book icon, it makes sense to use these keys to trigger shortcuts that move through the book. However, if you have a FileMaker Pro layout so large that you must scroll to see it all, these keys in their unmodified form move you around the window. So we have defined Alias Keystroke shortcuts that use Command-Page up for moving to a previous record and Command-Page down for moving to the next. And we have Sequences that use Command-Home to move you to your first record and Command-End to move you to the last.

These Move-to-first-record and Move-to-last-record Sequences utilize (and overcome) FileMaker's awkward method of moving to a particular record. If you click on the field under the Book icon, type in a record number, and press Return, you will go to the record of that number. But that's a lot of clicking and typing, especially if you go to either the first or the last record often. You can also select this Go To Record field by pressing Esc (of all things!) but this only works if you don't have a field currently selected in your database, so it's not consistently useful (and then you still have to type in the record number and press Return).

A Click shortcut with several variations can help you overcome this deficiency. First select Record One Shortcut from the QuicKeys menu (or trigger your shortcut for the same—see "Record One Shortcut" in Chapter 13, *Shortcuts That Control QuicKeys*). Click on the field beneath the Card icon. In the Click edit dialog box that appears, name this shortcut Click card field and assign it whatever keystroke you like, possibly Command-Control-G for go to, or Command-Control-J for jump. Click OK.

Next select the shortcut and copy it. Create a Sequence. Paste the Click as the first item and then create a Text shortcut containing the single digit 1, followed by return. You can call this Sequence something like First Card Jump. We use Command-Home as the trigger.

FileMaker doesn't let you type end or last or anything like that to take you to the last card, but it does let you enter an arbitrary large number. So copy the Click again, make a new Sequence, paste the Click in, and then define a Text shortcut containing 9999999 and a return. When the return is entered, this number will change to the actual highest record number. We trigger this Sequence with—you guessed it—Command-End.

Filling in Forms

You can use QuicKeys effectively for completing repetitive forms or orders. FileMaker is quite good at providing automatic and semi-automatic field fill-in with auto-entry, lookups, and popups. Even so, in many cases QuicKeys can, with one initiating keystroke, type for us a series of entries in a series of fields. Even the tabs that move the cursor between fields can be included in the QuicKeys Sequence. Data entered by QuicKeys can go on to trigger subsequent FileMaker lookups.

The key to efficient use of such macros is to realize that while individual records may be quite distinct overall, nonetheless, sometimes there are subsets of information that tend to be entered together. In an order-entry form, it may be that most customers who buy item 1023 usually also buy items 2204 and 2310, so it makes sense to enter all three with a Sequence shortcut, even if once in a while it is necessary to go back and change or delete an item. On a personnel form, perhaps once a new employee is designated as an engineer, she automatically becomes salaried and first shift and an E is used to begin her employee number. QuicKeys can enter all this for you.

If you need to transfer several items from one record to another (perhaps the address needs updating for multiple customers at one company), QuicKeys is very good at taking advantage of the FileMaker Paste From Last Record function, which can paste from one record to another without repetitive movements back and forth. For example, if you have four fields whose contents often repeat from one record to the next, you can create a Sequence shortcut with four identical Alias Keystroke steps that press Shift-Command-' (apostrophe), FileMaker Pro's keystroke for paste from last record and move to the next field.

QuicKeys can be useful in deleting information, too. Perhaps you keep Last Order Date information in a database, and the duplicate record has been imported from an order entry file to update the order history for this customer. QuicKeys can copy from the Last Order Date field, mark the record for deletion, move to the previous record, tab to the Last Order Date field, highlight and paste, and then clear the temporary field.

Temporary QuicKeys

In addition to fixtures like those described above, there always seem to be recurring data-editing situations where a shortcut or two can be created just for a specific short-term task and then disposed of. Since recording a shortcut is now so easy, temporary tasks invite temporary macros, even strange and convoluted ones.

For example, in imported addresses from an outside source, some data may appear in a wrong field. The source may have mixed up the Title and the Organization fields. They can be rearranged easily using FileMaker equations if the reversed ones can be identified all at once. Otherwise, a little shortcut can be activated selectively as you encounter a reversed situation during manual scanning.

To make a temporary QuicKey easy to identify later for deletion, you can use a unique naming scheme (like putting X in front of each one) or a unique key combination. We suggest using Command-Control-Option-Shift, which makes it easy to edit out later. Even just Command-Control-Option (all lined up) will work nicely.

Sending Apple Events to FileMaker Pro

FileMaker Pro supports a healthy number of Apple Events. If you aren't familiar with Apple Events, refer to Chapter 16, *Apple Events and Scripting*. Sending Apple Events to FileMaker Pro is similar to sending Apple Events to other programs except you can't send to a remote FileMaker Pro application.

All of FileMaker's events are contained in two suites: the Required suite, and a catch-all suite that supports a subset of events from the Core, Table, and Database suites. The Apple Events Examples folder on FileMaker Pro's Utilities disk provides good online documentation for how to work with these events. You can use Apple Events with FileMaker to retrieve data from cells or set cells to particular values. Or, with the doscript Apple Event, you can play a FileMaker Pro script that you already have within the program.

Couldn't be simpler: when FileMaker receives a doscript Apple Event, the FileMaker script named in the event is played. For example, a company may have a FileMaker Pro database set up that contains its customer accounts. Every week the company treasurer executes a

Sequence shortcut that queries the FileMaker Pro database, first executing an internal FileMaker script named 60 Days Overdue that makes a subset of those accounts that are 60 days or more overdue. Then subsequent steps in the Sequence transfer pertinent data from FileMaker Pro to cells of a spreadsheet. It is then made into a chart of age of receivables. The first step of the Sequence is a DoScript shortcut that looks like Figure 22.4.

Figure 22.4
DoScript shortcut

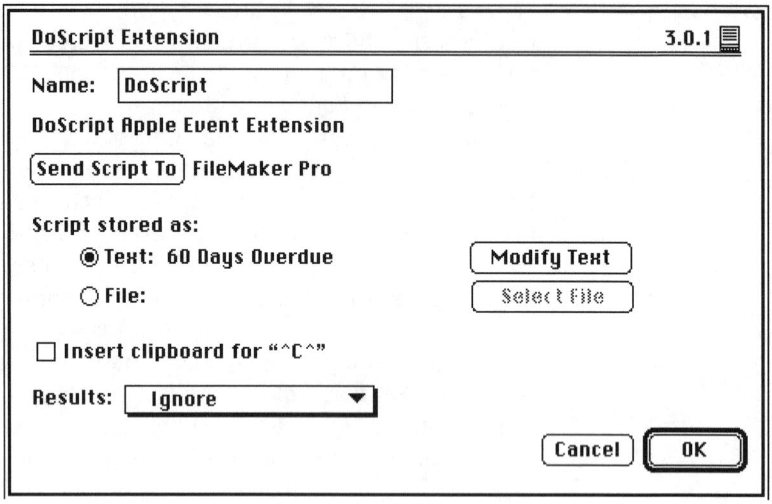

The name of the FileMaker Pro script has been entered as the text the script is stored in. When the Sequence that contains this DoScript step is executed (and FileMaker Pro is running), then the FileMaker script is executed.

Controlling FileMaker Pro with AppleScripts

You also can control FileMaker Pro at a lower level, using AppleScripts. As we suggest in Chapter 16, *Apple Events and Scripting*, even if you end up sending your AppleScript via a QuicKeys AppleScript shortcut, you'll probably want to develop and debug your script first with a script editing program like Script Editor. Just to give you the feel of this capability, check out the following simple script.

```
tell application "FileMaker Pro"
  Get Data of Cell "Company" in the 333rd Record in ¬
  Layout "Main" in Database "Zap.fmp"
end tell
```

Even an AppleScript novice can tell what this script does. You can package this script in an AppleScript shortcut and send it with a keystroke. Back comes the data in that cell.

Triggering Shortcuts with Apple Events

We've already mentioned that FileMaker's internal scripting language offers a wide variety of tools for automating tasks within the program. However, there are times when it can't perform an critical operation, but a QuicKeys shortcut does the job nicely.

Fortunately, the designers of FileMaker (and QuicKeys) have included the ability to trigger a QuicKeys shortcut from within a FileMaker script—by using an Apple Event. And if you want to get fancy with this capability, you can actually create the needed QuicKeys shortcut within a FileMaker script, using QuicKeys Script, and send it to QuicKeys Toolbox for execution.

Playing an Existing Shortcut

We know a conference company that has a good example of calling a shortcut from within a FileMaker Pro script. Every day, this company receives many registrations for their conferences, and the information is entered into a FileMaker Pro database. At the end of the day, the company's operations manager (let's call her Marci) finds the records for that day's registrants, prints out their invoices, and then prints out addresses on envelopes on another printer.

Marci's FileMaker Pro script can do all these steps except one, switching to the envelope printer; FileMaker doesn't have a command to select printers through the Chooser. For that, she has her script send an Apple Event to QuicKeys Toolbox to trigger a Choosy shortcut. Here's how she did it.

In the edit dialog box for her FileMaker script, Marci double-clicked on Send Apple Event in the Available Steps scrolling window. The step moved into the right-hand window containing the steps for her script. Double-clicking the Send Apple Event step there evoked the Specify Apple Event edit dialog box (see Figure 22.5) with the doscript option already chosen in the Send Event pop-up menu.

In this case, she didn't want to send a doscript, but instead a playbyname Apple Event—she knew it was that particular Apple event by previously using the QuicKeys Apple Events Shortcut edit dialog box to determine the Apple Events that QuicKeys Toolbox could receive (see Chapter 16, *Apple Events and Scripting*). She chose the Other option from the Send Event pop-up menu and a Specify Event edit dialog box appeared. She entered QKy2 for the event class and QPNm for the

Figure 22.5
Specify Apple
Event edit dialog
box

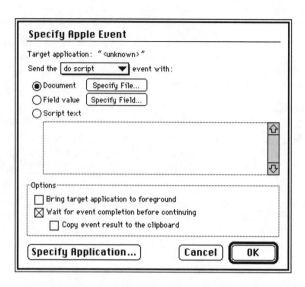

event ID (see Figure 22.6) and clicked OK. Marci found these codes using the Apple Events edit dialog box, and entered them very carefully, because she knew they were case-sensitive.

Figure 22.6
Specify Event edit
dialog box with
playbyname codes

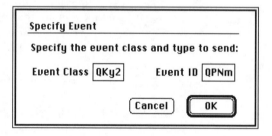

Next she clicked the Script Text radio button and entered the name of the shortcut (Pleiades, the name of her printer) in the text edit box. She then clicked the Specify Application button so she could tell FileMaker to send the Apple Event to QuicKeys Toolbox. An open edit dialog box appeared from which she navigated to QuicKeys Toolbox (it's in the Extensions folder in the System folder) and selected it. She kept the Wait For Event Completion Before Continuing option, as it was already selected.

The completed edit dialog box looked like that in Figure 22.7. When she triggered her FileMaker script, Pleiades was selected in the Chooser.

Figure 22.7
Completed Specify
Apple Event edit
dialog box

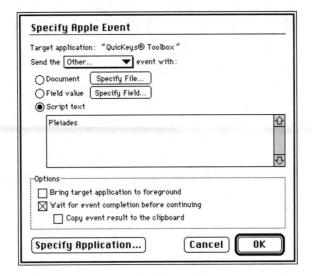

But be careful about checking the Wait For Event Completion Before Continuing Option checkbox. We've found that there's some sort of conflict between FileMaker waiting for an Apple Event completion, and QuicKeys waiting. So sometimes you get an unintended pause when you send multiple Apple Events to QuicKeys Toolbox, or when you trigger a QuicKeys Sequence with a playbyname Apple Event from FileMaker Pro. Unchecking the Wait For Event Completion Before Continuing Option checkbox has kept our procedure from getting stuck.

Playing a Shortcut Written from within FileMaker

But what if the shortcut you want to trigger from a FileMaker script doesn't exist? Maybe your FileMaker script is running on multiple machines, or you just don't trust Marci not to delete your essential shortcut. You can write the shortcut in QuicKeys Script and use a doscript Apple Event to send it to QuicKeys Toolbox for execution.

The process is very similar to the previous example, but you choose doscript from the Send Event pop-up menu, and instead of the name of the shortcut to play in the Text edit box, you enter the QuicKeys Script that defines the shortcut. To define a Choosy shortcut that changes the printer to Pleiades, the script looks like that in Figure 22.8.

The easy way to create scripts in QuicKeys Script is to record them in Apple's Script Editor (see "QuicKeys Script" in Chapter 16, *Apple Events and Scripting*). But simple ones like the Marci's Choosy script are pretty easy to write from scratch. You won't find documentation for

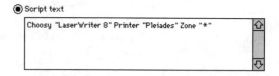

Figure 22.8
QuicKeys Script for
Choosy that
switches to
Pleiades

QuicKeys Script in your QuicKeys manuals, but if you made a full installation of QuicKeys you will find extensive documentation in the QuicKeys Script Info folder in the QuicKeys Tools folder.

Joe Kroeger contributed a significant portion of this chapter. Joe is editor of The FileMaker Report, *a journal for FileMaker users. Box 1300, Freedom, CA 95019; 408-761-5466.*

23 QuicKeys and QuarkXPress

The first thing to know about using QuicKeys with QuarkXPress is this: in order for Menu Selection shortcuts to work, you almost always need to select the Search All Menus option in the Menu Selection shortcut editing dialog box. Otherwise (we don't know why), QuicKeys can't find the menu items.

Bring to Front and Send to Back

The most important keystroke shortcuts missing from QuarkXPress are those to invoke the Bring to Front and Send to Back commands.

We believe that these commands are so important (especially in QuarkXPress, which is forever making boxes opaque) that they need single-modifier Command-based keystrokes—like Command-F and Command-B. Unfortunately, these keystrokes are already taken (for the Find and Frame commands). So using Alias Keystroke shortcuts we redefine the keystrokes for Find (to Command-H, as in change) and Frame (to Command-E, as in edge), neither of which is used for anything else in QuarkXPress. Then we use Command-F and Command-B for the Bring to Front and Send to Back commands.

Alternately, you can get around the problem by using the shortcuts used in Adobe Illustrator—Command-+ and Command-- (hyphen).

QuarkXPress 3.1 also has Bring Forward and Send Back commands, which move the item one layer forward or back. You access these commands by holding down Option while selecting the menu item. The obvious keyboard shortcuts are to add Option to the Bring to Front and Send to Back commands. Remember to select the Option checkbox in the Menu edit dialog box so QuicKeys holds it down when making the menu selection.

Styles and No Style

XPress lets you assign keystrokes to styles, but you can only use certain keys—the function keys (F1 through F15) and the numeric keypad keys, with any combination of modifiers. If you want to use a more mnemonic keyboard combination, use a Menu Selection shortcut to choose the style from the Style Sheets submenu of the Style menu.

You absolutely must assign a shortcut to No Style, because QuarkXPress doesn't let you assign one. We use Command-Option-N (and we use it all the time).

Section

Section, under the Page menu, is where you set the starting page numbers for sections. Since we use this command at least once per document, we've assigned the keystroke Command-Option-S.

Clone in Place

One thing we're *forever* wanting to do in XPress is clone an item—make an exact duplicate of the object right on top of the original. Figure 23.1 shows a Sequence you can build to do just that.

Figure 23.1
Sequence to clone an item in place

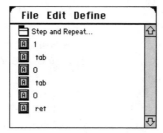

This Sequence only works if you have selected an item or items (if you don't, you get an alert box which tells you it can't find the Step and Repeat menu item). When you invoke this Sequence, it calls XPress' Step and Repeat command, enters 1 for the number of copies and 0 for the two offsets, and then presses Return. You can replace all the Alias Keystroke steps with a single Text step, if you want.

We use Command-= for this shortcut, since that's the clone shortcut in Aldus FreeHand (and it's FreeHand that made us want this command in QuarkXPress).

Use the Numeric Keypad

We grew up using Microsoft Word on the IBM, so the numeric keypad cursor movement keys from that program are second nature to us. We've set up Alias Keystroke shortcuts to make the numeric keypad work as we like (see Figure 23.2).

Figure 23.2
Numeric keypad
Alias Keystroke
shortcuts

🅰	pgdn	[3]	⇧
🅰	⌘-pgdn	⌘-[3]	
🅰	pgup	[9]	
🅰	⌘-pgup	⌘-[9]	⇩

■ ■ ■ ■ ■
Selecting Tools

In the previous version of this book, we explained a devious way of using Real Time shortcuts to select tools in XPress. Earlier XPress versions made it necessary. Now you can use Click shortcuts to select tools, but this solution is still not ideal, because it depends on your never moving the Tool Palette. The Tool Palette is unnamed, so you can't target that window by name. Instead, just make sure the clicks are positioned relative to the screen, keep the Tool Palette in the same place, and select away. Using a Click shortcut in any of XPress's other floating palettes can work, even if you move the palette, because you can target the window names in the Click's Window edit dialog box.

We use unmodified function keys to select tools. F1 is the Item tool, F2 is the Content tool, and so on.

■ ■ ■ ■ ■
**Moving
Through the
Tools**

Okay, what if you're used to the standard Command-Tab and Command-Shift-Tab to move down and up through the tools? That's great (especially for toggling between the Item and Content tools), but Command-Shift-Tab is a lot of keys. So how about Command-` for moving up through the tools? It's intuitive, because it's right above the Tab key. Steve likes to use Command-` to close windows, though, so he uses the function keys to choose tools, and the standards, Command-Tab and Command-Shift-Tab, less frequently.

■ ■ ■ ■ ■
**Changing
Page Views**

QuarkXPress' keyboard-click combinations are the best ways to zoom in and out on pages, but sometimes you want to just press a key to go to a certain magnification. QuarkXPress has shortcuts for 100% and Fit in Window, but not for its other menu zoom items. So we created shortcuts (see Figure 23.3)

Figure 23.3
Zooming shortcuts

📋	200%	⌘-2	⇧
📋	50%	⌘-5	
📋	75%	⌘-7	⇩

The percentage shortcuts all use the keys at the top of the keyboard, leaving the numeric keypad keys free for other things. Thumbnails uses N because it's about the only key left that's included in that word.

The only conflict in this set of keys is Command-2, which normally inserts a Previous Page # token in text. We've remapped this to Command-Option-2 using an Alias Keystroke shortcut.

Sizing a Box to Fit a Picture

XPress has a great keystroke—Command-Shift-F—that scales a picture to fit in a picture box (add Option to maintain proportional scaling). What it doesn't have, though, is a command to fit a box exactly to a picture. Figure 23.4 shows a sequence written by Glenn Fleishman (Steve's thunder lizard of a managing editor) that does just that.

Figure 23.4

Sequence to fit a box to a picture

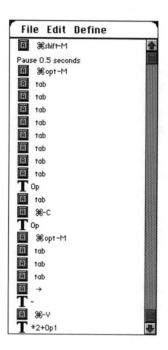

Remember that to enter a Tab keystroke, you *may* need to hold down the mouse button while pressing Tab. Also note that the 0p and *2+0p1 Text steps each end with a carriage return. Aside from that, we won't bore you with all these simple steps. It's how they all work together that's interesting.

QuarkXPress and Apple Events

QuarkXPress has arguably the most complete and robust implementation of Apple Events of any program on the market. Not only does it have a pretty good selection of events, but its object classes are remarkably flexible (if you don't know what object classes are, check out Danny Goodman's *The Complete AppleScript Handbook*).

Execution Contexts

Even more interesting, though, is that XPress' internal scripting language is not a proprietary collection of commands—it's AppleScript. Why does this matter? Maybe it doesn't, but if it does, it's because of contexts. You can execute an AppleScript in various contexts.

If you run an AppleScript in Apple's Script Editor (in the Script Editor's context), the Script Editor calls on the AppleScript system extension to interpret the script, then sends messages to XPress as called for (most of those messages are either set or get commands—that set object properties or ask what properties different objects have).

If you execute the AppleScript via QuicKeys' AppleScript shortcut, it's executing in QuicKeys' context: QuicKeys calls on the AppleScript extension to interpret the script. The message sending, however, is quite different. When the script wants to send an Apple Event, QuicKeys sends it to QuicKeys Toolbox, which sends it on to XPress—two steps. When you're querying XPress, there's even more traffic: send the query to QuicKeys Toolbox, which sends it to XPress, which sends the answer back to QuicKeys Toolbox, which sends it to QuicKeys. It gets slow.

Now suppose you send the whole AppleScript to XPress, unexecuted, using the doscript Apple Event. XPress executes the script (again, with the interpretive help of the AppleScript extension), but all the message-sending is internal—and fast. Plus, the entire script is run in the background, so XPress doesn't redraw the screen until the script is done.

What does all this mean? If you use AppleScript shortcuts to control XPress, use the following form (replace italic text with your own).

```
script ScriptName
  tell application "QuarkXPress®"
    Put the script here
  end tell
end script

tell application "QuarkXPress®"
  do script {ScriptName}
end tell
```

Alternately, use the DoScript shortcut, effectively bundling the script up in a package to send off to XPress for execution. This has the added advantage of letting you include the contents of the Clipboard in your script at runtime (via the Include Clipboard for ^C^ checkbox).

Of course, you're always better off writing and debugging AppleScripts in Apple's Script Editor and then pasting them into QuicKeys when they're perfect.

AppleScript and DoScript Shortcut Examples

We can't begin to delve into all the possible uses of AppleScript and QuarkXPress here. Figure 23.5 shows a quick example of how to use the AppleScript shortcut with XPress, however. Figure 23.6 shows a similar script in a doscript shortcut.

Figure 23.5
AppleScript shortcut to rotate boxes in QuarkXPress

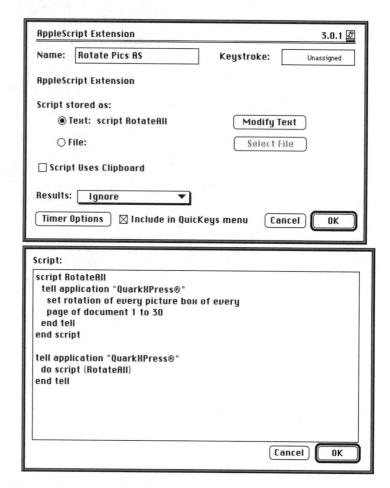

318

Figure 23.6
The same script in
a DoScript shortcut

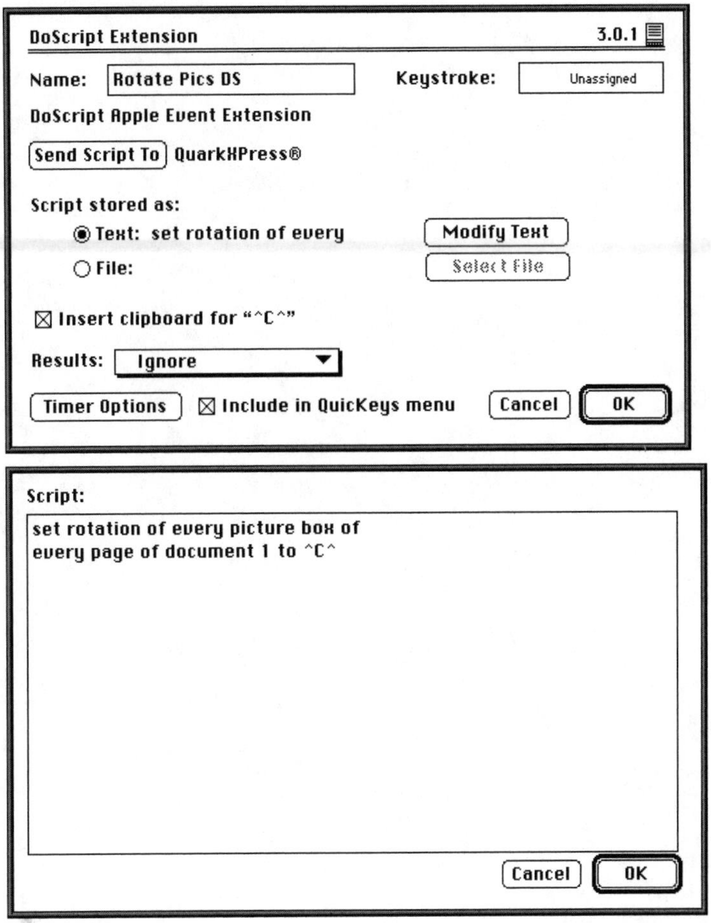

DoScript Extension   3.0.1 ▤

Name: ⎡Rotate Pics DS⎤   **Keystroke:** ⎡Unassigned⎤

DoScript Apple Event Extension

⎡Send Script To⎤ QuarkXPress®

Script stored as:
    ◉ **Text:** set rotation of every   ⎡**Modify Text**⎤
    ○ **File:**   ⎡Select File⎤

☒ **Insert clipboard for "^C^"**

Results: ⎡Ignore ▼⎤

⎡**Timer Options**⎤   ☒ **Include in QuicKeys menu**   ⎡Cancel⎤ ⎡**OK**⎤

Script:

set rotation of every picture box of
every page of document 1 to ^C^

⎡Cancel⎤ ⎡**OK**⎤

Appendix: Resources

Adobe Systems, Inc.
PageMaker
411 First Ave. S., Suite 200
Seattle, WA 98104
206-622-5500

Aladdin Systems, Inc.
StuffIt Deluxe
Deer Park Center, Suite 23A-171
Aptos, CA 95003
408-685-9175

Altsys Corporation
FreeHand
269 West Renner Road
Richardson, TX 75080
214-680-2060

CE Software
QuicKeys
Box 65580
West Des Moines, IA 50265
515-224-1995

Claris Corporation
FileMaker Pro
5201 Patrick Henry Dr.
Santa Clara, CA 95052
408-987-7000

CompuServe Information Service
5000 Arlington Centre Blvd.
Box 20212
Columbus, OH 43220
614-457-8600

Hooleon Corporation
Keyboard enhancements
Box 230
Cornville, AZ 86325
602-634-7515

Microsoft Corporation
Microsoft Word
Microsoft Excel
One Microsoft Way
Redmond, WA 98052
206-882-8080

Multicomp, Inc.
FlipNotes
Universal F-Key template
Box 2761
Abilene, TX 79604
800-541-4351
915-675-5944 (fax)

Quantum Computer Services, Inc.
America Online
8619 Westwood Center Dr.
Vienna, VA 22182
703-448-8700

Quark Inc.
QuarkXPress
300 S. Jackson, Suite 100
Denver, CO 80209
303-934-2211
800-356-9363

Index

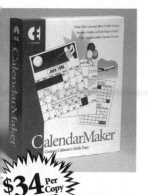